toddling to ten

toddling to ten

Your common parenting problems solved

 **the** **netmums.com**
guide to the challenges
of childhood

with Hollie Smith

headline

First published in 2008 by
HEADLINE PUBLISHING GROUP

6

Cataloguing in Publication Data is available from the British Library

Paperback 978 0 7553 1607 6

Typeset in Clearface Regular by Palimpsest Book Production Limited,
Grangemouth, Stirlingshire

Printed and bound in Great Britain by
Clays Ltd, St Ives plc

Headline's policy is to use papers that are natural, renewable and
recyclable products and made from wood grown in sustainable forests.
The logging and manufacturing processes are expected to conform
to the environmental regulations of the country of origin.

HEADLINE PUBLISHING GROUP
An Hachette Livre UK Company
338 Euston Road
London NW1 3BH

www.headline.co.uk
www.hodderheadline.com

Contents

Introduction

Your baby is on the move . . . first a shuffle, then a crawl. Before you know it, he's pulling up on any available furniture – a table top, a chair leg – or *your* leg. Your beloved baby is almost a toddler. Way back when you were a brand new mum you had imagined that the early baby days would be the hardest, that once the unpredictable, inconsolable crying and the sleepless nights were done with, and your baby had grown into a cute toddler, life as a mum would get easier. Wrong! What actually happens is that once you've seen off one lot of problems your child enters a new phase of life and starts presenting you with a fresh set. And so it goes on. From toddling to ten – and beyond, but that's another story – our children are more or less constantly providing us with something or other to fret about.

At Netmums, we have found that time and time again it's the same issues being raised by parents with children in this age range: tired and stressed parents worrying about how to get their children to eat, to go to bed, to stop kicking, shouting and screaming when something doesn't go according to plan, to do as they are told (at least sometimes). This is where *Toddling to Ten* comes in. Taking the 35 most common problems faced by parents with children in this age range, it offers practical and achievable solutions without being judgemental or prescriptive. We've painstakingly researched each issue and asked relevant experts to contribute their opinions. But, perhaps most importantly, the book gives the solutions that have worked for the people who really count: other parents.

Ordinary women at the coalface of parenting have lots of great ideas about how to tackle the basics of child behaviour because they've already tackled them themselves. Advice from one's peers is invaluable because if there's one thing that should serve as consolation to anyone experiencing the difficulties of parenting, it's that you're not alone. Whatever the problem your child has thrown at you, you can be certain that many other mums or dads have been through it, or are going through it, too.

The pressure to be perfect parents is intense. It doesn't help that we are faced with mountains of conflicting advice and parenting experts promising one-size-fits-all solutions. When we are just about holding it together and trying not to resort to shouting, crying or throwing things about, like our children do, what we need most is sensible, sympathetic and guilt-free guidance and support, which acknowledges just how complicated family life can be and offers advice on achievable ways forward. Friendly and reasonable, understanding and full of ideas, we're confident that *Toddling to Ten* is exactly that.

Siobhan Freegard
Founder, Netmums

Meet the Team

In *Toddling to Ten* Netmums has carefully researched the most common problems that modern parents face and set out to find realistic and achievable solutions to them. It offers sound, sympathetic and up-to-date advice on each issue. The book utilises the considerable knowledge of several dozen relevant experts, all of them highly experienced in their field. In particular, it calls on two 'regular' experts – clinical child psychologist Dr Angharad Rudkin and mums' life coach Patricia Carswell – both of whom make a very significant contribution throughout.

Then, of course, there's the advice and anecdotes of those other 'experts' – the members of Netmums.com, who know from experience that often there is no single solution to the challenges of childhood, and nothing quite as reassuring as the support of other mums who have already been there and done it.

Hollie Smith

Hollie Smith is a journalist and mum of two young daughters. She has written about family, health and women's issues for magazines such as *Woman*, *Best* and *Red*, and for newspapers such as the *Daily Mail*, the *Daily Mirror*, the *Express* and *The Times*. When not writing and being a mum, she finds cycling, singing and the odd glass of red wine give her some release from the stress of those two things! A member of Netmums for the last five years, she is a firm believer in the importance of friendship, support and solidarity among mums.

Dr Angharad Rudkin

Dr Rudkin is a Chartered Clinical Child Psychologist who has been working with families for almost ten years. She also trains and supervises other professionals in their work with children. Having grown up in Wales and Oxford, she now lives in Hampshire with her family and motorbike. Her website, aimed at helping women to overcome stress, can be found at: www.sistersofstress.co.uk.

Patricia Carswell

Patricia Carswell is a mother of two and a life coach who works exclusively with mothers and pregnant women. She runs antenatal courses preparing mums-to-be for the emotional challenges of becoming a parent and has a regular antenatal group. Her website can be found at: www.coachingformothers.com.

Toddler wobblers: How to cope with tantrums

The Problem

Mia has this ability to make us behave like children ourselves, neither of us wanting to give in, so it becomes a battle of wills. There's a tactic we use if one of us senses that the other is at breaking point, we'll intervene and take over. That's not really for the children's benefit, it's for ours. When a tantrum is in the air, however, no matter what you do to avoid it, it will happen. So you just let it happen and then it's over and you're friends again. They need to get it out of their system. Maybe the solution is to grit your teeth (or put some headphones on) until it's over: the hard part is to remember that when the tantrum is brewing or when it's actually happening. It sounds easy, yet it's so difficult.
Claudia from Bedford, mum to Sophia, five and Mia, three

It's normal when they go nuts

Let's get one thing straight about tantrums: they are completely normal. The chances are you won't know a single small child who doesn't throw a wobbler at least once in a while. There's scant consolation to be had when

your child is in the midst of a major paddy, but one thought is worth clinging onto: virtually every other mum will know what you're going through.

Why do they do it?

Most of the time, tantrums come from nowhere and that's one of the
reasons they're so maddening. Or else they're triggered by the smallest of
things and the stamping, screaming and sobbing that follows is totally
disproportionate.

Experts agree that the most likely cause of tantrums is sheer frustration: toddlers have well enough developed brains to know what they want
and what they're feeling, but they don't yet have the language skills to
express it or the physical ability to carry it out. They aren't able to reason
or rationalise in the way an older child can, and they don't have a grip on
what consequences mean. They tend to act without thinking about what
will happen next, and when they're in tantrum-mode, they can't see an easy
way out of it. When you're two, you live for the moment – and you've yet
to acquire any anger management skills.

The Problem Shared

What the Netmums say

I use 'time out' or the naughty step when we have tantrums but I've
come to realise those things aren't for the kids' benefit at all – they're
entirely for mine. Those minutes apart from my 'challenging' children
are lovely! Time for me to get a break from the madness and, most
importantly, time to calm down. If they're playing up because
they're too tired to think straight, it's obviously time for bed.

Get help from your partner whenever you can. It's always good to
have some back-up to enforce consistency because it's impossible
to keep up with all those warnings and praisings alone.

Jacqui from Charnwood, mum to Zachary, five and Reuben, three

We've tried everything when it comes to dealing with tantrums – ignoring bad behaviour, praising good, reward charts, bribery and shouting. We've never smacked, although I don't know how I've stopped myself at times.

What seems to work best with Imogen is being consistent. If we say no, we mean no. I think it's important to try and understand what's triggered the tantrum. In Imogen's case, the main cause is tiredness – she can come out of school and the slightest thing will set her off. On the other hand, when she's good, she's the sweetest child ever!

Lisa from Wolverhampton, mum to Eloise, eight and Imogen, five

One of the best things I've ever learned is that it's a good thing when children push the boundaries – it shows they have spirit and are developing the way they should be. And they act up with you because they're secure in your love. I always used to bear that in mind and it helped me brave the judgemental tuts and stares in the supermarket, and not feel I was a dreadful mother.

Distraction has always been my best weapon. Failing that, ignore them. Kids will take bad attention over no attention every time, so don't give them the chance to really get under your skin.

A tantrumming child is beyond reason, so don't try. And definitely don't bribe, because that's just making a rod for your own back. Identify their potential triggers – places, times and circumstances. Supermarkets are the most obvious hotspot. Boredom is often a trigger when you're shopping, so chat to them to keep them involved. Always make sure they're not hungry and don't take them to places they hate when they're tired.

Sometimes you still end up mid-aisle with a bored, hungry, tired toddler screaming blue murder. I've found it's much easier to distract if you get down on one knee and talk to Ethan at his level. It's logical I guess. If I was being dictated to by someone twice my size, I wouldn't feel that kindly towards them, either.

Crissy from Kingston-upon-Thames, mum to Isabelle, eight, Aimee, six and Ethan, four

Amy threw her worst ever tantrum in Claire's Accessories. She kept picking hair slides off the displays, earning us some dirty looks from the assistant. When I told her we were leaving, she went mad. It was a classic tantrum – she was puce in the face, lying on the floor, kicking and screaming – and the assistant was looking at me with contempt. I managed to get Amy out of the shop, but she carried on outside, in the middle of the shopping precinct. Nothing I said or did could calm her down. I was tired and in the end, I started crying myself. This absolute angel with her own kid in a buggy came up and gave me a hug. 'We've all been there. It's just a bad day,' she told me. It was probably one of the nicest things anyone's ever said to me.
Lorna from Winchester, mum to Amy, five and Izzie, two

I don't get many tantrums from Rebekah-Eve now: if she does throw one it's usually because she's hungry so the problem's solved by feeding her! But Amy-Jayne can really throw them, when she can't get her own way or if Bex is getting all the attention. She'll stamp her feet and growl at me like she's possessed! I don't take much notice of her when she does this, although sometimes I make it into a joke and talk back to her in the same growly voice, which gets them both laughing and stops things before they escalate. I think that's the key point, learning to tune into your child and predicting when the tantrum is going to kick in. If you can turn things around before they explode, it makes for an easier life for everyone.
Helen from Folkestone, mum to Rebekah-Eve, four and Amy-Jayne, two

I find just saying 'you are upsetting me' or 'you're disappointing me' can turn Shannon around. Ignoring works, although sometimes she'll take to hitting her sister or throwing something, which obviously I can't ignore, for safety's sake. We use the 'naughty step' a lot, but she has the most wicked temper and has been known to hit the wall so hard we felt it shake. In these cases, I need to pause and take a few big breaths before confronting her. Shannon's little sister has started to imitate her, so if she disagrees with me she'll cross her arms, screw up her face and

walk away with attitude. It's so funny, you have to stop yourself from laughing.
Zoe from Kings Lynn, mum to Shannon, five and Kacey, three

Mollie used to have some terrible tantrums. I remember going to a local toy store with her and my husband and, as we passed the section with the Teletubbies, she decided she wanted one – in spite of the fact she already had one at home. When I said no, she collapsed on the floor, screaming and kicking. I tried distracting her, but she'd got to the point of no return. In the end we left her there and hid in the next aisle, watching her. When she realised nobody was actually watching, she stopped straight away. I think just letting them thrash it out is the only thing you can do.
Mary from Bristol, mum to Mollie, five and Connie, two

We regularly have tantrums – from which TV channel to watch, whether he's eating his tea or not, which direction to go in the supermarket. At times it's embarrassing but mostly people are sympathetic, although I do get annoyed when he has a tantrum after I've told him off for snatching a toy from another child and a kindly play leader finds a similar one for him, as it feels like he is being rewarded for his tantrum. I have been known to get on the floor and scream with him or tickle him until he giggles out of it.
Claire from Worksop, mum to Luke, three

I've always found ignoring a great way of diffusing a tantrum. The tone of voice makes a big difference too, so even if you feel like crying, keeping your voice upbeat can stop things escalating. Sometimes, nothing you can do will alter the course of a tantrum. You can give them all the attention in the world, loads of positive reinforcement, ignore anything bad, say yes to every single demand, and then they will have a tantrum about the sky being blue. That's why music and other rooms were invented – so that we can put *ourselves* in 'time out' and sing very loudly!
Emma from Orkney, mum to Sophie, 16, Hugh, 11 and Jack, five

The Problem Solved

Prevention tactics

Heading off tantrums is your best bet for a quiet life. Most kids have flash-points that rear their heads repeatedly so you can learn to spot the signs that trouble's brewing. It may seem indulgent to spend your life tiptoeing round your little volcano, desperately trying to avoid situations that might bring on a mighty strop, but if it saves on stress in the long run, *indulge away*.

Tantrums can be sparked off or made worse by practical factors like tiredness or hunger, which is why they're common towards the end of the day. A well-timed rest or a snack might be all you need to keep the peace.

If you can move in with a distraction before the tantrum is unleashed, then do. Firmly suggest a change in activity or cheerfully veer the conversation round to something new. Just make sure your suggestion is more appealing than the matter in hand. Distraction is also useful with a full-blown tantrum. Even the most enraged small child can be brought down from a dark cloud by the possibility of something more interesting and less exhausting.

Anger management

Put yourself in your child's shoes. If you've got your head round how it feels to be a small, clumsy bundle of frustration, it's easier to forgive them when they go into a psychotic tailspin. That said, if a thumping great tantrum comes at the end of a bad day, or when you're tired, or ill, or already in a bad mood, empathy can fly out the window along with the remnants of your sanity, and the only distraction that comes immediately to mind is a high-volume swear word or the kicking of a convenient piece of furniture. Experts tell us that losing it yourself is the *least* useful reaction to a tantrum, and we all *know* that, as it's perfectly obvious. But small children rattle your cage. It's a fact of life. When it happens, count to ten and remind yourself that they're too young to know better, that they're not like this all the time, and that it will all have blown over in about three and a half minutes. If necessary, and if you know they're not in danger, or likely to cause anyone else any harm, walk away.

Ignorance is bliss

Sometimes, you have to batten down the hatches and wait for the storm to pass. If you refuse to show interest in a child's tantrum, in most cases they become bored or too tired to carry on. But don't let them wallow too long in their own misery – move in to smooth things over as soon as it's viable. Even if they push you away initially, they'll eventually calm down to a point where a hug, a stroke, or some kind words can help draw a line under the whole episode. Sulking about it or holding it against them for ages afterwards is pointless and sets a poor example of mature, adult behaviour. Praise them for their efforts in calming down. But if the incident kicked off because they weren't allowed to have or do something, stand firm: just because tantrums are to be expected and completely natural, that's no excuse for encouraging them by allowing your child to see how successful they can be!

When will it end?

Mums of older children look back on tantrums with a fond chuckle. If they get you down, remind yourself that they are part of a behavioural phase that *will* pass. When you've got the Terrible Twos and the Threatening Threes out the way, you can allow yourself a sigh of relief. By the age of four or five, their skills will have caught up with their intentions, and they realise there are better ways of getting what they want. Which is not to say that children aren't capable of some real snorters after the age of five, and beyond – the difference is that they'll probably have a good reason and you can talk them round more easily.

Psychologists often point out that tantrums are a positive developmental sign, because they are an attempt by children to express themselves, and that's an important communication and social skill. So you could try thinking of them in those terms!

What the experts say

The child psychologist

From the Terrible Twos onwards, children are learning that they are distinct from adults and therefore can exert their own ideas which is why, often at this age, their favourite word is 'no'.

Every child has their frustration button set at a different level: for some it takes the slightest thing to set them off, others can tolerate more. But all young children are basically selfish – they don't have the ability to put themselves in others' shoes. Tantrums are a normal part of growing up and a normal developmental stage. It's only by working through these stages that children can move on to the next one. We all learn from our 'mistakes' and children learn a lot from the consequences of their actions, so you need to let them know – calmly – that they're not acceptable. If tantrums are responded to in a way that reinforces them, i.e., by shouting or screaming back at them, then the child learns that it's an appropriate way to express their feelings. And if a child has done something unacceptable or broken a rule prior to, or during, a tantrum, then it will need to be followed by its natural consequence, whatever that may be in your family.

Reacting to a tantrum with your own tantrum will not work! You need to be the calm one in these situations, although of course, that's easier said than done. Some children will hate being touched while they're in a very emotionally aroused state, so you need to learn what your child prefers. Similarly, talking to someone when they're very cross is not going to work. Wait until they've calmed down, then maybe you can talk with them about what happened, in a constructive, non-blaming way. Small children will have tantrums regardless of the example they're set, but that doesn't mean they won't also be influenced by the reactions they see in their parents, so try and keep your own temper in check as much as possible. It may be normal behaviour for children to throw themselves to the ground when things don't go their way, but it's not so acceptable in grown-ups!

Generally by the age of four or five, children are learning

'appropriate' ways of behaving in nursery or school and will have better understanding of themselves and situations, so they'll be less likely to resort to tantrums. But they can go on for a while. Let's face it, some people never grow out of them.
Dr Angharad Rudkin, Child and Adolescent Mental Health Service

The mums' life coach

For many mums, the public tantrum is a nightmare. It brings out our fears about whether we're doing a good enough job of raising our children and is made worse by the thought of how other people might be reacting.

If you can see other mothers staring when your child's in the middle of one, remember they're probably just thanking their lucky stars that it's not *their* child this time. If you're unlucky enough to come up against someone who's openly disapproving or critical, do your very best not to react to them, however hard that might be. It's always helpful to have a reply up your sleeve which you've thought about when you're feeling calm – what comes to mind in the heat of the moment probably won't be so constructive! Have a think now about what you could say in this situation and try it out in front of the mirror.

If you have a very explosive personality, you may worry that your toddler has learned the art of the tantrum from you. Rest assured that tantrums happen to most toddlers, regardless of their mother's temperament. He might copy how you react afterwards, though, when everyone's calmed down, so focus on that as an area where you might lead by example. A hug goes a long way, for example, and its meaning is understood by even the smallest toddler. If your child is old enough to understand, you might find it helpful to apologise and explain why you acted as you did; it could be an opportunity to show that you understand your toddler's strength of feeling. Don't forget, though, that children move on quickly, so don't leave it too long.

On the other hand, if you're very calm by nature, you may find your child's tantrums baffling. Try to understand them by thinking about a situation that really riles you. Now imagine how that feels on a day when you're desperately tired. Tune into the feeling and magnify it a hundredfold – you'll get the idea.

Some mothers feel so frustrated and angry when their child is in a rage that they're shocked by their feelings. If you've found yourself hating your child at this point, don't panic and convince yourself you're a bad mother. It's normal to feel extremes of emotion towards your children – often those closest to us provoke the strongest feelings in us, both positive and negative, so your anger can be a sign that you care about them. Your feelings may come from frustration that things aren't going as you want them to, or from anxiety about your child's behaviour.

Remind yourself that it's the behaviour you hate, not the child. And if you've had a really bad day for tantrums, wait till your child's asleep and go and watch him sleeping – it'll remind you what you love about him.

Don't forget to show empathy to other mums. If you're watching someone else's child having a tantrum, don't tut or stare dis-approvingly (even if your child is one of those rare non-tantrum throwers). Be kind, give them a smile, and leave her in peace. One day you might need the same understanding.

Patricia Carswell, www.coachingformothers.com

The Problem Summarised

- Tantrums are normal, natural and healthy. Small children throw them because they can't help themselves!
- It's okay to feel upset and angry yourself when they happen. But it's helpful if you can avoid showing your child those feelings.
- Try the following tactics in this order when it comes to tackling them: avoid, distract, ignore, walk away. Keep calm, if you can. Get down to their eye level.
- Don't give in to their demands, or they'll assume tantrums are acceptable.
- Once they're over, move on.

Food fights: How to deal with fussy eaters

The Problem

My son will go weeks without eating much, sometimes just a slice of toast a day. Then, all of a sudden a switch flicks and for a couple of days his appetite is enormous and he'll eat anything I serve. He's skinny, but he's lively and developmentally sound, so the doctors refuse to send him (and me!) for help regarding his strange eating habits. Apparently, I just have to put up with it.

Rebecca from Hemel Hempstead, mum to James, four

Don't worry . . . it's just *another* phase!

The vast majority of young children are picky about what they eat. In fact, the fussy phase is yet another completely usual developmental stage. Children go through a whole series of these periods of growth within the first ten years of their lives and, as they can result in some challenging behaviour, it helps to bear in mind that they really *are* positive steps up the ladder of life. Fussy eating, for example, isn't just your child trying their utmost to annoy you. It's a sign that they're learning about tastes and choice, and working out how to assert themselves. While some children have restricted tastes well into their teens (and even into adulthood), the majority will grow out of it as they get older and more open-minded, usually after they've started school, become exposed to different eating habits, and are influenced by their less-fussy peers!

Until then, the business of getting our kids to eat well can be tricky, bordering on the hopeless. It's not helped by the desire to 'feed up' our children ingrained in our very instincts as parents. On top of that, we're faced with mounting pressure to make sure the food we get down our kids is *good* for them. Quite rightly, too – but it can make life hard when you'd be grateful to get *anything* down them at all. It's no wonder mealtimes can become a battleground, and food, a child's weapon of choice.

Start as you mean to go on

Children are more likely to accept a variety of good foods if you introduce them from weaning onwards. Many little ones are so delighted with the novelty of solids, they'll eat anything and everything for a while. However, even the most open-minded junior gourmet can, and will, change his mind. When they're old enough to have an opinion – i.e., as soon as they can talk! – children start announcing they don't like this, that and the other, because they've worked out that biscuits, crisps and chocolate are more enjoyable options. (And even if you work hard at avoiding or limiting those items, there'll be countless occasions when they encounter them outside the home.)

There may be a deeper, darker reason: they realise that refusing food is one of the few ways they can gain the upper hand over their pesky parents. Small children are amazingly manipulative when they put their minds to it. They know it's the grown-ups who are ultimately in control. And that's why they'll take whatever small opportunities they can to overrule! They're constantly nudging at the boundaries we set and forever seeking ways to get attention, positive or otherwise, from the adults around them – it's a way for them to test our love and develop their own abilities to cope in the world.

The Problem Shared

What the Netmums say

I've never pushed Damsie to eat, or made a big deal out of it. She usually refuses to eat the home-cooked food that I spend ages preparing, and on the rare occasions we have processed food, she gulps it down. I was a fussy eater as a child and I remember mealtimes being a misery. I'm hoping by ignoring it she'll just decide to eat one day. It's very frustrating and I want to cry when I have another full plate of food to throw away. On an average day she'll eat two Weetabix with hot milk, a small packet of crisps, an apple, orange and banana. For dinner we might have a roast, and she'll just eat the Yorkshire pudding. She's just had her three to four year check-up and the doctor told me that although she was underweight and short, I'm doing the right thing. But what is the right thing?
Claire from Plymouth, mum to Damsie, three and Cammie, four

Harry refused to eat vegetables a few months ago. I tried bribery and threatening, all to no avail. I gave up for a while (he eats fruit, so I wasn't overly worried) then I decided that he would get a sticker for every 'portion' of fruit or veg he eats, and it seems to be working.

There are other ways of getting them down him. I make vegetable soup, which I blend so it's not lumpy, and he'll eat a bowl of that. I also make fruit crumbles or sponges, which he likes with ice cream.
Michelle from Rochester, mum to Harry, four and Charlie, two

I always planned to be easy going about food. My husband was a fussy eater as a child and lived on spaghetti on toast for years, apparently! Even now his mum thinks it's her duty to tell Mark to 'eat up' every two seconds, which I hate because it's so stressful.

If Mark doesn't like what he's served, I just tell him calmly it's all there is, and if he wants to leave the table I let him. As long as they see the dinner table as a happy sociable place, they'll soon feel they want to join in.

I admit that when he goes on one of his three day 'fasts', I can feel anxiety rising, but by the time he reaches the third day he'll eat *anything* I serve him. I also occasionally provide a favourite meal in front of the telly, to take the pressure off and for a bit of fun. Making faces or pictures out of food and getting Mark to help prepare it is really helpful, too.

Jennie from Ipswich, mum to Mark, two and Stephen, one

When we get home from school, I put out a big plate of fruit. We regularly try a new one – and we'll all have a little bit and try to describe the taste. For our evening meal, I put out a big serving dish with lots of different veg on it, and the children help themselves. They seem to love being able to pick and choose the ones they'd like, and they eat it all. They're taking responsibility for what goes on their plates and they enjoy that freedom. There's no pressure and so the eating experience is more enjoyable.

Tracey from Leicester, mum to Adam, six, and childminder to five others

I think there's just a 'fussy gene' that some children have and there's not that much you can do about it. All my three were weaned on the same things at the same time and have the same healthy diet. Laura and James have always eaten everything, but from the start Ben has been picky about what he'll eat. With two other children at the table, it's not worth making it a battle. He eats from all the food groups, albeit in a limited way, and he gets close to his five portions of fruit and veg. I doubt that at the age of 20 he'll be fussy – my brother was just the same and he'll eat anything now.

Lisa from Amersham, mum to Laura, seven, Ben, five and James, three

Bethany has always refused to eat meat, vegetables, pasta and rice. She lives off chips, Yorkshire pudding, jam on crackers, bread (but only toasted, with chocolate spread on), salt and vinegar crisps, apples and yoghurt. I've spent hours trying to get her to help cook the meals but she won't. I've taken her to the doctors to see if they could help, but they told me she would grow out of it. She only weighs 3 st 4 lbs and can fit into age three to four clothes.

Now my son is taking after her, even though he was a good eater and would eat anything you put in front of him. I've restricted the amount of biscuits or crisps they're allowed to eat and they only get chocolate bars as a treat. But Bethany has gone for days without eating when I haven't let her have what she wants. My partner didn't start eating properly until he was about 14, so I'm hoping she'll be the same.

Emma from Swindon, mum to Bethany, seven and Robbie, two and stepmum to Owen, 18

Having a faddy eater is soul destroying, frustrating and at times downright annoying. Stacey's 14 now and still as fussy as ever. She was fine as a baby but at ten months she was put on a hyperactivity diet and then she began refusing everything. If you tried to make her eat, she'd gag until she choked. Meals out were a nightmare and during lunch hour I'd get phone calls at work asking me to collect her from school because she was screaming.

As she's got older she's been a bit more prepared to try things without the hissy fits. When I got her to eat a jacket potato, I felt like I'd climbed a mountain! I can only live in hope that when she's older she'll get fed up with being different to her friends or not being able to go to a nice restaurant because there's nothing on the menu she'll eat. On the positive side, she's healthy enough and has no tooth cavities, spots, or anything else that would indicate a poor diet.

Vix from Lymm, mum to Stacey, 14 and Ethan, four months

My kids eat what I put down in front of them, or they go without, it's that simple. I don't have a problem with giving the kids sweet things, in fact I love baking, which I think is far healthier than most of the sweet rubbish they'll buy with their pocket money. There are a few foods they don't like, however I normally put a small spoonful of whatever it is on their plate, which I ask them to eat. Basically, they get a lot of what they like as long as they agree to try new foods and eat a wee bit of what is good for them, which they may not like. It works for us.

Cassandra from Motherwell, mum to Aiden, eight, Anya, six and Andrew, eight months

The Problem Solved

If at first . . .

You can help them develop their taste for new foods by giving them lots of opportunities to try them. It's true, there are few things more galling than serving up a pan of lovingly home-made fishcakes only for them to remain whole on the plate, stone cold, half an hour later. And your response is vital: if you make a fuss, get angry, or try and force them to eat something, they are less likely to put the phase behind them as they grow. The way to respond when a child rejects food is to ignore it. Remove the offending item from the menu for a while, and concentrate on other things you know they enjoy. But don't make a big deal about it and don't give up – quietly serve those fishcakes again a few weeks later. You may end up chucking them or eating them yourself once more. But there's every chance that, sooner or later, they'll give them another chance and realise just how delicious they are. Perseverance is key.

Show them how it's done

If we teach our children that meals are something to be lovingly prepared and enjoyed with others, with any luck they'll end up with a healthy attitude to eating that lasts a lifetime. True, we don't all have the time or inclination to be a domestic goddess: if you're stumped for inspiration, there are loads of great ideas for fast but healthy foods in the Netmums cookery book, *Feeding Kids*, and in the Netmums family meal planner (in the food section of the website).

As parents, we are the most influential role models our children have in all areas of behaviour, and how and what we eat is no exception. So we may need to take a good look at our own eating habits. Do you eat all *your* greens? And do you snack on fruit, rather than biscuits? Do you always sit down for breakfast, or do you eat a bowl of cereal watching television? We can't really expect our children to do something if we don't do it ourselves. Just sitting down at a table, eating the same meal together as a family or with friends whenever possible, is one way to provide a great example.

Sweetie psychology

There are different theories on the psychology of 'treats', but most experts seem to agree that you shouldn't offer chocolate or sweeties as a bribe for eating up their greens or other sorts of good behaviour, because they'll start to recognise the sweets as highly desirable rewards, and the greens as something so awful they deserve a prize for getting through them! However, it *is* good for children to understand the difference between unhealthy and healthy foods, and that the former should be enjoyed in moderation, so feel free to pass those messages on – in a non-obsessive way!

Small people, small appetites

Some children appear to have the appetite of a small bird, or are so single-minded about the sorts of food they're prepared to eat, it becomes a massive worry for their parents.

Fortunately, most children under the age of ten need surprisingly small amounts of food to get by – and in fact, what most parents consider to be a very restricted diet is often far more full and varied than they think. If you're concerned that their drastically restricted diet may be affecting their growth or development, their general health, or their concentration, get them checked by a doctor. But don't be surprised if you're sent home with the news that they'll grow out of it.

In a small number of cases, a child may have a problem that goes beyond perfectly normal 'fussy eating' and a GP may refer them for specialised help. There's more on this in the factfile, p. 22.

Tricks and treats

If you want a child to eat their lunch or dinner, make sure they're hungry when they come to the table. Keep snacks healthy and light, and don't give them too soon before dishing up. That said, many children are natural 'grazers' who prefer to eat little and often – although the ideal is to have three proper meals a day with a few small healthy snacks to keep hunger at bay in between, children can be fazed by large platefuls of food. So if you've found that the only way to get good food down them is to let them nibble here and there, carry on. It's amazing how much goodness you can get down them this way: handfuls of nuts or seeds, a chopped apple, mini oatcakes, or tiny squares of bread and butter.

Don't be too obsessive about eating at the table, particularly if it's become a conflict zone. Changing the routine or scenery can be a good appetite booster: if you don't fancy your chances of a conventional sit-down lunch, try sandwiches in the park, a teddy bears' picnic on a washable rug in the bedroom, or a meal out in your favourite café.

Eating in front of the television isn't considered conducive to good eating habits and it's probably not to be encouraged on a regular basis. However, the occasional 'TV dinner' will do no harm, and some mums find it's a way of sneaking a healthy meal into them without them really noticing!

What the experts say

The mums' life coach

When your child won't eat what you've put in front of him, it's easy to become anxious. Feeding your child is one of the most primary functions of a parent, and when this goes wrong you may feel like you're failing on a pretty fundamental level. It doesn't help that the health of the nation's children is big news in the media.

In most families there's an unwritten rule that your kids' interest in your cooking will be inversely proportional to the amount of time you've spent on it. Sometimes it seems that the longer you take preparing delicious, home-made meals, the more likely they are to end up in the dog's bowl or in the bin!

It's important to keep a sense of perspective. By all means do what you can to provide a healthy diet and aim for that magic target of five pieces of fruit and veg a day whenever possible, but never force it. You can't make them like broccoli and beansprouts. And making every mealtime an all-out battle won't give them a positive attitude to food in the long run.

Your children will learn their attitudes to food from what they see at home. Ask yourself what messages about food you're passing on. Are you cheerful and matter-of-fact about mealtimes or are you obsessing about your own diet and constantly worrying about food? They'll learn from your actions as much as your attitudes. If you're munching on chocolate bars while you serve them salad, the contrast won't be lost on them. Equally, if you're fanatical about healthy food, it might just turn them off. Remember that food is supposed to be fun as well as nutritious.

When your children are past that irrational pre-school phase and are old enough to negotiate with, consider going through recipe books with them, and working out what they like; once they've agreed on something they're not in a strong position to refuse it once it's made. Of course, there are no easy solutions if your children all like and dislike different things, and some compromise is inevitable – if you only prepare things that everyone likes, you could end up with a very restricted diet.

Patricia Carswell

The nutrition expert

Very many young children go through phases of being fussy about what they'll eat – it's so common as to be normal. For most of them, especially those who've been brought up on a healthy diet from the start, it won't cause nutritional problems as it's often a short-term thing. It can be due to psychological reasons, when food is often a way for a small child to show his or her feelings, or get attention, or it could be down to a physical problem such as teething, illness or tiredness. And it can be that the child doesn't like that food. As adults we all have a few foods we really don't like, and it doesn't matter, because there are plenty we do like. So you should concentrate on the foods they do enjoy. Over the weeks or months ahead introduce different foods if you can, to replace the ones they don't like, preferably from the same food group, e.g. replace one fruit with another.

Serve good, healthy, natural foods, avoiding those that have been processed and have lots of additives, and cook from scratch where possible. Go easy on the sugar and salt and watch out for the 'bad' fats. Trans fats, which are found in commercial products and contain polyunsaturated fats that have been hydrogenated, or chemically altered, are best avoided, and saturated fats, found mainly in fatty animal produce, should be kept to a minimum. Let your child see you eating and enjoying these foods, so that they'll eat and enjoy that food without even thinking to question it. Food and eating is a wonderful thing as well as a necessity and it is a parent's responsibility to get across a sense of pleasure, wonder and interest in them. So get them involved in choosing, preparation and cooking as much as possible. It's also a good idea to chat to them about the origin of food, for example, asking where milk comes from or what a banana tree looks like.

The good thing about eating today is that there's so much choice that if your child won't touch a certain food, there'll always be another which offers similar nutrients. So, bone up on the food groups – protein, carbohydrates and fats – and try to make sure they're getting a reasonable balance from them all. Vegetables and fruits are very important as they provide vitamin C, fibre and a range of compounds vital for health. Ideally, they should eat fruit and veg of different sorts and colours, to get a mix of nutrients. But if they'll only eat one or two, then that's better than nothing. If strong taste is a problem, e.g. cabbage or sprouts, swap for a milder vegetable. Some children don't like the chew factor with vegetables – disguise them by finely chopping into pasta sauces or stews, or blending into soups. *Judith Wills, www.thedietdetective.net*

The child psychologist

Fussy eating is a perfectly normal developmental stage, when children are learning that they don't actually have to do everything Mummy and Daddy say! A parent's job is to protect and nurture their child and if they reject this nurturing, it can feel hurtful. Children are astute and can be mean when they know something is really important to their parents – it's a good way to try out their power over them. The more parents plead, the more likely the child will dig in their heels, too, so it can become an emotional battleground. Then both parent and child approach dinner time with a feeling of dread and tension, making another argument more likely.

As for healthy foods, children will reject them for the same reason as adults do, because unhealthy stuff tastes better. The quick fix that we get from a biscuit or chocolate bar is more addictive than the sensations from eating an apple. What's important is that the child is given the opportunity to eat a balanced diet that includes both, so that they don't get dependent and crave the bad stuff.

If your child is going through a fussy eating stage, try to remain calm, and *don't* take it personally or start scolding the child. Trust in the fact that the child *will* eat when they are hungry and won't starve to death. Children have great self-regulating capacities – they'll eat when they're hungry and are happy to go without when they're not – so you need to be as flexible as possible about their eating habits. Remember, it takes two to have a battle. If you don't even enter the field, then there is no battle to be had.

Dr Angharad Rudkin

The Problem Summarised

- Being picky about food is very common among children, particularly in pre-schoolers. The majority will grow out of it.
- Setting a good example is the best way you can encourage your child to eat well.
- Try not to get stressed and don't make a big deal out of it when they won't eat. But don't give up. Keep on presenting them with new foods.
- If the dining room's become a battlefield, shift the scene elsewhere.
- Even the fussiest of eaters will be healthy enough. But if you're worried, seek advice from your doctor.

Factfile: Kids' Eating Problems

Occasionally, a child who won't, can't or doesn't eat much may be diagnosed with a problem that requires medical intervention. These include:

- Selective Eating: Sometimes called perseverative feeding disorder, this is just an extended or extreme form of fussy or faddy eating. It occurs when a child is excessively selective about what they eat and are unwilling to try new foods, beyond the pre-school stage when it's considered a normal developmental phase. They may be healthy, in spite of it, but if it's an issue for more than a couple of years and/or their diet is so limited that their growth and development is threatened, they may need some professional help to change their eating behaviour. A common method of treatment is to very gradually increase their exposure to small amounts of different foods.
- Restrictive Eating: This occurs when a child has a very small appetite and is simply disinterested in food. It's usually harmless, unless it persists for several years, in which case their growth may be affected.
- Food phobias: Fears that are linked to eating or certain foods, which lead to the sufferer avoiding the thing they fear. Common examples are fear of vomiting, choking or swallowing while eating.
- Food Avoidance Emotional Disorder: A rare problem, where emotional issues affect eating or appetite. Sometimes confused with anorexia but different in that sufferers may actually want to eat, but don't know why they can't.
- Anorexia Nervosa and Bulimia Nervosa: Complex eating disorders driven by a preoccupation with weight and body shape. Childhood-onset cases are very rare, and prompt diagnosis and treatment is all-important as these disorders can have a serious effect on a child's physical and psychological well being.

Pyjama dramas: How to have easy, peaceful bedtimes

The Problem

We were never strict about bedtime with Rebekah-Eve, and I suppose some people would say we made a rod for our own backs. She'd always fall asleep on the sofa and we would put her in her cot when we went up to bed. When her sister was born we decided to make sure she went into her own cot at a sensible time, 7 p.m. Rebekah-Eve was intrigued by this and wanted to go up herself, so we encouraged it. She then decided she wanted to go into our bed rather than hers, and watch her favourite DVD, so we allowed this and now she goes up every night at the same time as her sister, and falls asleep in our room. Once she's asleep we transfer her into her own bed.

Helen from Folkestone, mum to Rebekah-Eve, four and Amy-Jayne, one

Goodnight, sweetheart

Bedtime, or at least, that bit of the day that comes *after* bedtime, when your children are tucked up in their beds, fast asleep and silent for the first time all day, is a wonderful thing. Don't feel guilty for relishing it. All adults need some purely adult time – for most of us, evenings are the only time to get it. And consistent, sensible bedtimes aren't just good for tired parents, they're very good for tired children. We all need a decent night's sleep to function properly during the day, and children need even longer than the rest of us to recharge their batteries because they're growing rapidly, and because childhood is an especially tiring business.

When should bedtime be?

Different children have different needs and not all families have the same schedules. But as a general rule, children aged 18 months to five years need ten to 12 hours sleep (while they are still napping, they may also need up to two hours in the day) and those aged five to ten should be getting between nine and 11 hours.

Bounceback kids

It's common for children of all ages, and for all sorts of reasons, to kick up a fuss about going to bed, or to re-appear *after* you've tucked them in: research suggests that 20 per cent of two-year-olds and 12 per cent of eight-year-olds have settling difficulties. (See *Solving Children's Sleep Problems* by Lyn Quine (Beckett-Karlson, 1997.) Even children who've previously been easy to settle can start to rebel: they suss out that there's a whole other world of fun outside their bedroom door at night, or they're less tired than they used to be. There are various techniques you can employ to help with this situation. But whichever you choose, commitment, consistence and perseverance are key.

Different strokes for different folks

Plenty of families don't bother with routines, set bedtimes, firm rules about who sleeps where, or even the premise that children need significantly earlier nights than adults. This is often the case for working parents who feel they'd never spend any quality time with their kids if they didn't keep them up late. If that's the way you choose to live your lives, don't let anyone else make you feel guilty about it. As long as your children aren't too tired to function properly as a consequence, and you accept that once you let them get used to such a situation you may have your work cut out to change it, then carry on.

The Problem Shared

What the Netmums say

Right from the beginning we've followed a very strict routine. I'm a strong believer in parents needing time to themselves to talk, cuddle, and do adult things without children running around the place. Both our girls are in bed by 7.30 p.m. at the latest and it doesn't make any difference whether it's a weekend, holiday, birthday or Christmas. They don't even question it. It's bed, book and lights-out.
Mary from Bristol, mum to Mollie, five and Connie, two

We never had a structured bedtime routine with my older two. When Andrew arrived we knew we had to be more organised, so when he was a few days old, we implemented bedtimes for all three of them. But I still have problems with the older two. They're in their bedrooms by eight but Aiden will read as long as he can get away with it and Anya will play until she's actually tired. As long as they're not bouncing off the walls and making a racket, we leave them be. They're generally asleep by 9 or 10 p.m. Andrew's a star – as long as he has his bath, he goes down without a peep.
Cassandra from Motherwell, mum to Aiden, eight, Anya, six and Andrew, eight months

Jamie's had the same routine since she was a little baby: bath or shower, teeth brushed, story, sleep. As she's got older it's got later, she used to go to bed for 6 p.m. at one point but now we take her up at 7.30 p.m. After brushing her teeth and a story she's tucked up by around 8 p.m. On a weekend when there's no school to think about, we let her stay up until 8.30 p.m., but on those nights she doesn't get a story. She knows it's just allowed at the weekends and has never been a problem in the week. I just hope that as she gets older it stays the same!

Lisa from Hull, mum to Jamie, seven

When James was younger bedtime was so much easier than it is now. I suppose we expect him to get on with it – wash himself in the bath, clean his teeth, put pyjamas on, and his dad is just around to supervise. But it often ends up with Dad getting angry and then James messing about and prolonging things even more. Once he's in bed there'll be an argument as to whether there's time to read, write or listen to a story tape. If he'd only get on with getting ready for bed there'd always be time for these things!

Nicola from Stockport, mum to James, seven

Our routine includes a bath around 5.30 p.m. every other night, wind-down time at 6 p.m., then at 6.30 p.m. they go upstairs and get undressed, go into their bedrooms and do some colouring for half an hour and then at 7 p.m. it's lights out and sleep. We stick with it at weekends, too. The only time I relax it is during the holidays or on trips away.

Jane from the Wirral, mum to Jake, six, Libby, five and Emma, three

My eldest went to bed at 6.30 p.m. before her brother and sister were born. Now she's a little older she feels it's unacceptable to go to bed at the same time as them. So when her sister was born her bedtime was delayed by half an hour and then by another half an hour when her brother was born. The time gap in between them all going up gives us a good steady bedtime routine and by 7.30 p.m. everyone's in bed. I do think all children need a good night's sleep and my children are so used to their routines – they all get a full night 99 per cent of the time and *usually* go to bed without any trouble.

My husband and I are also keen on having our own time. It's nice to have those few precious hours without the children for watching a good programme, listening to music or being romantic.

Frances from Halifax, mum to Sophie, seven, Emily, two and Jacob, one

My daughter tends to go to bed between 9.30 p.m. and 10 p.m. She's a good sleeper and is happy and well behaved during the day, so a slightly later bedtime doesn't seem to disturb her. As for time with my husband, we both agree that we would rather spend more time together as a family than send our daughter off to bed. He often doesn't get home until late from work so if she went to bed early, he would never see her apart from the weekends. After dinner we play a few games with her, read some stories and then it's bath time and bed. She enjoys extra cuddles in bed and we talk about what we are doing tomorrow and then say goodnight.

Kathryn from Stockport, mum to Sarah, three

Emily goes to bed between 8.30 and 9 p.m., listening to an Ibiza Chillout CD which has been helping her sleep since she was a baby! Lucy goes at around 8.30 p.m. She puts on a DVD and within about ten minutes she's asleep. Korben also goes to sleep watching a DVD, around 8 p.m. And Tyeran goes to sleep on the sofa or in his bed. OK, the sofa is not ideal but it works for us, my hubby will carry him to bed and he never stirs whilst being moved. I know TVs and DVDs in bedrooms are frowned upon by some people but the children settle happily with them. We don't have strict bedtimes, but the children are sensible – they'll all go to bed when they're feeling tired. Even Tyeran understands he has to sleep or he won't be able to cope with nursery.

Andrea from Derby, mum to Emily, nine, Lucy, eight, Korben, six and Tyeran, four

My son loves his bed (like his mum) but we did have a few problems recently when we changed from cot to bed. He would get out of bed, open his door and go to the top of the stairs to call for someone – quite clever really as he was still wearing his sleeping bag! I just used to go up and without talking, pick him up, put him back in bed and walk out. He did this for about three or four nights, but persistence paid off, and he hasn't done it since.

Cathy from Plymouth, mum to Jacob, two

The Problem Solved

Same time, same place

We hear a lot about routines and how children thrive on them. The truth is that most parents find they do indeed make life easier and children happier, and never more so than at the end of the day. Establishing an unchanging time for lights-out and a comforting ritual leading up to it, early in a child's life, is the best thing you can do to smooth the path to easy bedtimes in the future, because once a child knows they can expect a certain thing to happen every day at the same time, they will soon accept it as inevitable. And if you never offer little ones any other option, they won't even realise that there's something more exciting happening, elsewhere, past 7.30 p.m. Bedtime routines can be established when they're still small babies, but it's never too late to start one. It will almost certainly be worth your while: structured bedtimes not only lead to peaceful evenings, they're also an important step towards an uninterrupted night's sleep. If a child is comfortable and happy in their own bed at the start of the night, they're more likely to settle again if they wake up later on.

What makes a good bedtime routine?

A bath, milk, a book or a quiet game, songs, and a cuddle or any combination of those are all popular ways to fill that calming-down period just before bedtime. Some parents – especially those who've been working during the day – find it's a useful time to swap news and views with their little one. The main aim is to do exactly the same thing at the same time every night. The drawback for parents is that the repetitive nature of a bedtime routine can become tedious. You just have to keep reminding yourself that once you've tucked them up, you can creep downstairs, pour a glass of wine, and tune into your favourite TV programme in peace.

Right on cue

Sleep associations are something that experts talk about a lot. They're all the things that children link in their minds to sleep, bed and bedtime, and so if you want those to be problem-free, you have to make sure their sleep associations are positive. A relaxing, consistent bedtime routine is a good sleep association in itself. So is a specific 'cue' that always signals the time for lights-out: for instance, a particular song or phrase such as 'Night night, I love you.'

It's all too easy to fall into the trap of bad sleep associations. For instance, if your little one will only fall asleep with you lying down next to him, that's what he associates sleep with and that's what he'll demand each time. That kind of commitment is draining for you, but more importantly, it means that every time he wakes up in the night, he'll need you to settle back to sleep again (there's more on this in the next section).

If you want them to stay in their own beds at night, make sure that's where you settle them at bedtime so that they associate their own bed with comfort, security and sleep. A favourite object such as a cuddly toy or a little blanket will usually develop into a pleasant sleep association. But if you want to avoid them becoming reliant on theirs and having to prise it out of their hands when they start school, let them know it's just for bedtime. And make sure it's something you can duplicate if necessary. Otherwise if it goes missing, like Teddy, you'll be stuffed.

Get back to bed!

When a child gets out of bed after you've put her in it, you need to lead her firmly back, tuck her in, and leave without stopping to chat. If she does it again, you have to repeat the process, and keep repeating it until she gives up and drops off.

If it becomes a persistent problem, and rewarding them when they *do* get it right hasn't helped, you can try one of several established methods such as controlled crying or gradual retreat. In brief, controlled crying means leaving them to cry or grumble, returning to check them at regular intervals. Eventually, they'll accept that room service has been discontinued and give up the fight. It's tough, and some parents can't bear it. But it's usually effective and is comparatively quick – it can take as little as a few days, but more normally a week. Controlled crying doesn't really work once they're in a proper bed and able to get in and out at will. You can do something similar if you put a stairgate across their door, but you do need to make sure their bedroom is completely safe.

The more gentle 'gradual retreat' method is effective for all ages and isn't so distressing, but it does take longer and it requires a huge amount of patience. For more about this method, see the factfile below.

For older children who won't get back into bed there is a tougher method: door-shutting. This is appropriate when they've made the move from a cot to a bed – usually between two and three. It involves holding their bedroom door shut for a few minutes at a time and warning them clearly that you will continue to do so until they get back into bed.

It goes without saying that you should only attempt these methods once you're sure they're not genuinely in need of help or are scared, poorly or in pain.

Bedtime for older kids

The rules don't really need to change that much for children who've passed their fifth birthday, although their bedtime inevitably will. They tend to be extra tired for a while when they've started school, and inclined to snuggle up and drop off without argument. But as they grow up, they'll start to be livelier come the evening, and will naturally want to push their bedtime back. The other factor is that they stop waking up so early in the mornings. It's bliss when you realise you need to start setting an actual alarm clock because your little human one has ceased answering that job description, but the flipside is that you're likely to have their company for longer at night, instead.

Pre-bedtime routines will also change as they grow up, but it's still a good idea to stick to them, and that hour beforehand should remain 'quiet' time, devoted to gentle playing, reading or some appropriate TV. Computer games aren't a great choice, because they leave the mind buzzing for a while.

Once you've negotiated a later bedtime, stick with it just as you would with a two-year-old. If you're happy for them to read in bed or play quietly in their rooms beforehand, or for them to take responsibility for turning their own lights out, keep an eye on them to make sure they're not overdoing it. (And if they have a television in their room, be particularly vigilant.) If they stay up late for a special occasion or because life's more relaxed on weekend nights, make sure they know it's back to business as usual next day.

Older or younger siblings can complicate things – having separate bedtimes may not be easy to enforce, but it's only fair and democratic. And older ones have to understand that smaller ones need peace and quiet if they're to settle.

If there's one element of those early bedtime rituals that's worth clinging on to as they grow, it's the goodnight cuddle or kiss. Over time they'll drop their warm milk, and stop asking you to read to them. But until the day they leave home, they still need to feel loved as their head hits the pillow.

What the experts say

The child psychologist

Getting bedtime routines up and running from an early age is certainly key to good bedtimes. They allow the child, over time, to learn their own body signals about tiredness and they will have a good idea of what to do about it.

I think if the family are happy to spend the evenings together then that's fine, as long as the children are getting enough sleep. Although sometimes it becomes easier to have the children around rather than have to think of something to talk to your partner about, so just be careful if you think that you're slipping into this routine! And keep an eye on how the child seems as a consequence; for example, are they struggling to get up in the morning, always yawning, their schoolwork going downhill? If so, it may be a good idea to establish an earlier bedtime and a routine leading up to it. You can always relax it during the weekend.

Routines are just as important for older children and bedtimes can be modified through discussion with the child themselves. In fact, it's a great area for practising negotiation skills, and giving the child a sense of having some control over the rules. With younger siblings, it just has to be agreed that their bedtime is earlier because they need more sleep. Sticker charts are a good way of offering an incentive if you meet with any resistance.

Dr Angharad Rudkin

The sleep therapist

A bedtime routine is fundamental to healthy sleep habits throughout life, not just childhood. It makes settling easier because it introduces the expectation that sleep is approaching, provides familiarity and security, and sets boundaries. A routine also helps ensure they go to bed at the right time and get the amount of sleep they need. Children with routines can usually self-settle very quickly. And routines are just as important, perhaps more so, for older children, because that's when they will start to push the boundaries.

If you have a child that's getting out of bed after being settled the first thing to check is whether you've got the routine right, and a consistent bedtime. Are they either overtired or not tired enough? Are you sure you're not rewarding their behaviour? How are you responding when they get out of bed – do you let them sit with you for a bit, pick them up, cuddle them, or talk to them? You have to lead them or send them back to bed quickly and without intervention – this is known as 'rapid return'. Stay firm, but don't get angry, because it doesn't work. Say 'no, we're going back to bed'. You may need to do it several times. Of course, it's not always as simple as that. If it's still not working you'll have to look at using a technique to help them settle. Controlled crying (and we prefer to call it 'controlled checking') and gradual retreat (which is the method we favour most) are the two best known. You do have to get these techniques right though, so if you're going to try them, you need to research the subject very thoroughly, and be prepared to commit to them totally.

When it comes to laid-back attitudes to bedtimes, you have to use your judgement. Kids do need less sleep to function well as they get older, and different children, just like adults need different amounts of sleep. So you just have to weigh up what yours need: it'll be obvious if they're not coping because they're tired. And if they *are* obviously tired because they're going to bed too late, then you'd have to ask, is this being fair? If a child has consistently late nights and they can't make up that sleep debt, they're potentially sleep deprived.

Mandy Gurney, Millpond Sleep Clinic, www.mill-pond.co.uk

The Problem Summarised

◆ Children need lots of sleep. A sensible, consistent bedtime will help them to get it.
◆ An unchanging bedtime routine encourages them to settle happily – and sleep through.
◆ Be aware of the 'sleep associations' you establish: some are good, some are not so good.
◆ If you want to get a child back to bed, be firm, calm and consistent.
◆ More complex sleep training methods can be effective (but need careful research).
◆ Older children want, and need, later bedtimes, so be flexible.
◆ If you prefer to let it all hang out at bedtime, make sure they're getting enough sleep.

Factfile: Gradual Retreat

Gradual retreat is one of the most popular sleep techniques. It's gentle, so there's no distress involved as with controlled crying, but it's effective. It takes a little while for it to work – up to a month – and a huge amount of patience and commitment on your part.

When you put the child to bed, or back to bed, sit on a chair by their side. It's vital not to engage in conversation or interaction of any kind: stay as quiet as you can and if they need comforting, do so quickly and silently. After a couple of nights, move your chair back a few feet, and again, you are quiet and unresponsive if they try to engage you. Every few nights, move your chair back a few feet until, in theory, you can place it outside the room altogether and they can go off to sleep without you in the room at all. They know you're there, but they don't need your attention. Eventually, they don't need your presence, either.

You can use the technique if they're not settling at bedtime and equally, if they are waking in the night, although obviously it's harder to do when you've been woken yourself. That's when you have to remind yourself that the effort you make now will pay dividends in the future.

Midnight mayhem: How to get them back to sleep when they wake in the night

The Problem

Neither of my daughters has ever been a good sleeper. Carly still occasionally wakes in the night and I find her on the floor next to my bed wrapped in her quilt. Until recently Paige used to wake every night, just for reassurance. She still does sometimes but has been sleeping a lot better since starting school full-time. I've never ever used controlled crying. I'm not against it, I just know that I couldn't leave one of my babies crying. I'd prefer to go and settle them quickly.

Michelle from Stevenage, mum to Carly, eight and Paige, five

Waking up is hard to do

The majority of children sleep solidly through the night by the time they are toddling. However, a significant number of kids still wake up for one reason or another – an estimated 20 per cent of two year olds, and five per cent of eight year olds.

To a certain extent, parents who are used to being woken find they adapt to the disruption. But we all need a good night's sleep if we're to function normally the next day. There's not a parent out there who won't have suffered from sleep deprivation at some point and it's a *nightmare*. At best, broken nights make you tired and irritable. At worst, they affect your relationships, your working life and your sanity.

Sleep cycles and bad habits

The key to a whole night's sleep is your child's ability to settle again by themselves once they've woken. If you've already put in the work on good bedtime habits and positive sleep associations, in theory you'll reap the benefits because if they wake in the night, they are far more likely to re-settle without help from you.

Sleep is made up of different stages of deep sleep and light sleep, which occur in several cycles throughout the night. Most people wake up during periods of light sleep, but immediately turn over and go back to sleep: babies and many small children are less likely to, because once they're awake they may realise there's something else they'd quite like, be it refreshment, or a little bit of company. Then, when they've got whatever it is they want, they'll try it on the next night, and again the next – the result is a habit that's hard to break. But we all reach a point when we're no longer up for providing 24-hour room service, and you have to make sure they know it isn't available.

Fortunately, it's amazing how well they can settle into good sleep habits once the bad ones have been broken.

The Problem Shared

What the Netmums say

By morning, both girls are in bed with me and my husband is in my eldest daughter's bed. This usually happens any time after midnight. My husband sometime gets fed up with having to change beds but we both work, and at least we get some sleep this way.

I don't like the thought of controlled crying and if my girls feel safer in my bed and sleep better that's all that matters to me, and I think

my husband has just got used to it now. They'll grow out of it in their own time, but until then, if they're happy, I'm happy.
Joanne from Dagenham, mum to Megan, six and Isabel, two

My eldest son slept through the night from 12 weeks onwards and even now, aged almost eight, he can be relied upon to never wake up before morning. My second was brought up exactly the same way yet he was the world's worst sleeper. At first it was eczema keeping him awake from three months, then he was lonely, I think. We ended up with him in bed with us and at times I was in the depths of despair. But I knew that I'd done the same for both boys so how could it be anything I'd done? I think it's down to personality. Leon is a very loving and intense sort of child. I think he needed to be with me, even though it drove me nuts! He sleeps well now. Looking back I wished someone had just said to me, this is the way it's going to be, it's just for a short time. It would have saved a lot of heartache.
Julie from Southend, mum to Jude, eight, Leon, five and Madeleine, two

In my opinion controlled crying is cruel. The littlest member of the family put in a dark room and left to cry, sob and often scream? It may work for some, but not my family. I tried it once and it was just heartbreaking. Tyeran still comes into our room at around 4 a.m. most days and that's fine with us. We co-slept with all our children for at least the first year and then at one they went into a bed in their own room, my husband or I went to sleep with them, then either left or stayed with them all night.
Andrea from Derby, mum to Emily, nine, Lucy, eight, Korben, six and Tyeran, four

Conner shared our room until he was two, so getting him to stay in his own bed through the night was a battle. Now he's in his own room with a stairgate on the door, and he wakes maybe once in the night, sometimes not at all. When he does wake we just go in, tell him it's still bedtime and walk out. This usually works straight away, but if it doesn't, we just keep repeating it until it does.
Tracy from Watford, mum to Conner, two

Rebecca still wakes up at least twice every night, usually once for the toilet (because she won't go by herself) and the rest of the time for no particular reason. It does grind you down by the fourth or fifth time. Dan was the same until he was about seven, so I'm into my 12th year of broken sleep. I can't remember what a full night's sleep is like.

Allison from Cramlington, mum to Rebecca, nine and Dan, 12

The Problem Solved

Excuses, excuses

Sometimes kids wake up with a perfectly genuine need that you have to attend to. But more often than not, night waking is a habit, or a bid for attention, and there's no reason for you to be dragged from your warm bed in the small hours.

Some little ones persist with a demand for milk in the night – it may have become their sleep association and that's what they need to resettle. But after 18 months they're long past actually needing it and unless you enjoy creeping down to a cold, dark kitchen to get them their dairy fix, it shouldn't be encouraged. Whether you drop it suddenly and go 'cold turkey', or attempt to wean them off gradually by cutting the amount down gradually, they'll almost certainly object and you'll probably have to employ a sleep technique, too. If it's thirst that's bothering them, you could let them take a small non-spill beaker or cup of water to bed with them – although once they're out of nappies at night, you may need to avoid that if they're to get through the night without a wee. If they do wake needing the loo, and have got to grips with the potty or toilet, encourage them to go without disturbing you. Leave the landing light on if it helps, and praise or reward them when they're successful. You can help them get through without the need for a toilet trip by making sure they've emptied their bladders last thing, and keeping pre-bedtime drinks to a minimum.

Don't give in to demands for a midnight snack. If they've had a decent supper, they should be more than capable of surviving until breakfast!

Frights in the night

A child who is scared has a legitimate reason for waking his parents up, and fears of the dark or monsters in the closet are normal. A nightlight or the presence of a familiar toy or comfort object can ease their worries. Indulge them if they need a piece of furniture moving because of the shadows it's casting, or their wardrobe doors shut in case the monster jumps out. If they've seen something scary on television that day, be sure to discuss it well before bedtime: if it wasn't real, make sure they understand that.

Nightmares are a perfectly common part of childhood. They aren't necessarily caused by something stressful or worrying, but it's worth talking them through with your child – particularly if they're recurring – to make sure something isn't playing on their mind. If you do suspect anxiety on their part, don't attempt to have a conversation about it just before bedtime.

Night terrors are different. They tend to affect boys more than girls, are most common between the ages of two and six, and often run in families. They occur in deep sleep, usually during the first part of the night. Though the child's eyes may be open and he seems to be awake, he won't be. A child having a night terror will look frightened or distressed – he may thrash around or shout out – but in fact, they know nothing about it and won't recall it in the morning. The only person they're scary for is the adult who witnesses it. Don't try to wake a child who's having a night terror. Just talk soothingly to them and stay with them until they're back in a normal sleep zone again.

The causes of night terrors aren't entirely understood. However, it's believed that factors such as stress or overtiredness may make a child more *receptive* to night terrors occurring, so it's worth ensuring that any underlying anxieties are ironed out, and a calm, early, consistent bedtime routine is in place for children who are affected. If they're having very regular night terrors at the same time each evening, you can break the pattern by watching out for signs that they're becoming agitated and waking them before the night terror kicks in. Otherwise, it's not something that should cause too much worry and there's no medical treatment. Although they sometimes occur in adulthood, in most cases, children will grow out of them.

Remember, the ideal is for a child to feel happy and safe on their own, in their own bed, so unless they're really traumatised, try not to stay with them until they've dropped off: they might wake later and panic that you're not there, then cry out or come to find you again.

Getting tough

So, you've established that your little night owl has no good reason to be hooting. Don't jump up to attend to her: give her a while and she may just settle herself. If she comes into your room or downstairs, lead her back to bed, firmly, quickly, and without stopping to chat. Repeat as many times as necessary – it may go on for some time.

Persistent problems will need to be tackled with a technique such as controlled crying, gradual withdrawal or door-shutting (see pp. 29–30 for more information on these techniques).

Crowd scene

Virtually all parents give in and allow their child into bed with them in the middle of the night, at one time or another. Sometimes, when everyone is exhausted, or if the child is ill or inconsolable, or none of the usual methods of getting them back to sleep are working, it's the only option when you're desperate for some sleep (assuming, that is, you *can* sleep with a small wriggling human close by). If you don't want it to become a habit, you have to make it clear that it's a one-off.

For some parents, co-sleeping with toddlers or even older children is a deliberate habit. If it's your choice, and if it genuinely suits *all* parties, it can be a happy arrangement. The biggest risk is that you'll struggle to turf them out when you decide it's time to reclaim your bed. And also, your sex life may suffer. But equally there are many for whom bed sharing doesn't appeal, or for whom it's already become an unwelcome habit. If your child comes into your room at night, you need to find the willpower to drag yourself from under the duvet, take them gently by the hand, and lead them back to their own beds. If they're genuinely disturbed or scared about something, stay with them for a while.

If they're seeking sanctuary in your bed for no other reason than that they like it in there, you have to be firm, take them back, tuck them in, and leave either silently, or with a few firm, quiet words: 'This is Lily's bed. Night night.' Be prepared to do that again, and again, until the habit is broken. Give in once, and you're back to square one. If they persist, it's time for a 'technique'.

Medicinal measures

Some medicines with mild sedative properties are available over the counter and can be useful as a short-term measure, over a couple of nights, when all else has failed and everyone needs to get a good night's sleep for their own well-being. But they're not advisable, or even particularly helpful, for long-term use. If you've got a major sleep problem, you need to change it permanently.

Getting help

Sometimes, bad sleep habits are so ingrained that a solution seems out of reach. When it gets to that point, it may be time to call in the professionals. A doctor or health visitor will refer you – or you can refer yourself – to an NHS or private sleep clinic, which offer guidance and help in teaching babies and young children to sleep, with ongoing monitoring and support.

What the experts say
The mums' life coach

This is an incredibly painful subject. A child who won't sleep can push the whole family to their physical and mental limits. There's no fatigue quite like that numb-from-the-neck-up, living-dead exhaustion that comes from struggling with a sleepless child. It can reduce an otherwise sane, happy person to a wild-eyed, irrational shadow of her former self.

Rule number one is to ignore all those people who cheerfully inform you that their child slept through the night from two weeks. It may be true (though I do think a bit of selective memory is often involved in this kind of boast) but it's not helpful. As many parents have found, the solution isn't always obvious. What works like a dream – no pun intended – with one child may be completely ineffectual with another. It's essential to find a way that sits comfortably with your own values. Perhaps you feel strongly that your child needs to be able to make it through the night alone, however tough a process it may be to get them there. If so, you may well find a well-established method such as controlled crying can work for you. Maybe you're keen on maintaining a lot of contact with them and don't believe in letting him cry; for you an intuitive approach will feel more appropriate than one based on firm theories. If you try to adopt a method that goes against what feels right, you can be sure that your misery and discomfort will rub off on your child and everyone around you. Whatever you decide to do, it's worth doing it consistently. Experience shows that babies and children respond well to consistency and predictability; so experimenting with a particular sleep theory one night and a different one the next will only confuse your child.

Be prepared for your children altering their patterns without warning. Some seem to operate in cycles, and many change without any apparent reason. And if all else fails, remember that one day you'll be dragging them out of bed to have their lunch. Sleepless nights can be gruelling and seem to go on for ever, but they do eventually come to an end.

Patricia Carswell

The sleep therapist

Whatever your child associates with going to bed at bedtime, they will have to re-create in the night when they wake. Children that settle on the sofa or in mummy's bed or with mummy lying down beside them will have to wake you to re-create that, so if you want them to sleep in their own bed through the night, make sure that's where you put them at bedtime.

When a child cries or demands your attention in the night, and you know that he is not unwell or scared, don't jump out of bed immediately. It's OK to ignore it for 10 to 15 minutes, and you might just knock it on the head very quickly. Of course, if it doesn't resolve itself, then you need to look at a sleep technique.

When it comes to bed sharing, it's a case of each to his own. If parents want to do it, they have to understand the implications: if a child has never learned to sleep by himself, at some point, when you want them to, you might come across problems.

For older children, you can use rewarding systems for positive behaviour. But the goals have to be achievable and realistic, you can only work on small changes at once – if you're in the middle of a gradual retreat programme, you might offer them a reward if they manage to stay put while you're sitting by their side, and then again the following night, when you've moved a foot away. One thing that works well is to introduce the 'sleep fairy', who brings rewards for children who don't get out of bed or disturb their parents at night. It doesn't even have to be a big reward – sometimes it can just be 'fairy dust' left in a box in your room (they may be frightened by it if you leave it in their room), which they find fascinating.

Overcoming a sleep problem is hard work, and it requires patience and commitment. When you're tired, the temptation is to think in the short-term. But with sleep problems, you have to think ahead. Ask yourself, do I really want to be doing this in six months' time?

Mandy Gurney, Millpond Sleep Clinic (www.mill-pond.co.uk)

The Problem Summarised

◆ Sleep deprivation causes serious problems. But it's not something you have to live with. There are solutions.
◆ It's not uncommon for kids to wake in the night, well beyond the age of two.
◆ Children who wake may have a good reason. You need to rule these out first.
◆ Bed sharing's fine. But it's a hard habit to break!
◆ Read up on the subject if you're tackling a major sleep problem. You'll find some recommended further reading on p. 388.

One for me, one for you: How to help them to share with others

The Problem

We were at a breastfeeding support group recently. Mark had taken his helicopter, as there aren't many toys there, and another little boy picked it up and began playing with it. Mark started to complain, but I just told him he had to share. Then the boy's mum insisted he give it back. I told her it was fine, and that Mark had to learn, but she still told her son to give it back. I *wanted* him to share it, but this boy's mum wouldn't let him! What are you supposed to do in a situation like that?

Claire from Shaftesbury, mum to Mark, two and Sarah, six months

Start sharing young

It goes without saying that sharing is an important skill: in adulthood, we need to do it all the time. If it seems to you that your little one is terrible at sharing, don't worry: little ones *are* terrible at sharing. Like so many things, sharing is a social skill which doesn't come naturally to them, and needs to be taught.

There's no harm in starting to pass on the message about sharing as soon as they're old enough to snatch a toy or split a bag of chocolate buttons. But don't be surprised if it doesn't sink in straight away. As a concept, it may take them a while to get the hang of it!

Some things aren't for sharing

Of course, some possessions are sacrosanct to a child and you cannot expect them to share them: a little one may not wish to hand over his precious cuddly toy to a green-eyed pal, and an older child won't want their clumsy younger sibling to get their mitts on something fragile or valuable.

Learning to respect other people's possessions is an equally useful lesson for life.

The Problem Shared

What the Netmums say

Children have a very narrow outlook on their little lives – everything around them is theirs. They really cannot share until they get older, although you can help them. I'm a teacher and the little ones in the reception class don't know how to share, it's something you have to teach them.

When I take Kristian to mum and toddler groups I keep a close eye on him. If he has something and someone takes it off him, I ignore it, unless it's done in a nasty way. If he takes something I always give it back. It is not as if they really want the particular toy, it's just that they see everything as belonging to them.

Penny from Newport, mum to Kristian, two, Jessica, 15, Amy, 17 and Craig, 26

If my daughter wants something someone already has, I always try to direct her to another toy that's similar. If she has something and another child wants it, if it can be shared I try to sit among them and help them take turns. However, if she has something that can't be shared and another child tries to take it off her, I try to intercede and say that *she's* playing with this at the moment, and then suggest they play with another toy. I started doing this when Kerala seemed to be constantly having toys taken from her and none of the other mums were stopping their children from doing it. She'd started to hate going to mother and toddler group, and who could blame her? I don't let her take her own toys to groups like that because they are hers, and I feel she has to be prepared to share in that sort of situation.

Deborah from Enfield, mum to Kerala, two and Chase, four months

Grace knows she has to share. I've encouraged her to look at her toys before her friends arrive to play and we talk about what they might play with. If there's something she's not keen to share, then we put it out of the way. When she's at other people's houses, she expects them to share with her, which can prove difficult. I always talk to her and the other child, reminding them that it belongs to them and that Grace will just play with it and give it back. I think at times, for children that aren't used to sharing, it's difficult for them to understand that their belongings aren't going to be taken away. If I say, 'You can play with it when Grace has finished,' I make sure that she gives it back after a few minutes.

Louise from Newcastle Under Lyme, mum to Grace, four

As with everything in life, sharing is a learning curve from the minute they're born. When it comes to possessions, it's still an uphill struggle with all three children, especially if they want the same thing at the same time. Fortunately there isn't a lot of bickering in our house as things are often resolved quickly – they've learned between them how to resolve things and I'm constantly surprised how willingly they'll share things like sweets with each other.

Frances from Halifax, mum to Sophie, seven, Emily, two and Jacob, one

Whenever mine took a toy from another child I gave it back, and when they wanted a toy someone else had, I tried to let them sort it out themselves. I've also turned the tables on them: if they grabbed something I would take something of theirs. They're pretty good now, but maybe it's easier when you have siblings. I imagine only children find it harder.

Jane from the Wirral, mum to Jake, six, Libby, five and Emma, three

I set out from the start to 'model' sharing which I think is something a lot of mums do, whether consciously or not. We share our food with them. I let them 'share' my special things (jewellery, creams, lipsticks), and ask them to share theirs. We also talk about how nice it is to share and how we all have a nicer time if we do. The issue was tested when my youngest was finding her independence and was grabbing her older sister's toys. We had a rule where their special bedtime toys were theirs and theirs alone, and the rest were to share. I intervened with disputes and helped them (or at times *made* them) share and they soon seemed to learn. When they had friends to play I used to ask them which toys they wanted to put away (only one or two special things) and which they would choose to get out in the lounge to share. This seemed to work well as it settled any disputes before they arose. I didn't even have to do this for long before they did it themselves and now they're older it isn't really an issue at all.

Nicola from Edinburgh, mum to Hannah, six and Feena, three

The Problem Solved

Divide and conquer

It's easier to teach little ones about sharing when there's more than one thing to share. So practise sharing with a boxful of crayons, a bucket of bricks, or a plateful of chopped fruit (sweets may be more of a challenge!). Ask them to help you divide it equally. Point out that sharing reaps rewards: perhaps if they share their things, their sibling/friend will share their stuff later on. And praise them lavishly when they've been generous. Talk about how nice it feels to have made someone else happy by sharing.

Time shares

Single objects are trickier. If you take something away from a child to give to another, they may assume you're taking it from them permanently, hence their reluctance to let go.

Make it very clear the other child wants a short play, and then they'll return it. Give them a time slot and let both children know that's how long it will be – if you have an alarm on your watch or even a timer knocking around, that can help. Meanwhile, you could ask your child to help find another exciting plaything for his friend to have once his turn is up – encourage him to see it as a win/win situation, rather than a win/lose situation that he's just lost! Giving him responsibility will make him feel he has some control over the situation. It'll also distract him from the fact that his best mate has just walked off with his spaceship.

Non-negotiable items

When a possession is precious, agree upfront that it doesn't have to be shared. You may want to have a rule that it can't be flaunted, or you may decide that whoever wants it and can't have it has to accept that, in which case, you need to have something equally desirable on hand to offer as a distraction. Bear in mind that nothing is quite as desirable as an object they can't have – if it's about to cause a fight, you may have no choice but to put it away altogether.

If you've visitors, ask your child in advance if there's anything they don't want to share and allow them to hide it, making it clear that everything else is available for all. But set a limit – if they want to put away 85 per cent of their toys, it won't be much of a play date.

Share and share alike

As with all those other important social skills, you can best lead the way by example. Use the word 'share' whenever you can and demonstrate how easy it is to do: offer them half of *your* biscuit, rather than giving them one for themselves (healthier, too, for both of you!); and allow them to play with *your* possessions sometimes. (Although, obviously there are limits here –

you may not want them having a picnic with your heirloom china, or making magic potions from your expensive moisturiser, and that's fair enough.)

It can be harder for only children to learn about sharing because they don't have to do it so much. If you have just the one child, you may need to be extra-enthusiastic when it comes to modelling sharing, and give them lots of opportunities to practise it.

What the experts say

The child psychologist

Sharing is an essential skill to develop, as it's one of the main tools for successful relationships as a child and as an adult. It also involves compromise, which is another important skill.

Young children find sharing hard because they don't actually have the mental capacity to put themselves in another person's shoes. For example, if they're playing with a toy and another child comes up and takes it, they're not able to think, 'Oh well, maybe I've been playing with it for too long and it's their turn to play with it now.' This sort of thought process requires a 'theory of mind' that children don't tend to get until a bit later, aged around eight (although they often seem to lose it a bit in adolescence again!). Instead they think: 'Oi, I was playing with that and enjoying myself. Get off!' What's important is that at this point, whenever it seems appropriate, adults intervene with some teaching, for example, telling them that the other child was not trying to be mean, it's just that they wanted a turn, and letting children know that it's a good thing to share and that this will be rewarded. If they're having none of it, let them know there may be consequences if they don't choose to share – they'll have to leave playgroup, for example, because no one will be that keen to play with them. If they make the 'right' choice, you give them a big hug, and praise them for it. If not, you need to follow up on those consequences. Having an opportunity to talk about it later on is useful to help it all sink in.

As children get older, you'd expect them to have learned this lesson and be applying it the majority of the time. If an older child is reluctant to share, it may be that they were never taught how to, or when they do share it hasn't been noticed or rewarded, or they don't have much chance to practise it, for example if they're an only child. As with younger kids, it's a question then of intervening, teaching and rewarding when it happens. Let's face it, none of us like to share certain things, but if we learn that this is a good thing to do and people will think we're nice for doing, then there may be more motivation.

Of course, it's not essential that everything is shared. It's important for a child to grow up learning that there are some things that belong to someone else and that are very precious and are not expected to be shared. These boundaries should be enforced in families just like other rules. If the thing in question is something like a family computer, then rotas can be drawn up to help.

Dr Angharad Rudkin

The mums' life coach

It can be so frustrating watching your otherwise sweet-natured child clutching furiously on to his toys, or snatching them from another child with That Look on his face. What you have to remember is that a small child's world really does revolve entirely around him – and it's not his fault. It takes years for children to see the world through other people's eyes, and for some it comes more naturally than others. Think about the context in which you talk about sharing. If it's only ever mentioned when you're asking your child to part with a beloved toy, it's not going to have good associations. Some mums introduce the idea over a less contentious issue. 'Would you like to share your broccoli with Teddy?' might be greeted with more enthusiasm than, 'You've got to share your new truck with that boy you don't really like.' If sharing is a regular and agreeable habit, it'll be less shocking when your child is asked to share something precious like a toy or a biscuit.

There will be times when it might not be reasonable to expect your child to share. The toy in question might be fragile and the child wanting to borrow it might be rough, or perhaps the other child is being domineering and making unfair demands. This can be delicate

if the other child's mother doesn't see the problem, but it can be a chance to teach your child some invaluable skills involving negotiation and compromise.
Patricia Carswell

The Problem Summarised

- Little ones can't share. They don't know how! But they can be taught.
- Some possessions are precious, and they shouldn't have to share them.
- It's much easier to teach sharing when there are lots of things to share.
- Failing that, have something else to hand as a distraction.
- Model sharing. Show them how it's done, by doing it all the time.

Fighting talk: How to rein in aggression

The Problem

Until recently, Rosie took great delight in slapping her dad or me if she didn't want to do something. I would take her to the naughty step and explain that what she was doing hurt and that she needed to think about what she had done and stay on the step until she was sorry. Often she wouldn't stay and I ended up (after several attempts) threatening to take her to her bedroom or shutting the door on her, at which point she would usually say sorry. My husband is not as patient. He tended to shout and this would escalate the situation. It's been a long hard slog to get through and I don't think how we dealt with it has had much to do with it stopping, it's just run its course.

Melanie from Derby, mum to Rosie, three

Small, but scary

When your child is aggressive, either in a one-off situation or during a prolonged phase, it's easy to assume that your parenting skills must be at fault. Research suggests that it's the number one concern for up to a third of parents, so if it's a worry for you, you're not alone. But the truth is, aggression is normal, and it certainly isn't necessarily a result of bad parenting.

Young children behave aggressively because they haven't yet learned they mustn't. It's a natural outlet for frustration if they can't get what they want, be it your attention, or a particular toy they've got their eye on. And as with sharing, they have to be taught that aggression is socially unacceptable.

Older and wiser?

By the time they've been at school for a couple of years, children should be more or less in control of their impulses, so if they're still prone to violent outbursts, or if they develop such a tendency, it may be an indication that they're insecure about something else in life. Occasionally, repeated violent behaviour is linked to disorders such as Attention Deficit Hyperactivity Disorder (ADHD). There's more on this in the factfile on p. 79.

Boys will be boys

It's a fact of life that boys tend to be more aggressive than girls, although it's not clear whether that's due to nature (the male hormone testosterone may play a part) or nurture (adults are more likely to encourage or reinforce rough behaviour in boys as they assume it's 'normal'). Parents of boys may have to accept they have a harder task on their hands when it comes to dealing with this particular problem.

The Problem Shared

What the Netmums say

My daughter went through quite a bad, pushing stage soon after her brother was born (I don't know if it was because of that). She would run up to other children for no reason and push them over, repeatedly, and it got very embarrassing. I reacted by getting hold of her and firmly telling her that it was not acceptable behaviour and always made her apologise, but it didn't seem to make much difference. We made a sticker chart with a few rules, and every hour she was good she got a sticker. At the end of the day if she had mostly stickers she got a treat – not a present, just a nice activity like painting or baking. That seemed to make quite a difference. I think the main thing though was following through on threats. If she was pushing at other toddlers I would tell her she had one more chance and we were leaving and then if it happened again we left. I think you have to carry out what you've said you will. It seems to have passed now, apart from the occasional scuffle, but I'm not sure if it was just a phase or if the things I did really helped!

Heather from Fife, mum to Rachel, three and James, one

My eldest boy is quite placid and has often been at the end of aggressive behaviour when playing with friends. At first he used to cry, but never really hit back unless forcibly pushed. We've always encouraged him to assertively tell the other child that he doesn't like their behaviour and to just walk away and ignore them. Situations like this soon resolve themselves. Of course he's no angel but he has shown himself to be confident when aggressive situations arise, possibly because he's been able to talk and express himself from an early age.

At the other extreme, his younger brother has turned out to be a perpetrator of pushing and hitting. We've found this harder to handle and have had to use consistent discipline of time-out and separation from his brother. Interestingly, his language skills have taken longer to develop. Also, the pushing and hitting often happens when he's hungry or needs a nappy change, so we try and stay one step ahead.

Shauna from Marlborough, mum to Callum, five and Oliver, two

We had a really bad time with my youngest son, who was born 13 weeks early. He would bite, headbutt the wall, kick, and pinch. We were so worried he was going to injure himself, his brother or someone else. We didn't know why he was doing it or what we could do to stop it. If he ever did anything that was hurting himself or anybody else we'd pick him up and hold him, he would then pinch, scratch or kick us – my husband and I sometimes ended up with scratched faces and cut lips.

He was diagnosed with speech delay and hearing problems as a result of being premature, and since that happened and he's been getting help with his speech, he's a different person as he can now communicate what he wants, whereas before he could only point at what he wanted or grunt and nobody knew what it meant. We still get the occasional outburst but he's now a typical toddler and it's over just as quick as it started. He's stopped harming himself by headbutting the wall, his brother is no longer scared to stand up to him, and I will gladly take him to play with other children.

Amanda from Manchester, mum to Benjamin, five and Joseph, three

Daniel hasn't been aggressive in a nasty way, but he is very boisterous with other boys. Personally I think it's a way of expressing feelings they don't understand or even just their way of saying: 'Hello it's really nice to see you'. If it gets too much I pull him off. It's definitely slowed down over the last couple of months, as he's started to understand more of his feelings.

Elizabeth, from Watford, mum to Daniel, five

The Problem Solved

Keep calm!

It can be very hard to keep your cool when dealing with an aggressive child. But doing just that is key: if you erupt too, it's just reinforcing their belief that it's reasonable behaviour. Using physical force on kids is a bad idea at the best of times, but in response to aggression, it makes no sense at all.

Dealing with aggression: a step-by-step guide

1. When a little one lashes out with kicks, pinches, slaps, bites or pushes, react as swiftly as you can by getting down to their eye level, taking hold of their hands and issuing a quiet, but firm 'no' or 'calm down'. Repeating the words can have a calming effect.
2. Explain why their actions are wrong.
3. Appeal to their sense of empathy by pointing out that they've hurt their victim, and asking how they would feel if it was them. Ask them to apologise, but until they're old enough to mean it, don't insist on a 'sorry' for the sake of it. It's probably more important that they understand that what they did was unacceptable than try to make amends for it.

Diversion and dispersion

Keep an eye out for aggression triggers (hunger, tiredness and boredom are probably the top three), and act in advance if you feel a violent outburst coming. It's that old distraction ploy coming into its own again!

Plenty of fresh air and lots of exercise can help offer an outlet for aggression, and regular bouts of well-controlled rough-and-tumble play may be useful.

Appropriate ways of dealing with aggression

When you're dealing with an aggressive child, bear in mind that there may be good reasons for their behaviour – don't be quick to dish out severe punishments until you've made sure that there are no deep-seated motives for their actions.

Issuing 'time out' is probably the most appropriate response as it gives everyone involved a chance to cool down. There's more on this in the fact-file below. Explain clearly why their behaviour's wrong – even if they are old enough to know perfectly well for themselves. Help them to understand why they must say sorry, if you are keen for them to do so – an apology is of limited use if they don't actually mean it.

At times like this, you might want to help them call on their 'emotional literacy' skills, or set about overseeing some 'restorative justice'. These approaches are being used increasingly in schools to help children deal with difficult feelings such as anger and resentment, and situations involving conflict. There's more information in the factfile on p. 121.

The influence of television and computer games is a complicated and controversial issue. But research certainly suggests that the violent sort can provide a negative example for children, so be vigilant about what's on their screens. There's more about it on p. 287.

Lead the way

Almost inevitably, a child who grows up in an environment where aggression is the norm will go on to repeat that sort of behaviour. Use every opportunity to encourage and reward gentle and loving behaviour, and do your best to react gently yourself when dealing with a frustrating situation.

If rough justice and raised voices are routinely bandied around in your home, you can't really expect anything better from your children.

What the experts say

The child psychologist

Children do need to be taught that it is wrong to hit, shout and threaten and that there are negative consequences. It's perfectly normal in younger ones, but if older children are still being aggressive it could be because they have difficulty expressing themselves verbally and communicate how they are feeling by their behaviour. It may be that there are adults modelling aggressive behaviour in the family so the child is learning that shouting and throwing things is an acceptable way of showing you're cross with someone. Or it might be that the child is troubled by something, for example bullying, or a split in the family, and is being overwhelmed by feelings which lead to outbursts. These can be prevented by encouraging them to articulate their feelings. Talking about stuff you've seen on television – when a character from a programme is going through a particular experience or feeling that they can identify with, for example – is one way of prompting such conversations.

If you've talked to the child, examined your own (and your partner's) way of dealing with anger, discussed the matter with their teacher and found nothing that might explain the aggressive outbursts, then it might be worthwhile asking your GP for a referral to your local Child and Adolescent Health Service, so they can be assessed for an underlying cause.

Dr Angharad Rudkin

The mums' life coach

If your child is being aggressive towards others, you may well experience very mixed feelings. You may be appalled at his behaviour and worry that it's the fault of your parenting. At the same time you may feel instinctively protective towards your child as you're aware that other people are angry and disapproving of him. You may even become defensive, wondering if the whole thing's being blown out of proportion. All of these feelings are perfectly natural, but it's important not to let your emotional reaction govern the way you handle the situation. Do your best to remain calm, and deal with it as you would any other issue that arises. Don't feel pressured to discipline your child in a way that feels wrong to you, just to placate others.

If it happens at school, it's usually wise to speak to the teacher and work out a strategy together for dealing with it. The teacher is more likely to be patient and give your child the benefit of the doubt if he or she feels supported by you. If another child is involved, you may find it helpful to speak to his parents, to avoid any misunderstandings.

If your child is the victim of another child's aggression, you'll probably be very upset, especially if he's in pain and has teeth marks or visible bruising. You may find yourself feeling angry towards the offending child and, quite possibly, his mother or whoever was in charge, either for letting it happen or for not responding strongly enough. However you decide to handle it, remember that you're setting an example to your child. If you want to teach him to be understanding and forgiving, then shouting and criticising – however tempting – may not be the best way to demonstrate it.

Patricia Carswell

The Problem Summarised

◆ It's normal for young kids to be aggressive but they need to be taught it's unacceptable.

◆ By the time they're about seven they should have aggressive impulses under control.

◆ Beyond that, aggressive behaviour may be a sign that something's bothering them.

◆ Encouraging them to articulate their feelings is all-important.

◆ Aim to respond to aggression calmly yourself.

Factfile: Time out

Most parents find this an effective consequence to issue when things go belly-up, not least because it literally removes an angry or frustrated child from a heated situation (and you from them), and allows them space and time to think their actions through. The idea is to take or send them to a particular place in the house and leave them alone there for a while. It needs to be somewhere they don't want to be, with no distractions available – their bedroom is probably not a good choice, as they may be more than happy to while away a few moments with their toys and books. Equally, don't shut them away somewhere that might actually be scary for them. Warn them what you're going to do, so they have a chance to opt out of the consequence by altering their behaviour. If you're going to do it, do it immediately. It won't mean anything later in the day and anyway, it's not particularly fair to suspend a punishment, even if it is tempting to shout: 'Wait 'til your father gets home!'

Once they're in time out, tell them clearly and calmly how long they must stay there. One theory is to leave them there for one minute for each year of their age: much more than that and you may be pushing your luck, so it's probably a fair rule to go by. It's not much use as a consequence for the under-threes, because at that stage they don't have a grasp of the concept, although it can still be a useful way of calming a situation down. Little ones shouldn't be shut in a room though, if it scares them. Better perhaps to stick to a 'naughty step' or another spot where they don't have to be too far away from you.

How do you make a child who's feeling defiant stay put? It's not always easy. You may have to be firm and very persistent about making them stay or ordering them back, but once you've introduced time out as a regular consequence and everyone understands how it works, they should start to accept it.

Once they've finished a period of time out, draw a line under the episode and move on. Some parents like to conclude it with a hug, to smooth things over. If it's worked, and they've calmed down, apologised or adjusted their behaviour accordingly, give praise where it's due.

Tall tales: What to do when a child tells lies

The Problem

James seems to know what lying is now. I've dealt with it by issuing time out, although that only worked for a while. I've now explained to him that if he lies, he will get punished for that, as well as whatever he did wrong in the first place. He seems to have got the message – he knows that if he's done something wrong and he's honest about it, it will mean one punishment rather than two! I've also told him the story of 'the boy who cried wolf', and that was helpful too.

Rebecca from Hemel Hempstead, mum to James, four

First, the good news

Guess what? Lying is yet *another* positive developmental phase and virtually all kids do it at some point or other. When children fib, it's a sign that their language is developing and they're learning to use their imaginations. Of course, that's not to say we should all start interpreting our kids' tendencies to tell porkies as creative genius. Lies – other than the white sort, usually employed to save someone's feelings – are not something that go down that well in the adult world.

Why do kids tell fibs?

There are different sorts of lying and different reasons for why children do it. In little ones, it can be down to genuine confusion between truth and fiction. Sometimes children lie by way of boasting or bragging – they talk about something as if it's real because they wish it was. And sometimes they lie for the heck of it, to test your reaction or earn your attention. But mostly, children lie to avoid getting into trouble. You can't really blame them, but you do need to point out it's wrong and teach them that honesty is the best policy. Doing so early on is probably sensible – children are rubbish at lying when they're little but they can grow startling adept at it, so if you learn to pick up on their fib-signals from the start you might find it easier to sniff them out later, when their lies are so convincing they might deservedly scoop a BAFTA for their performance.

The Problem Shared

What the Netmums say

Kami has just begun to learn about lying and how to do it. She seems to be a pro, as well! Thus far, it's only about little things. Sometimes I can be standing there and see her do whatever it was (say she throws something) and I say, 'Kami, did you just throw that book?' And she'll say: 'No, Mommy . . . it was Daddy!' I'll then tell her that I saw her do it, that I know what she said was a lie, and ask her if she'd like to answer the question again, because it hurts my feelings for her to lie to me. She usually says she was only kidding, then she'll go on to admit she *did* do it and say 'sorry' for lying.
Kearsten from Dudley, mum to Kami, three

I think the most common reason for lying is because they know they're about to be in trouble. What they don't always realise, and what I keep saying to my oldest son, is that lying just gets them into more trouble! I think they'll still try it if they can get away with it though.

Jemma from Carshalton, mum to Jack, eight and Alex, two

My youngest son tells 'fibs' sometimes. If I ask him something and I know that he's lying, I say: 'I know that you are not telling the truth and I'm going to ask you once more and hope that I get the real answer.' Then I give him my stern face. Usually this does the trick; if not then he gets 'time out' and I tell him that he's there because I know he told a fib, and he's invited to come back when he's ready to tell the truth. We watched *Chicken Little* [a Disney movie about a young chicken who creates panic in his home town when he wrongly claims that the sky is falling down, and is later met with disbelief when he announces, quite truthfully, that aliens have landed!] and I thought that that was a good example of what can happen if you tell fibs so we had a chat about it. He seemed to get the message!

Rebecca from Poole, mum to Jaymes, eight and Joshua, seven

My little one sometimes lies, more so since he started school. Mostly it's just small stuff, but on occasion it's been bigger stuff, to try to get him out of being in trouble for something he's done. I explained to him that I will be more angry and upset if he lies to me than if he tells me the truth – then he usually owns up. It doesn't work all the time, but seems to be helping generally.

Jacqui from Southend, mum to Joe, five

Keyah understands more about people's feelings now and will sometimes lie to spare them. For example her three-year-old cousin Kursharn drew a picture of a house, and Keyah told her it was great. Then she whispered to me that she'd told her that so she would feel glad, and in fact she thought it was rubbish! She'll also occasionally tell lies to make things sound more interesting. I tell her that there's no need to make things up and it's best to say what actually happened.

Paula from Kempston, mum to Keyah, six

Lying was a big problem for me with Carianne. She lied to get attention, as she's a twin and also because I've had a new baby. Inspired by the boy who cried 'wolf' story, I pretended not to believe her when she *was* telling the truth, and she got upset, so I explained that because she kept lying I would never believe what she would say. Harsh, I know, but it seems to have worked so far.

Amanda from Arnold, mum to Robbie, eight, twins Lewis and Carianne, five and Phoebe, six months

The Problem Solved

Liar, liar

If your child is clearly lying to avoid recriminations, the worst thing you can do is to let them know how cross you are about it. If they think they'll be in even more trouble when they've come clean, of course they're going to make up the wildest excuse they can, so try and keep your temper at bay. Avoid making accusations, and putting them in a position where they might lie in the first place: i.e. don't say 'Did *you* do this?' (especially if you know full well that they did). Avoid strong, emotive words like 'lie' or 'liar' if you can. Better to say: 'Please be honest with me,' than 'Don't lie to me!' As ever, praise them if they get it right, and admit to something they've previously denied.

Honesty pays

Technically, you should carry on regardless of the inevitable consequences of whatever it was they were lying about – if that's your intention, don't try and tempt the truth from them beforehand by promising you won't be cross or that you aren't going to punish them, or it'll just make a liar of you! Sometimes, if they've shown honesty, you might want to consider being lenient by way of reward. But you'd need to make it clear that's what you were doing – and it probably only works as an incentive to truthfulness if you drop it into the equation once in a while.

The language of truth

Talk up honesty, and when they do lie, discuss with them why it's not a good idea. Ask how they would feel, if someone lied to them. Fables of old and children's literature is riddled with assorted liars who almost always have to learn the error of their ways – for example, the Boy Who Cried Wolf, Pinocchio, and the eponymous child from Hilaire Belloc's very funny, and rather dark poem 'Matilda' (although given Matilda's gruesome end, probably not to be recommended for very young or sensitive children). When you're reading cautionary tales like that together, talk the issues through afterwards. It's a good way of helping them sink in.

Eat your carrots and you'll see in the dark

Be conscious of the fibs *you* tell, particularly to your children. Think about it – how often do you lie to get them to do something or to avoid the more truthful but complicated explanation? It works when they're very small, but eventually they'll get wise to it – and then it's *you* that's standing there with your pants on fire.

When fibs mean more

Most fibbing is basically harmless and needs no more attention than gentle dissuasion on your part. But if lying becomes a persistent habit, or if the lies they are telling are downright hurtful or offensive, then you'll need to issue more serious consequences – and look for an ulterior motive. Lying, like so many other forms of 'bad' behaviour, can be a smoke screen for more deep-rooted feelings. If something's troubling them, you need to find out what.

What the experts say

The child psychologist

Fibbing or 'white lies' are an essential oil for the cogs of social interaction. Without them we can find ourselves in a bit of social trouble, as seen in very small children or in children with Autistic Spectrum Disorder, who don't know how to lie and will tell you the truth, even if it's that you're fat, hairy or stupid! This kind of bluntness and honesty doesn't go down well with most people. So children learn from quite an early age to sometimes not tell the truth. And this is fine.

Lying does require an ability to understand what the other person is thinking, and so will tend to emerge around six to eight years. Before that, if a child is lying it may be that they genuinely can't differentiate between their fantasy world and the real world.

If a child is lying a great deal it may be that they are actually unhappy with their lot at that time, and are trying to avoid certain consequences or are trying to mould their life into the shape that they want. At these times, the most important thing is to try and work out why the child is lying, without being confrontational.
Angharad Rudkin

The mums' life coach

No one likes to be labelled a liar, and it's upsetting for any parent to think their child has been lying. But the truth is that most of us lie a little bit in adult life nearly every day. 'No, it was no trouble at all' (when you went out of your way to do a favour). 'No, it doesn't make your bum look big (when it's desperately unflattering). And we lie to our children, too. 'What a lovely picture – yes of course I can see what it is'! Or even, 'Let's put your tooth under the pillow and see if the tooth fairy brings you anything.'

What we have to do as parents is first of all work out where we draw the line ourselves. It's a personal thing – we all have different levels of comfort and morality. Think about your own feelings towards the difference between fantasy play and false stories, and between little white lies to save hurting people's feelings and, say, lies told to get out of trouble. It's only when you get this straight in your own mind that you can find a consistent approach to teach your children.

If your child does understand the difference between truth and falsehood and is still telling lies which go beyond what you feel comfortable with, ask why he's doing this. Is he scared of getting into trouble? Is he trying to impress someone? Is he escaping from reality by making up fantasies? Generally you'll find that there's a reason.
Patricia Carswell

The Problem Summarised

- It's not necessarily a bad thing when kids lie. In little ones, it's a positive developmental sign!
- Little ones tend to lie because they don't always understand the difference between truth and fantasy.
- More serious lying in older children may be an indication of a deeper rooted concern.
- Don't threaten trouble when they lie: it's unlikely to get you the truth
- Be honest yourself. If you tell lies, they'll soon suss you out!

Naughty, naughty: How to tackle disobedience and bad attitudes

The Problem

It must be an age thing as my eight year old is a nightmare. What really bothers me is that he's only like it at home. Sometimes he's like a demon possessed! I've tried ignoring his bad behaviour, taking away his favourite possessions, grounding him. Nothing seems to work. He can be a very well behaved boy for a few days and then he just erupts. When it's happening it really gets to me. I know I shouldn't, but at times I've been so angry I've thrown things around the room. I don't know why he's like this. I've tried to talk to him but he doesn't let me in.

Yvonne from Mauchline, mum to Lee, nine, Marc, three and Sean, six months

All kids are bad sometimes

At some point or other, your child will almost certainly cock their thumb to their nose and defy you altogether. Children move in and out of naughty phases according to their age and what's going on in their lives. But typically, there'll be regular displays of disobedience when they're very little (because they don't know any better); followed by a tendency towards compliance (when they're old enough to understand there'll be consequences other- wise); then a flip back to the dark side (when they're growing up and they want to test you). It's par for the course. Accept that, and you're halfway to dealing with it.

How *dare* you!

There are few things more infuriating than a person who is half your size and 30 years younger than you refusing to do as you bid them. If you've coped OK with tantrums, fussy eating, sleepless nights, lying, fighting and a stubborn refusal to share, chances are you'll come undone when they start defying you.

Irritating though disobedience can be, it's perfectly normal. You are not a failure if your child is naughty; in fact, they'd be weird if they didn't stick their heels in once in a while. Of course, that's not to say you shouldn't act on disobedience and bad attitudes when they rear their heads. Let it go, and things may get out of hand. Times may have changed, and so – thankfully – has the way we discipline our kids. Modern thinking is that our energies are better directed at being posi- tive about their good behaviour rather than negative about the bad. And that's quite right. But even in this liberal day and age, parents are still in charge, and can still reasonably demand respect for their authority from their children.

The Problem Shared

What the Netmums say

The only way to stop my daughter being naughty is to totally ignore her. And it's hard, as she will hold on for as long as is humanly possible! Walking out the room works best, as although you know what destruction is occurring it's better when you can't see it. And I always make her clear up/rectify anything that she has done. Then we'll play together, so she knows I love her.

Nicola from Berkshire, mum to Eloise, three and Sophie, one

We use the naughty step in this house. It works really well with Callum. It was a bit of a battle at first, but it works first time now. He's even been known to put himself there before I can tell him off!

Shelley from Bushey, mum to Callum, three

The only thing that I've found which doesn't require taking a hard line and usually works is time out. You put them somewhere where they don't like to be put and leave them to think about what they've done and how they are going to apologise. It usually works with my daughter. If I stay in the situation and try and talk to her I usually lose my patience then end up feeling guilty. Mums are prone to guilt, and time out is guilt-free.

Claire from Penge, mum to Miriam, two

We've tried everything with my eight year old. He now has pocket money and I use a behaviour chart which lists five things he must stick with each week, for example, doing his homework without moaning, keeping his room tidy, not answering back, emptying the dishwasher when he's asked. He has the chance to earn £5 a week, and he's at the age where he wants money to buy computer games, so he has the incentive. But if he gets three crosses he loses out and unfortunately he does lapse. Last week he got nothing. I don't know what else to try. He doesn't have a favourite toy or book, so he doesn't mind if something gets taken away from him. Are all children like this? Is there a cure?

Jemma from Carshalton, mum to Jack, eight and Alex, two

I've tried everything to get good behaviour from my son, who has been diagnosed with ADHD. With help from my health visitor we tried so many different types of behaviour management including star charts, ignoring bad behaviour, time out, but all to no avail. In the end I sat down with my son and explained how sad I was that his behaviour was so bad, so often, and how happy I would be if it improved. I really laid it on thick, with lots of emotion. Then I explained that I was only going to ask once, then there would be a punishment; however when I noticed the tiniest act of kindness or helpfulness, I told him how happy it made me. At his age, my happiness/sadness mattered so much more, and making him feel able to control my emotions by his behaviour obviously worked! I guess if he hadn't started out such a loving, caring and sensitive child, I might not have been so lucky.

Melanie from Warwick, mum to Adie, 11, Charli, nine and Tegan, six

We take pocket money away when they misbehave. They start the week with the chance of £5 but not doing as they are told loses them 50p a time. Rebecca rarely loses more than £1, whereas Dan is invariably down to £3 or less a week. He pushes the boundaries for everything and always thinks he can get the last word.

Allison from Cramlington, mum to Rebecca, nine and Dan, 12

Wait until they want to ask *you* for something, or take them places, or give them stuff . . . and completely ignore them. Take an hour to answer if they take an hour to do what you ask. I ask them how it feels and it turns a bad situation around. They usually think twice about ignoring me when I ask them the next time. Always be one step ahead of them and if you can't, then just play their games using their rules. It makes them see how inconsiderate they are and jolts them up a bit. I've found this only works well with the older kids. Younger ones get too confused and upset.

Leigh from Manchester, mum to Jack, four and foster mum to Toby, 12

I don't value 'obedience' very highly as a virtue. A child who's 100 per cent obedient is one who can't think or stand up for herself. Of course there are times when my daughter doesn't do what I want. There are usually natural consequences which teach her much better than any punishment I could dream up. If she doesn't tidy her toys in her bedroom, it gets so crowded that she cannot play in there. If she doesn't go to bed on time, she'll be so tired the next day that I'll cancel the play date we had planned. If she doesn't put her coat on, she gets cold. If she is rude to me I will feel cross and may not feel like reading to her later. I do tell her when she is doing something that winds me up, and sometimes I mention possible consequences of what she is doing. Also, I don't set myself up for a fall by creating conflict if I don't have to. It's clear by my words and tone of voice whether I am making a request or giving an order. If it's just a request, she doesn't have to do it. But if she's consistently unhelpful then I may remind her that when she doesn't help me, I don't feel like helping her.

This has worked really well, so far at least. She's a cheerful, cooperative kid most of the time. She doesn't always do what I tell her. But that's OK. I don't always do what she tells me either!
Sara from Oxford, mum to Catryn, seven and Ellie, seven months

The Problem Solved

Take a deep breath . . .

Experts say we have to keep calm when dealing with defiant behaviour and disrespectful children: after all, they're growing up, experimenting with boundaries, setting you a test, feeling their way round life, and generally exploring their independence.

If you feel your temper rising when you're being provoked by a child, take a moment to yourself before dealing with the situation. Breathe deeply, and try counting to ten. If necessary remove yourself, mentally or physically, from the situation for a little while. Try and remember that they'll be looking for an emotional reaction – and who wants to give them the satisfaction?

Once you're calm, issue any 'consequences' you see fit as soon as possible, so they can associate it with their behaviour.

A game of consequences

Most parents have read enough childcare manuals and watched enough parenting reality shows to be familiar with all the recommended forms of punishments for naughty children. 'Consequences' is the rather more forgiving term that's favoured these days.

The thing to bear in mind is that sometimes some of them work, and sometimes some of them don't. Likewise, one form of punishment can be effective with one child, but not with another. For example, some kids don't have a problem with 'time out' at all, as it's a good excuse for a daydream! And age is relevant: remember that where pre-schoolers are concerned, enforced consequences aren't usually much cop because they're too young to actually learn from them. Better to focus on the 'natural' consequences of a small child's actions.

It's wise not to get too hung-up on particular methods of discipline. Don't feel bad if they don't always seem to work in practice – you can carry out the instructions in the manual to the letter, but sometimes, your kid will still coolly get off the naughty step the minute you put her there. Working out which consequences are the most effective, most often, is generally just a question of trial and error.

Time out is popular. Docking of pocket money or removal of privileges, be it a favourite possession or a special event that's looming, can also be effective. If you make use of a star chart or other reward system, warning them that they're losing out on the chance of a sticker, or whatever the incentive is, can pull them up.

One thing is certain, if you say there will be consequences, you need to make sure there are, because if your threats turn out to be empty ones, they won't think twice about repeating the behaviour next time.

Count to five

Remember that, unless the deed is already done, they're entitled to a warning first and the chance to rectify a situation before you act. Tell them very clearly what will happen if they carry on. Giving them five seconds for a re-think can be all you need to avoid a clash at all. Try counting backwards from five to zero rather than the other way round – somehow, it's more dramatic!

The bottom line

A word on smacking: most people these days agree that as a form of punishment it's not only dubious (it's illegal to hurt a child in such a way that could leave a mark and many campaigners would like to see a total ban), it's not actually very effective. If you feel so mad you want to hit them, just walk away.

Letting it go

Those age-old parenting maxims 'Don't Sweat the Small Stuff', and 'Pick Your Battles' can be reassuring when you're at the end of your tether. You can't possibly punish everything and the stress involved for everyone means it isn't worth trying (unless you've already threatened those consequences, in which case, of course, you need to follow them through).

Let them know they've done wrong and you're not happy. But the world won't end if, sometimes, you let it go. Wait until they do something wonderful, instead, and then make a big deal about how great they are.

A serious problem

Persistent or extreme naughtiness can be an indication of deep-rooted unhappiness, or, in a small number of cases, a symptom of a behavioural disorder such as ADHD – see the factfile, below. If you feel your child's behaviour at home is out of your control, it may be time to seek some specialist help through your GP. Where trouble is occurring at school, you will need to seek the support of your child's teachers, who may well enlist the services of an educational psychologist.

What the experts say
The child psychologist

As with everything else, it is important to remember that children will go through various stages of being cheeky, disobedient or uncompliant. They go through these stages due to their age and their brain and emotional development at that time, life events, and peer influence.

Children are all born with different temperaments. Some are placid, while others have a real drive to always be the last one to speak. The important thing to remember is not to panic if your child is disobedient, or going through a disobedient stage. If it's a real change in them, then don't come down harshly: try and find out what's happening for them, as irritability can be a sign of underlying sadness that a child is unable to talk about.

If a child grows up in a family where the rules, boundaries and consequences are clear then they'll know what will happen if they disobey these. Of course, it's not always easy to be consistent if you're tired or stressed, as parents often are. At these times, a child may pick up on the tension it causes and be worried or uncertain about what it means, which they might deal with by behaving badly.

As with everything else, attitude needs to be modelled by the adults around. Taking some bad-mouthing from a young kid isn't easy to cope with, but the thing for adults to remember is that this is *not* an adult talking to us in a disrespectful way – of course, in that situation we would retaliate and shout back – this is a child, just learning about the ways of the world. Rise above it, don't take your anger out on the child, and stay calm. This child needs to be shown and told what to do and say in a situation in which they feel frustrated and cross.

As for smacking, it doesn't work! If you rule by fear there's going to be a time when that child realises they can fight back. Then you're stuck as an adult trying to supervise and control your child's behaviour by force – which is an impossible situation. Ruling by respect and consideration is infinitely more effective and beneficial for the child.
Dr Angharad Rudkin

The mums' life coach

Nearly every child does things they know they shouldn't from time to time. A level of disobedience is normal and nothing to worry about. Children will want to test their boundaries, and whether you come down on them like a ton of bricks or let it go, it's going to happen. Equally, a bit of attitude is to be expected, as they experiment with growing up and testing your limits. Most children don't wait until their teens to get to the 'whatever' stage.

Don't make other children the standard by which you judge your own. Find your own standards – keeping up with the Joneses' kids is the fastest shortcut to misery. Decide what you think is acceptable and stick to it. So Bobby next door never puts a foot out of line? Ignore it – we all know children who've gone wild later on. If your child has behaved badly, do your best to distinguish between the behaviour and the child. 'That was a stupid thing to do' will hurt less than, 'You stupid boy', and will reinforce the fact that it's the actions and not the child that you're cross with.

Patricia Carswell

The Problem Summarised

- All kids are naughty sometimes. It's very normal and not usually a cause for worry.
- Just because it's normal, doesn't mean they should get away with it!
- Punishments or 'consequences' don't always work. Sometimes you have to experiment to work out what's effective.
- Give them a warning. Be clear about it when you find something unacceptable.
- Aim to be consistent. When you've threatened consequences, follow it through.
- Let some things go. Don't sweat the small stuff!
- If they are seriously naughty over a prolonged period of time, there may be an underlying unhappiness causing it.

Factfile: Attention Deficit Hyperactivity Disorder (ADHD)

ADHD is a condition which affects the parts of the brain responsible for attention, impulses, and concentration, and can result in a range of 'disruptive' behaviours, including hyperactivity, impulsiveness, mood swings, and difficulty in concentrating. It's thought to affect 3 to 7 per cent of school age children and is most commonly picked up in children aged five. A combination of causes are likely, with genetics a significant factor.

ADHD has nothing to do with bad parenting or other social factors such as a poor diet or a stressful family background, although it's possible that these things can exacerbate it.

Once a diagnosis of ADHD has been made, usually by a child psychiatrist or specialist paediatrician, treatment will usually involve a combination of approaches, including behavioural therapy, or medication.

Ps and Qs: How to make bad manners good

The Problem

There's only one thing my son does that bugs me and that's coughing without putting his hand over his mouth, which he often does over our dinner. We're tackling this problem at the moment!

As soon as he was old enough to understand us and could talk we taught him to say 'please' nicely if he wanted something and 'thank you' if he was given something. We also get him to say excuse me or pardon me when he burps – although we sometimes have to remind him of this one!

Emma from Aberystwyth, mum to Nathan, three

What's the big deal about manners?

You might not think that bad manners are actually that much of a problem. After all, with so many other more vital parenting issues to keep on top of, is it *really* so important that our children eat correctly and say the right things? Is 'please' *actually* such a magic word? And would Grandma even care if she didn't get a thank you note after Christmas?

Well, yes, yes and yes. The extent to which manners are important will vary from home to home, and since we're a long way evolved from the 'seen and not heard' ethos of Victorian times, there's no need any more to be *obsessive* about social niceties. But even today, in a world where informality rules, manners do matter. Children are naturally inclined to be bad-mannered, and etiquette isn't usually on top of their agendas. But if we want them to co-exist successfully with other civilised folk, we have to teach them. It's part of the socialisation process.

The Problem Shared

What the Netmums say

I think that kids should be taught good manners and that the buck starts and stops at home. When we go out to eat, I've had comments on how well behaved my girls are and it makes me feel so proud. Obviously Rebekah-Eve's not perfect, but if she does forget to say please or thank you, she's reminded of the fact and if she doesn't say it, she doesn't get what she's asking for. Amy-Jayne doesn't speak yet, but when she hands me her cup I say thank you, and then thank you again when giving it back to her, so that she gets the idea early on.

Helen from Folkestone, mum to Rebekah-Eve, four and Amy-Jayne, one

Don't you think we parents can be bad at setting an example? I frequently see mums or dads not being very polite, but expecting their kids to be. I'm amazed how many parties my kids go to with gifts and don't get a thank you card. I've always made sure my children write to say thanks, or even just sign their name on a letter. They all ask to get

down from the table, even Maddy who's two. It's just nice and makes the world a better place. Yes, they do forget sometimes, as do I, but hopefully I'm giving them a good grounding.
Julie from Southend, mum to Jude, eight, Leon, five and Maddy, two

I always tell my little girl please and thank you, and I remind her to say it back when she asks for something and when she gets given something. She always used to say 'what' if we called out her name, but we kept insisting on 'pardon' and now she says that instead. She goes to nursery and has picked up some bad habits but at home we keep saying 'please, thank you, and pardon'. We're now trying to reiterate, 'May I please?'

She eats with a knife and fork, although sometimes she's allowed to use her fingers with things that are hard to use with a fork. As she gets older I'm beginning to introduce her to thank you notes. I write them and she signs them with her little squiggle. There may be a bit of a way to go yet before she understands!

It's nice when children have a good attitude and I think it does start at home. If they pick up bad manners elsewhere, then you need to keep banging the message back in.
Sarah from Quedgeley, mum to Paige, three

I like kids to use their manners and to have thought about what they're saying. I hold onto things until Jack remembers to say please if he's asked for something, and when I let go I tilt my head and give him a look until he says 'thank you'.

For the older kids, I tend to add a question along the lines of . . . 'and the words which you've forgotten are . . .?' Sometimes a quick prompt is all it takes.
Leigh from Manchester, mum to Jack, four and foster mum to Toby, 12

Last year, on holiday, we sat with an old couple who were amazed at how polite and well mannered our children were. They would go up and help themselves to the food and said 'please' and 'thank you' to the waiting staff in Spanish. The head waiter told us they were a credit to us.

We really can take them anywhere. I think one of the reasons they are so polite is because we lead by example. My husband and I always remember to say please and thank you when we talk to them, so they do so in return.

Andrea from Derbyshire, mum to Emily-Rose, nine, Lucy Mae, eight, Korben, six and Tyeran, four

I won't allow bad manners at all in my house. If my boys don't say please, thank you, or excuse me – and not just to adults, to each other as well – they are pulled up about it. If they've taken something without asking first they have to give it back until they say please and then thank you.

But some adults set a terrible example by not showing any respect or manners towards them. It doesn't take two seconds to say thank you to a little boy who has held open a door for you, and who is very proud to have done so!

Amanda from Manchester, mum to Ben, five and Joe, three

Instilling habits that are seen as good manners is such an easy one if you start it early. Making sure the children understand why they are doing what they're doing takes a little longer. James has always used versions of please and thank you, mimicking his older brother and sister. He'd still snatch toys – but at least he'd shout 'please' and 'thank you' as he did it!

Lisa from Amersham, mum to Laura, seven, Ben, five and James, three

I think good manners really depend on age. Joey doesn't sit at the table to eat very well but I no longer pressure him to do it, especially when we're eating out, as long as he's not bothering other people. If I do pressure him to sit still and eat then he's more likely to have a tantrum, which would bother other diners far more! As for please and thank you, these were among the first lot of words he spoke and always uses them properly; in fact, he also signs when he says please. Recently he's begun saying 'excuse me' and 'sorry' when he bumps into something or someone.

Ellie from Pembroke Dock, mum to Joey, two and Grace, nine months

My son is praised for his manners all the time by teachers and other adults. It does have to start with the parents and I have always been polite to him, saying please and thank you, excuse me, and sorry when I have needed to. I childmind, and have taught all my children to say please and thank you, an ability they sometimes lack when they first start! Another bugbear of mine is children that leave the table before everyone else has finished. Josh and all children I look after know that it's polite to wait for everyone. The world is a much nicer place when we all show good manners.

Carol from Rosyth, mum to Josh, six

The Problem Solved

Model manners

Take a moment to assess your own inclination towards good manners and, chances are, it'll be decidedly erratic. But – no surprises here – if we want our children to be well mannered, we need to be (permanently) well mannered ourselves. Showing gratitude and asking politely are the most basic of social skills and, whatever your view on manners, every child needs to acquire them, so 'please' and 'thank you', or at least something that passes for them, should be among the first words in their vocabulary. Even when they don't actually understand what those words mean (and it's common for little ones to get confused between the two), it's good for them to understand their importance, which if you reiterate them enough, they soon will.

Be liberal with other important verbal gestures like 'excuse me', 'pardon' and 'sorry' – the precise wording isn't important, but the sentiment is.

Dear Nana . . .

Thank you letters may seem like a bit of a chore after birthdays and Christmas, especially if they've had a party and 25 young guests need a written show of gratitude for their gift. But they are generally expected and, certainly where older relatives are concerned, usually much appreciated.

If they're not old enough to pen their own, write them on their behalf and get them to at least sign or add kisses, or exploit their creative abilities.

Table talk

When it comes to mealtime manners, you have to be realistic – remember, it's actually a cognitive challenge for little ones to master cutlery and eat without scattering food all over the table and floor. And even for older kids, keeping peas on a fork can be a tricky business, so be tolerant: unless you've been invited to dine with Her Majesty herself, children shouldn't be expected to perform like students from finishing school.

That said, there's no harm in encouraging good table manners as soon as they've mastered the art of putting food in their own mouths. And once they're old enough to eat carefully and politely, and to understand the various rules – whatever they may be in your house – you're well within your rights to enforce them.

What *are* the rights and wrongs of table manners? It comes down to what's acceptable in your family, but common no-nos are talking with a full mouth, getting down before others have finished – or at least until they've asked to be excused – and licking plates or knives (this last is a question of safety as much as good manners!) Sticklers may also quibble with elbows on the table, reaching for things rather than asking politely for someone to pass them, and using fingers instead of cutlery.

Pick your battles wisely. Decide what's really important to you and your partner and focus on those things by setting the right example. Let the rest slide. If you're eating good food, at the table, together, then you've already achieved great things. Doing it politely and tidily is just a bonus.

Say hello to your auntie!

Being able to converse politely and make appropriate social chitchat are all part and parcel of good manners. It can be embarrassing when children show a distinct lack of enthusiasm for doing so, but they can hardly be blamed – these things don't come naturally to the best of us, never mind to kids who have quite enough other adult skills on their learning to-do list. And sometimes when they seem bad-mannered, they're just being honest. After all, who *does* want to stand around politely passing the time of day with Auntie Janet?

Don't let insistence on politeness become a war of attrition. If you have to force them to do or say something, it won't mean much to them. Lead by example and they'll get to grips with it in the most natural way. Meanwhile, try not to be embarrassed by their lack of social graces.

I *beg* your pardon?

Burps and blow-offs aren't a problem in most families – in fact, some see them as a source of hilarity or even competition. At some point, there comes a time and a place where they are not appropriate, but kids will usually work out for themselves when and where. Meanwhile, decide whether, at home, farting is funny or foul, and try and stick with that.

There are all sorts of other disgusting personal habits which kids enjoy and – truth be told – they've probably picked up from observing the adults around them. If you don't like them picking their nose, tell them so, but don't make a big deal out of it, because it will probably have the opposite effect. If you're worried they'll do it at an inappropriate moment, during a visit from your mother-in-law, for example, have a quiet word beforehand.

What the experts say
The etiquette tutor

Society may be a less formal place these days, but manners are still important and if children are not taught when they are young, they will become bad-mannered adults. Just because they're children doesn't mean they're exempt: it's about setting up good habits for life. Having good manners means treating others with kindness and consideration, so well-mannered people find it easier to make social friends and business colleagues. And good manners help make the world a less aggressive place.

Children can be taught the words 'please' and 'thank you' right from the start – certainly once they've reached their first birthday. They can also be taught not to interrupt conversations or *demand* everything they want. Other basics include learning to pass food to others at the table, and not barging through doors or lounging on the sofa so that no one can sit down. Conversation is important –

talk to children and they will respond. I'd advise against too much TV, as it may stunt the development of good communication skills. [There's more information about television, and how much is 'too much', pp. 287–301.]

With table manners, they can start as young as possible, but it's important not to overdo things early on. Try and make it light-hearted. Teach them not to eat with their mouths open or speak with their mouths full, and to eat different foods politely rather than scream-ing *'I don't like it!'* They can be shown how to hold their cutlery prop-erly as soon as they are physically able. They should ask if they can get down from the table.

When it comes to burps and other 'noises' the best thing is to ignore it, if you can. Once children know they have an audience they usually play to it. One doesn't want to make them anally reten-tive, but that sort of thing is anti-social once they grow out of the cute stage.

Diana Mather, Public Image Inc

The mums' life coach

Most of us discover, once we've had our children, that we're quite old-fashioned. We want our children to say 'please' and 'thank you' and 'thank you for having me', and go to great lengths to make this happen. Who'd have thought you'd find yourself using that old chestnut, 'What's the magic word?'

Manners don't happen automatically, and it can be endlessly frustrating persuading children to behave politely. If the whole thing is wearing you down, stop stressing about the small details – the way they hold their cutlery and how often they say 'please'. Focus instead on the overall message you want to get across to them. Is it consider-ation for others? Treating others as they'd like to be treated them-selves? How other people feel about them? Once you've got them understanding the basics, provided you back it up with your own example, the rest should follow more naturally.

If you're really despairing, remember that the hard work usually pays off away from home. The child who grunts and eats with his fingers at home can be a model of good behaviour at his friend's house.

Patricia Carswell

The Problem Summarised

- Manners matter – even in today's world.
- Like most sorts of behaviour, they have to be learned.
- Leading by example is the way to do it: strive to be polite – *to* them, and in front of them.
- Writing a thank you letter is the least they can do if someone's shown them generosity.
- Make some allowances for the fact that they're kids: good manners don't always come easy!

New kid on the block: How to ease new sibling jealousy

The Problem

We talked about the new baby all through my pregnancy to get Louis used to the idea. When Henry arrived, we tried to keep positive all the time with Louis, even if he was being a bit naughty during the first few weeks. I found that he would poke his baby brother if he felt he wasn't getting attention, but this has mainly passed now. It's a juggling act. I would say take each day as it comes. I'm still discovering new ways of keeping the harmony even now.

Jane from Harlow, mum to Louis, two and Henry, seven months

The new arrival

OK, let's say your husband or partner leaves home for a couple of days. When he comes back again, he has brought with him a new wife. She is very fragile, unbelievably demanding, and she sucks up the majority of your husband's attention. But your husband is quite clearly enraptured by her. And rather than sharing your disgust at this situation, everyone else around you seems to think she's rather wonderful, too. You struggle bravely on with this situation in the hope that sooner or later she'll go back where she came from. But at some point it hits you: she's here to stay.

A crude analogy, perhaps, but it demonstrates how the arrival of a new baby in the family can totally stink for older siblings, particularly for those who've been an only child until then.

Aggression and regression

It's perfectly normal for children of all ages to feel a range of emotions when they're coming to terms with a new sibling. They may well feel displaced or threatened, jealous, insecure, anxious, or downright angry. But they may also be excited, interested and happy about their brother or sister, and that may make them feel guilty or confused.

Don't be surprised if a child shows a dramatic capacity for violence towards a new arrival. Equally, other sorts of less obvious bad behaviour can be a direct consequence of their feelings: defiance, rudeness, or killer sulks, for example. It may not kick in for the first few weeks, until they realise it's a permanent fixture. It's normal for them to respond with very few feelings at all, so don't be put out if they appear indifferent to the family's latest member. Regression is a natural response – they may want to try on nappies, sit on your lap, be fed by you. Unless they're pushing puberty when this happens, it's perfectly normal.

You can make it easier for them, but remember: whatever efforts you make, it's potentially a tough time for any kid. Take comfort that whatever discord abounds when there's a new kid on the block is unlikely to be lasting. By the time their first birthday has rolled around, no one will recall a time when they *weren't* part of the family.

The Problem Shared

What the Netmums say

We did it all by the book when I was expecting James. We read books with Rachel about the new baby, talked to her about it, bought her a gift from him and made sure visitors made a fuss of her too. So I was totally shocked when she began to viciously attack him – hitting, scratching, and pushing at him when he was just a few weeks old. And this wasn't when he was getting attention – one day I was baking cakes with her when the baby was asleep. We had a lovely time, then she got down from the table and scratched him across the head, drawing blood.

At first we tried ignoring it, then we put her in the 'naughty room' if she did it, but basically I think it just took time for her to adjust. James is nine months now and they're starting to interact and get on well. She still has her moments if her little brother grabs her toys but it's much better. It just goes to show that however much you prepare an older sibling, it's still a shock.

Heather from Fife, mum to Rachel, three and James, nine months

My eldest was two years and nine months old when his brother was born. Once he turned three we successfully toilet trained him, and then his classic trick was, when I was feeding the baby, going into the kitchen, coming back and then announcing: 'I've had a wee'. A lovely way to get mummy's attention! It didn't work though, and he soon realised I wasn't going to put baby down and run and sort him out. He only did it a few times.

Joanne from Manchester, mum to Benjamin, four and Oliver, one

There's a big age gap between my two, but I still felt it was important that my son didn't feel left out. After 16 weeks we kept him informed of everything that was going on. We asked him if he wanted to come to the 4D scan with us, and even asked if he wanted to be at the birth – thankfully he said no! He was the first person to be told she'd arrived, the first to get texted a picture, and the first to see and hold her. He is absolutely brilliant with her, and she lights up whenever she sees him. I still try and make sure that we have time just the two of us, even if it's just breakfast together. And my other half has taken him away on holiday so that it was something just for him.

Sam from Fareham, mum to Nathan, 12 and Lucy, eight months

Bethany was so excited when she found out I was pregnant, especially as I'd had a miscarriage before. I talked to her all the time about what would happen once the baby was born and she even came with me to the scan. I got her to choose a teddy bear for herself and the baby, and she also chose all his clothes and bedding, and a pram.

The first day back she got a little upset as the neighbours came round and wanted to see the baby and she felt left out, but after a little chat and hug she was OK. She was involved 100 per cent in helping with him if she wanted to. She fed him his bottle, changed his nappy, bathed him, played with him, read books to him, and even fed him his first solids. In fact I was glad I let her help as I had to go into hospital several times and if it wasn't for her, my partner wouldn't have had a clue how to make the bottles, what Robbie ate, or how to work the washing machine!

Now he's two and she's seven, and she still loves to help out looking after him. She's teaching him his colours, and how to count. Owen was 11 when Bethany was born and during his visits he was a great help, too. All three of them are close now, and it's lovely.

Emma from Swindon, mum to Bethany, seven, Robbie, two and stepmum to Owen, 18

Thomas was born with serious kidney problems which meant I've had to spend a lot of time in hospital with him and that's caused a lot of anger and jealousy from Charlotte. She never directs it at him, it's always at me. She's hit me and is rude and nasty to me. I know it's just frustration over not being able to control her life. She loves Thomas a lot and has never shown any sign of anger to him.

Other times I've been stuck in hospital with Thomas and she wants to stay with me which is very painful as I'd give anything to be home with her. It's been really hard but I've made time just for us when I can and talked to her lots about why I'm not always around. I don't think the answer is to pander to her by buying gifts, for example. She gets praise when she's good, but the best thing I can give her is my time, even if that just means a shopping trip or a shower together.

Victoria from Stockport, mum to Charlotte, six and Thomas, ten months

The best advice I can give is let them be as involved as possible. My son was almost 19 months when my daughter was born so he didn't really understand what was happening, but he's now two and helps me do everything from feeding to dressing her. He's never shown any resentment towards her; in fact it's better than ever now that she gets down on the floor and plays with him. He just randomly goes and gives her a kiss or a cuddle a few times a day. My other tip would be that if it's possible, try and spend some time alone with each child separately.

Rachel from Mansfield, mum to Rhys, two and Ava, six months

Jack was four when Harry was born. He was fine at home, although he wasn't keen on Harry and I being alone together. But at nursery, he would make himself sick all the time, so I would go for him. It was his way of getting my attention. His teachers realised what he was doing and they began to keep him at school. After about four months, it stopped.

Gem from Gateshead, mum to Jack, five and Harry, 15 months

We made sure that both my second and third babies came with presents! It worked really well, and Caitlin still loves her doll that her baby brother gave her when he was born. We did all the other stuff, too, such as letting the children be there for the scans, lots of feeling the baby in the belly, helping to choose names. But for us, the most special thing has been having home births for the last two. It meant that the other children were around and knew exactly what was happening and that the baby was coming soon. I had both daughters rubbing my back during contractions! When they woke up in the morning their baby brother was in the Moses basket at the end of the bed, and we made a real fuss of giving them presents from him. It was really lovely. It's important to make it a real family affair, keep the children fully informed and let them help as much as possible, without forcing them.

Michelle from Stoke, mum to Caitlin, seven, Shannon, six and Connor, two

The Problem Solved

Preparation, preparation, preparation

You can ease the shock of a new sibling by preparing your older one. Tell them as soon as is practical and let them watch and feel the growing bump, explaining how the baby is developing. Let them help get the nursery ready with you, choose new stuff, or sort through the hand-me-downs that you've earmarked for the baby. Be prepared for them to re-claim items they've long since grown out of, and never force them to hand anything over they don't want to.

Casually talk about how the new arrival will affect life at home, how routines will change, and what a lot of help, care and patience they will require. It's also worth getting hold of one of the many books that have been specially written on the subject. They may quietly take the story in, or they may be inspired to ask any questions and talk about worries that are forming in their minds. Another useful way to open up the subject – and to emphasise how much attention *they* got, when they were tiny – is to get out their baby photo albums.

Talking about potential names together is a nice thing to do. Some parents are even happy to let an older child decide independently what their sibling will be called: just make sure you're happy with everything that's on the shortlist! If they've no experience at all of newborns, visit any you know if you've the chance, to give them a taster.

By all means talk about how nice it will be when the baby's arrived, but don't overdo it, otherwise it'll be a major disappointment when the said infant gets home and turns out to be boring, noisy and smelly.

Make any major changes to your older child's life well in advance of the birth or delay them until much later – moving them to a new room, transferring them to a bed or potty training, for example. They'll have quite enough on their plate coming to terms with their newly extended family.

Birth-day presents

After the birth, it's a good idea to let your older child or children visit you and the new baby in hospital, rather than returning home with their new sister or brother. Lots of new babies these days bring presents for their older siblings – how much this is likely to act as a 'sweetener' is debatable, but a highly desirable gift may provide a useful distraction for a while.

Mother's little helper

Involving your older child or children with the new baby is universally reckoned to be a good idea – keeping them busy distracts them from negative feelings, and if they're taking part in the baby's care, they won't feel left out. Let them help according to their ability – fetching and carrying, fastening nappies, tucking them into their cots. All help has to be supervised – even much older children will need a close eye kept on them.

But I'm your baby, too

A new sibling may cause a young child to regress in an obvious way – they may dig out their old feeding bottles, insist you tuck them up in the baby's cot, or even try out his nappies for size. It will be a brief phase, aimed at reminding you that *they* were your baby first, and it's OK to humour them. If they revert back to behaviours they had got to grips with, wetting themselves for example, it may be a cry for attention, or a subconscious response to the big changes. It should right itself in a short time and you'll need to be patient and kind – the ever trusty sticker chart or a similar reward system comes into its own here.

Big up their role as older brother or sister. Emphasising how 'grown up', clever and responsible they are usually helps, especially if you point out the many benefits of being older: being able to watch TV, eat sweets sometimes, and enjoy outings without falling asleep. Avoid banging on about setting a good example – now and in the future. It may cause them to resent their seniority!

The love/hate thing

It's a worry when a new baby provokes a violent response, but when you bear in mind the strength of feeling an older child may have after a sibling's arrival, it's understandable. Sometimes it can be overt – a whack with a toy or a hard pinch – or it maybe a hug or squeeze gone too far as the love/hate feelings they're having manifest themselves. Never leave a baby alone with a young child, for even a moment. There'll come a point when a child is grown-up enough to be trusted for short periods, but you'll have to assess this for yourself. Meanwhile, don't take any chances!

You may find the violence is not directed at the new baby but at you, other siblings, or anyone who happens to be around. There's a delicate line to be trodden between making clear the violent behaviour's wrong, and making allowances for their unhappiness. Tell them it's unacceptable, in no uncertain terms, but be lenient for a while. Try and understand how hard a time this is for them. Be super-vigilant, so that, where possible, you can ward off any attacks before they happen. Encourage them at every opportunity to show gentle affection to the baby, by allowing them to stroke its head or give it kisses and (carefully supervised) cuddles. Don't forget that all-important praise when they are kind.

Time for them

There's not much getting round the fact that new babies sap the majority of your time and attention. But it's vital to give older siblings a bit of you, too. Spend as many precious moments as you can with them – and without the baby – and make sure they also get lots of positive attention from other members of the family, by way of compensation.

Even if you're busy, perhaps feeding the baby, pay them attention by talking to them, or encouraging them to sit quietly by your side.

Talk to them as much as possible, anyway. Keep them informed, and encourage them to express their feelings. Say you love them, and keep telling them you love them. At this point, it may be hard for them to believe that you do.

Other odd reactions

You may well notice other, less obvious, responses to a new baby by an older sibling. They may be generally badly behaved: showing off, being defiant and sulking are likely, and almost certainly down to a simple bid for your attention. Young children can seem completely indifferent to a new brother or sister. It's no cause for concern: they're getting used to the idea and will be responsive in their own time. Meanwhile, never force them to show interest, and continue to show interest in them.

What the experts say

The child psychologist

Having a new sibling can be a tricky time for little ones, especially if they're currently the youngest in the family. All children have feelings of displacement and jealousy, however old they are, but slightly older children are able to think it through and rationalise their worries. They often experience love/hate feelings for a new baby – they love the new addition because clearly their parents love him, too, and some enjoy treating the baby like a doll, giving it hugs and pretending to feed it. The 'hate' feelings come in when the child realises that they actually have to compete with this new addition for parents' time. As with any competition, humans feel resentment towards the very thing that they're having to compete with.

Most children react with some increase in difficult behaviour. They may become more demanding, particularly at separation times. They may also develop all sorts of tricks for getting their parents' attention, for example, claiming they feel sick, or stopping eating.

The important thing to remember at this time is that these feelings and actions are completely normal. Children are incredibly resilient little things and they will get through this difficult period. Also, sharing with a sibling and being secure within their relationship with parents, even when that parent is off changing their sister's nappy, is an essential thing to learn and will strengthen their relationship with you in the future.

For your own sanity and to minimise their feelings that their world really has gone upside down, stick to as many of the rules and boundaries you had before: for example, bedtime, dinner time. This is difficult in reality, but it helps the child to know that the world keeps on turning in its familiar way, and gives predictability at a time when there isn't much.

Finally, I doubt there isn't a day when mums and dads don't feel guilty about some aspect of parenting. Having another baby is not a hurtful thing to do – it's just another life event that an older sibling needs time to adjust to.

Dr Angharad Rudkin

The mums' life coach

Sibling jealousy is as old as the hills. It's a natural part of family life, and it's quite normal for an older sibling to feel a little miffed that he is no longer the star of the show.

The best way to deal with the arrival of a new baby is to plan ahead, both emotionally and practically. Remember that this is a new and important relationship in your child's life, which will take some adjusting to. Ask yourself what the new arrival will add to family life. And what will he or she take away, in terms of time, energy, attention and baby status.

Depending on the age of the older sibling, explain that the baby will need a lot of extra looking after, and that you will need the older child's superior knowledge and help in order to be able to care for him or her.

On a more practical level, plan ahead in terms of time. What can you do to ensure that you will have some one-to-one time with your older child after the baby is born?

If your older child doesn't seem to be adapting well, don't panic. Once things have settled down, the new baby will enrich the family in many ways, will be a companion for the older sibling, and will teach your older child many lessons about sharing, compromising and caring for another person. That's worth a few tantrums.
Patricia Carswell

The Problem Summarised

◆ The arrival of a new sibling can be a devastating time for an older child: loads of patience and understanding will be required. And it may take time.
◆ Prepare a child as best you can for their brother and sister, well in advance.
◆ Violent jealousy, regression and indifference are all likely reactions.
◆ Allowing them to help out with the new baby is a good idea.
◆ Try and keep the rest of their lives as normal as possible as they adjust to a massive change.
◆ Don't feel guilty: new siblings are a (wonderful) fact of life.

Special blend: How to help them adjust to life in a step family

The Problem

I dated my new partner away from home. Once the relationship got to a point where I thought it was stable, I introduced him to my boys. I felt this was very important. Of course my children still love their dad, and my partner will never replace him. At first, I was the only person to tell off my children and my other half was to consult me about any situations. It takes a lot of trust to put your children into someone else's care.

Anyway, it's all worked out great. The kids love him and even though I never asked them to, they are happy to call him Dad. My advice is take it slow, and make sure they always know they come first. *Ava from Birmingham, mum to Kai, eight, Ethan, six and Evan, 14 months*

There may be trouble ahead

Step families have come a long way since Snow White's time. Factors like rising divorce and remarriage rates mean they are now an ordinary fact of life. All the same, coping with a new family dynamic remains a potentially bewildering and stressful experience for a child. Whether you have to help them establish a relationship with your own new partner, or with their father's – not to mention all the other new family members those new partners may bring into the equation – it's a delicate business that will almost certainly require lots of love, understanding and patience.

Inside the mind of a child

Children who are trying to come to terms with life in a step family – or 'blended family', to use an increasingly popular term – may have all sorts of issues going on. Even if a significantly long time has passed since the break up of their original family unit, whether it was due to divorce or death, they may still be trying to deal with *that* situation. When the added complication of a parent's new partner arises, it's hardly surprising that a lot of kids don't respond positively: the boyfriend or girlfriend in question may be a perfectly delightful person, but their presence is still going to take some getting used to. Similarly, if a child has only ever known life with a lone parent, they're probably going to have something to say about it when a whole new person looms so significantly in their lives.

Keeping an eye out

Of course, some children take new family set-ups in their stride. But even if that appears to be the case, never take it for granted that they are OK with it: sometimes children are very adept at hiding the way they really feel. Unhappiness about family life can manifest itself in ways that aren't obviously linked: trouble with school work, poor sleeping or eating, moodiness, defiance or clinginess. None of these things are insurmountable, but a child who's affected by one or more of them will need your sympathy and support.

Plus points

Potentially, there are loads of positive things about step family life. Having an increased choice of reliable adults (step grandparents or step aunties and uncles included) to turn to can be a very good thing indeed. Step siblings, if they hit it off, can become great friends. Challenging though it may be, negotiating their way through the choppy waters of a changing family structure may help a child towards independence and maturity – it's good experience for the complex nature of grown-up life that awaits them. With any luck, there'll be more presents, too!

The Problem Shared

What the Netmums say

I was a single parent from the start with Charlotte, and she was four when I met my husband, Dave. They were slow to settle with each other. She wasn't scared of him but cautious, as she'd never had a male figure in her life. He was very good with her and took it at her pace. It was a while before he would stay over, as that was 'Charlotte's space'. She called him Dave up until the day of our wedding and the day after, he was 'Dad'. It was strange how quickly she changed.

I have always tried to talk to her about what is going on. From the day Dave met her, to us deciding to get married, and telling her all about her real dad, who she doesn't see and is now married with another daughter. It's not easy as often I've had to say things that she doesn't want to hear.

In the end, Dave is her dad and he loves her and cares for her as I do. I have no worries over that at all. They are good together, and I can see them growing closer all the time.

Victoria from Stockport, mum to Charlotte, six and Thomas, seven months

I had my first two by my husband while I was quite young, my third with a long-term boyfriend, and my fourth, Nicholas, with my fiancé, who also has a daughter, so I've had a lot of experience of being in a step family.

We've not actually had many problems with it, all four older girls get on well most of the time, and they all love Nicholas. I'm not sure what we did to make it work so well – I suppose the biggest thing is not making an issue out of it. Right back when I first met Nic's dad, the girls used to talk to him on the phone a lot, then we started meeting up for days out with the kids and it just went from there really. I've always been a very open mum and talk to them about everything. Now as a family we still do that and although we're very busy we make an effort to spend time with them all.

Bethany from Ripley, mum to Shannon, nine, Hannah, eight, Laura, five and Nicholas, 13 months

I think introducing new adults into a situation has to be done at a pace the child is happy with. Sophie was two when I met my husband. For the first few months of our relationship he would only come over when she was at her dad's house, and then slowly he would come for tea when she was there, or we would go and visit his family on a Sunday together. He thinks the world of her and loves her like he loves our sons. There are a few issues though – he can't get over the fact that she has never called him Dad. She's always had regular contact with her real dad and seen him a couple of times a year, so although my husband has been there full-time there was always someone else called Dad. He's been hurt by this through the years but tries not to see it as rejection. He's put the graft in with her and I think it will pay dividends in the long run. I know she respects him just as much as her real dad. In retrospect we should have spoken about this more at the time and realised how important it would be later on for him. I think I spent all my energy concentrating on making it OK for her and didn't think about his part in it all.

Emma from Orkney, mum to Sophie, 16, Hugh, 12 and Jack, six

Nathan was six when I split from his dad and I felt it was important that neither of us introduced new partners into his life too quickly. When my other half and I decided to move in together, a few years after meeting, we both discussed it with him to make sure he was happy about it.

My other half refers to him and considers him as his son, even though there's no genetic tie. He may not be his biological dad but it is him that takes him on holiday, who talks to him when there's a problem, and who would swing for anyone causing him harm.

I've never had any reason to believe that my son has an issue with his stepmum either. He always seems very comfortable with her. Both her family and my other half's have also welcomed him without any issue.

My son doesn't call my other half Dad. I know he'd be chuffed to bits about it if he did, but that's just the way it goes. He thinks sometimes that my son plays him up or is stroppy towards him because he's not his real dad. I've tried to explain that he is exactly the same towards me and it's just his age! But I know it upsets him sometimes.

We now have a baby girl, and the word 'half' doesn't even enter the conversation. She and Nathan are brother and sister, and that's the end of it.

Sam from Fareham, mum to Nathan, 12 and Lucy, eight months

The Problem Solved

Questions, questions

Getting inside a child's head is rarely easy, but empathy – in this and in so many other situations – is everything. It can be hard for a parent, particularly if they are in love and happy about it, to view a step family situation from their child's point of view. But they'll need to think hard about some of the questions they'll be asking: Why should I have to accept the authority of someone who isn't my real parent? What does Mum *see* in him? How am I supposed to get used to this shuttling back and forth? Why do I have to share my home with people I don't know that well? How come I'm getting less attention than I used to? Is it OK that I *like* my stepmother? Is any of this *my* fault?

Those are just some of the obvious questions. That's a lot of answers to help them find.

Slowly does it

All the experts agree that timing is crucial. 'Easy does it' seems to be the overwhelming piece of advice offered to anyone who's looking to introduce a new partner to their children or to take things further and instigate a whole new domestic arrangement. Of course, to a child, 'going slow' may mean taking a couple of years about it: an adult who's keen to get on with their life won't want to wait long to do so. It's a tricky one. There are no absolutes in this situation, no formal guidelines about how many weeks, months or years these things should take if a child is to cope with it OK. It probably comes down to a delicate balance between what feels right for the child and what feels right for the grown-ups. If the two things are mutually exclusive, compromise and negotiations will have to be made.

Sibling stuff

It's a common mistake to hope or even assume that step siblings will be the best of friends. It's often hard to form a close relationship with a brand new brother or sister, especially for older children who've got used to their place in the pecking order. Don't ever push it. Make sure, if you are setting up a new home which step siblings will have to share at any point, that they each have a space to call their own. Offer lots of fun stuff and time together as a unit: but if they don't want to play, don't make them. If step siblings don't get on, you may just have to accept that and help them cope with living together as best you can.

When a new baby turns up, that can be even harder. Imagine how difficult it is for a child coping with a natural new sibling: now magnify that several times over to get an idea of how it feels when your mum or your dad starts a whole new family. All the same rules for coping with a new sibling apply, with even more sensitivity required.

Dos and don'ts

Never be cross with a child who isn't happy about a family situation. Accept that they may behave in a variety of odd or difficult ways – and for a long time, too – and try to understand what they are going through. Cut them some slack if their behaviour is unacceptable, but remember they still need some boundaries, so don't let all hell break loose and ignore it on the grounds that they're 'still adjusting'.

Don't force them to accept a step parent as a replacement mother or father – particularly if the real deal is still on the scene (however unreliably). Encourage them to retain their relationship – if it's viable – with the parent, and extended family members, they leave behind (however acrimonious things may have become for the adults involved). Don't try and overcompensate by giving gifts: but do be as generous as possible with your time.

Keep talking. Work on that 'emotional literacy' by helping them to understand that it's OK to feel rubbish and better still to admit it. Remind them of the positives, whatever they may be.

If it's your ex that has moved on, your child may feel bad about being with him and his new partner, particularly if, in spite of themselves, they enjoy it. As hurtful and unbearable as this situation may be, you need to give them permission to be happy in their other family by letting them know that it's alright. And don't vent your spleen about their dad's partner in front of them: it won't help them come to terms with her themselves.

What the experts say
The family therapist

For a 'step' issue to arise at all it means that the original family has broken down, either by divorce or death, and that means the children involved are having to deal with loss, and, quite likely, in the case of divorce, not knowing who to blame. It's usual for children to 'take against' a step parent – even if she/he arrived on the scene much later and was not part of the original family breakup, because *someone* has to be blamed. Children often take this on themselves. They tell themselves: 'If only I'd been better behaved this wouldn't have happened', so it's probably with some relief that someone else can be blamed for the family turmoil.

Adults often cross their fingers and hope that because they love a new partner their children will too. In my experience, children are happy to go along on outings with a girlfriend or boyfriend, but their mood changes once a permanent arrangement is on the cards. Many children hold onto the belief – against all odds – that their family will get back together again and a stepmother or stepfather puts an end to that dream. Adults can fool themselves into thinking that the kids will love each other, but when there are step siblings the family order changes – the youngest may become the eldest, the eldest is no longer on top of the pile, and that can be very hard to adjust to. If it's down to you to help a child accept a new stepmother, you'll have to explain that things will be different, and acknowledge that the child will have mixed feelings. Children can feel disloyal about liking a stepmother. The best way to help them is to talk, talk, talk to them and listen, listen, listen. Kids often give oblique signals so it may not be easy working out their true feelings.

Adults should never tell themselves that 'kids are tough', that 'kids adapt', or that 'it's so common nowadays, they'll manage'. Each child has to be given the time and space to settle in their own way – however long it takes. Remember, it can take years to successfully build a 'blended' family.

Jill Curtis, www.family2000.org.uk

The child psychologist

The issues here are similar to those surrounding a new sibling – it's all to do with our roles in the family and how we perceive ourselves in relation to others. If there is a new addition to the family, whether it be a baby or a partner, it is a life-changing event for everyone and needs to be dealt with as thoughtfully as possible. This is often difficult around times of separation and meeting new partners because parents' resources tend to be taken up with their own coping and feelings. Your child is going to have confusing feelings and worries, as does anyone at times of change and uncertainty, and it will affect the way they behave for a while.

Give the child as much appropriate information as possible, for example, don't hide someone away when it's obvious that they're becoming a big part of your life. Continue to have good quality time with your child, without the new partner, and gradually invite the new partner to join in. Offer choice where possible – a major complaint of children is that they feel they have no control over what's happening to them. The same goes for step siblings – try not to throw them together immediately and expect them to get on just because they're the same age or they like the same music. Do it gradually and with as much information and choice as possible. Keep house rules as firm as possible, because it's at times of change that family members push the boundaries more than ever.

Difficult as it may be, try not to be disrespectful of ex-partners as this can confuse children. Mediation services can be useful for families who are finding things particularly difficult.

Dr Angharad Rudkin

The Problem Summarised

- Step families are an ever-increasing fact of life.
- Adjusting to step relationships can be daunting for a child and their behaviour may well be affected.
- Be sympathetic, but keep boundaries in place.
- Just because you feel positive about a new partner, it doesn't mean your child will.
- Don't allow your own bitterness about a situation to cloud your child's view of things.
- Take it slow: step families can take a long time to successfully 'blend'.
- Once settled, step families can be extremely happy units!

Factfile: Step family statistics

Experts use the term 'step family' to refer to a married or cohabiting couple who have at least one child between them from a previous relationship, who either lives with them or visits.

The 2001 census was the first census to specifically identify step families, and revealed that there are 0.7 million step families with dependent children living in households in the UK – that's around 10 per cent of all families. 0.4 million of the couples heading up a step family were married, and 0.3 million were cohabiting.

Other research suggests that there are as many as 2.5million children who are part of a step family set-up, either because they live in a house with a step parent, or regularly visit one.

More than 80 per cent of step families consist of a natural mother and a stepfather, so it's much more common for children to stay with their mum than their dad.

Analysis by the charity Parentline Plus showed that 11 per cent of people calling them for help wanted to talk about step family issues.

(SOURCES: National Office for Statistics; Parentline Plus)

He started it! How to deal with sibling squabbles

The Problem

It's usually my eldest that starts the fights in our house. The two younger ones get on fine on their own. He constantly has to tap them or pinch them – why I don't know. Even when I've caught him out he tries to deny it. It's not like he doesn't get the attention. He stays up later with us and he's forever sat chatting to me or his dad about his day. We try to do as much together as a family, but Sam often spoils it by starting the fights. It's very hard to cope with.

Dawn from Macclesfield, mum to Sam, 11, Sean, seven and Jade, four

Sibling rivalry is a *good* thing!

When you think about it, it's hardly surprising that brothers and sisters sometimes have complex relationships: brought up in the same small space, they're forced to share everything, from treasured possessions to their parents' love, and generally expected to love one another, even if the only things they have in common are genes and an address. If the siblings in your home seem to spend a disproportionate amount of time at each other's throats, don't worry, it's normal.

In fact, it's more than normal, it's instinctive. And it's useful, too. Sibling rivalry can help teach a child vital life skills, such as negotiation and compromise. And a little bit of competition can be a positive driving force.

Squabbling siblings = stress

Unfortunately, warring siblings can also cause a great deal of stress to their parents. For many, it's the worst aspect of having more than one child. When yours are at it, you may find yourself wondering: 'What will it be like when they're older and bigger?' And 'Will they *always* hate each other this much?'

Sibling conflict can affect a mum and dad's relationship too, as they're forced to enter the battle zone and may – consciously or otherwise – find themselves coming down on opposing sides.

All change

Conflict between siblings will probably come and go. One minute all is harmony, the next it's hell! Equally, they can move through longer phases of getting on or not according to their age, changes in the family structure, and all sorts of other circumstances. Age gaps, gender difference, and their position in the family may well influence how they get on, but these factors can't be changed, so there's no point worrying about them.

Don't assume their relationship as children will necessarily affect their liking for one another as adults: some brothers and sisters fight like cat and dog when they're young but grow up to be very close. Others get on fine, but drift apart when they're older. You can help to forge smooth sibling relationships, but you may have to accept that they are different people and may never truly see eye to eye.

The Problem Shared

What the Netmums say

My boys rarely get on. They squabble, fight and whinge at each other practically constantly. Thank goodness my eldest now goes to school which gives me (and them) a break from it! They physically fight, especially when one butts into the other's game. Max will bite if he's really pushed, and Daniel doesn't know his own strength, often pushing his little brother right over. To be honest, I think this will always be the case, until they leave home and start separate lives. Then I think they will quite possibly get on pretty well!

I do worry about it but I believe that it's normal, especially in boys (or am I being sexist?). I leave them to it to a certain extent, except I butt in as soon as they are being aggressive to one another, then whichever one was aggressive will be put on the naughty step. I've now had to introduce a 'naughty mat' as well, so when they've both been aggressive, one goes on the step, one on the mat.
Sarah from Milton Keynes, mum to Daniel, four and Max, two

My girls bicker, and I don't think they'd be normal if they didn't! If one of them is in trouble they blame the other one, if one is in a bad mood, they blame the other, if one is bored they wind the other one up! Sometimes I feel like a referee but usually by the time I've walked away to work out how to deal with it, I turn around and they're playing happily again!
Michelle from Stevenage, mum to Carly, eight and Paige, five

Mine fight, and they're only two! Katie and Kimberley both had bite marks down their arms last week but they still push, hit, bite and shout at each other. They're driving me round the twist at the moment. I've started a positive parenting course hoping to find some helpful tips. Saying this, they both love each other and when they're not fighting they're often kissing and cuddling. What's it going to be like when they're teens? I daren't even think about it!
Sam from Stoke, mum to Katie and Kimberley, twins aged two

Laura, my eldest can be very nasty towards her two younger sisters: she slaps them and punches them all the time. Chloe pinches now and again but usually it's her that gets hurt. Jazmyn's the worst. She bites, punches and hits out with whatever she can find: coat hangers, remote controls, the vacuum cleaner. She's totally changed since the birth of my youngest last year. It may well be down to jealousy, as Macy is very ill and needs 24 hour care. It's a very difficult household. I only cope with the help of antidepressants.
Katrina from Corby, mum to Laura, nine, Chloe, five, Jazmyn, three and Macy, one

My girls say they hate each other and even go so far as to put cereal boxes in front of them so they don't have to look at each other across the table. They never say anything nice and they're constantly screaming, shouting, hitting, tripping each other up, and slapping each other.

If I do have to referee a particularly bad dispute, they are usually both to blame. They dislike each other. Holly is very intolerant of Ruby, yet she puts up with anything from Lily and is otherwise generally caring. Ruby gives as good as she gets. Poppy manipulates the situation sometimes, and then the fights turn nasty, with two against one. The worst thing now is that they are starting to involve Lily in the disputes and when they fight she starts shouting too, even though she doesn't really know what for! I don't like her spending her young years in this environment. The only way I can stop the constant backbiting is to supervise closely, but when I have to make tea all hell breaks loose.
Danielle from Ashford, mum to Holly, 12, Poppy, ten, Ruby, eight and Lily, two

My two constantly wind each other up, snap at each other, tell tales on each other and physically fight if the opportunity presents itself. My other half and I feel like we are constantly in the middle of them, trying to get them to be nice to each other, or even just to tolerate each other. They'll squabble if one of them gets five pence more spent on them than the other and the constant bickering over who gets to watch what on television has led to it being banned altogether on numerous occasions. I'm sure that it will continue for a while longer yet and we will just have to ride it out. Eventually they'll realise they like each other!

Allison from Cramlington, mum to Dan, 11 and Rebecca, nine

Mine have recently increased their squabbling. I think it's because Emma has got to an age where she doesn't just do what Sam wants automatically. To start with I did get drawn in to sorting it out but I quickly realised I wasn't helping at all and was only succeeding in making one of them think I was being unfair, while the other one felt smug and, more importantly, I was upsetting myself and going round in circles. So now when the squabbling starts and the calls of 'Mum, Emma is . . .' or 'Mummy, Sam did . . .' echo out, I just tell them I don't care, if they don't want to be friends then that's really sad but not to bother me with it. It stops the bickering almost immediately.

Donna from Rotherham, mum to Samuel, five and Emma, three

Mine can be angels and play really well together, but the next minute be fighting like cats and dogs. When it's going well, I always tell them how well they're playing (I've found positive praise works wonders on my kids). I always can tell they're working into a fight, so I suggest something else, or get one of them to help me. If all else fails and time permits, I put them in the bath, or take them out for a walk.

Jane from the Wirral, mum to Jake, six, Libby, five and Emma, three

My son and daughter wind each other up constantly. Initially it stressed me out – I was an only child, and I didn't get it. Finally I figured I would just leave them to it unless things were getting really nasty. I don't listen to the tale-telling, I just tell them that if they are going to kill each other, can they do it quietly.

They can both be very aggressive towards each other, fighting and shouting and name-calling. They try and convince me that they hate each other which is why they don't get on. But it gets put into perspective when you walk into the living room to find the pair of them screaming and rolling around on the floor – and they tell you they are fighting to make their younger brother laugh!

Cassandra from Motherwell, mum to Aiden, eight, Anya, six and Andrew, eight months

Mine have always squabbled with each other. They moan if they think one of them has a bigger piece of cake, fight for the window seat, wrestle for the last biscuit, the usual stuff. Our last holiday was completely ruined by their constant fighting and bickering. Each day my husband and I had to referee the fights. Sitting in a car for two hours, with three kids elbowing, pushing, hair-pulling, pinching and deliberately farting on each other in the back, is just soul-destroying. Even our marriage became rocky as the kids' arguments led to hubby and me arguing over their punishments. It was the holiday from Hell. In fact, we were the family from Hell. We've vowed never to take them away again, at least, not until their behaviour improves.

Since getting home, the fighting and constant bickering has continued. I have no idea how to deal with them – all other methods of punishment have been exhausted. Chloe went to school recently with a whopping big bruise on the side of her face, where Jack whacked her.

It's reached the point where I hate being alone with my kids, seriously! So far, I haven't found the answers.

Christine from Kettering, mum to Holly, 12, Chloe, ten and Jack, eight

The Problem Solved

Possession of the ball

We've already looked at sharing and, with siblings, exactly the same rules apply. Sharing is hard for young children and has to be taught. Allow them to keep aside very precious things that they don't want to share. Help them negotiate timed turns. And avoid inevitable tussles over particularly desirable things in the first place: if you know from experience that they will both want the pink plate, make sure there are always two pink plates available!

Brothers with arms

You can't be with your kids at every moment, but whenever possible, you should pre-empt flashpoints. If you spot the warning signs, 'divide and conquer' – in other words, separate them before it all kicks off. Or offer a distraction – change the subject, introduce a new activity, or suggest an irresistible diversion. (Wave a bag of crisps in front of them, if necessary – not nutritionally ideal, but sometimes you have to weigh these things up, and a portion of salt may be better than a black eye.)

Sometimes, you have to leave siblings to sort out their conflicts themselves – even when they're small. More often than not, they'll come to a resolution on their own. And anyway, they are quite possibly fighting as a cry for your attention in the first place, so indulging them by rushing in with a response may not be the answer. Of course, if the conflict is becoming physical and there's a possibility of real harm being caused, you have to intervene. Separate them and put them in different places for 'time out'. Don't try and force them to 'make up' once they've calmed down, but do bring them together to talk about what went wrong.

Two into one won't go

Don't try and force togetherness if your children don't get on. Let them have their own space where possible – even if they share a bedroom, make sure they get to spend time alone in it if that's what they want. Allow them to have separate possessions, separate friends and separate activities. When you want to do things as a family, focus on the things they do have in common.

Point out that they don't have to be friends, but they do have to have respect for one another – it's a tricky concept, but they should start to get the hang of it once they're at school and forming lots of new relationships. You couldn't possibly jump on every insult, even if you heard them all. But very personal or hurtful abuse should be reined in: make sure you say so when something is unacceptable. Again, appealing to their empathy can be helpful. How would *they* like it if someone had touched on *their* raw nerve?

If they're old enough to make sense, encourage them to talk to one another. It may sound a bit touchy-feely, but it's really valuable if they can express the way they're feeling. This skill is called emotional literacy. And talking things through is a vital element of 'restorative justice' – there's a bit more about this approach in the factfile on p. 121.

Keep in mind that, usually, squabbles come and go. Warring siblings are often, ironically, also very close and even affectionate at other times. Praise them and acknowledge them when it's all going well!

Love one, love them all

When all's said and done, jealousy is probably the main cause of sibling conflict. If one of them has something the other has – whether it be an appealing new possession, or the tacit favouritism of one or other parent – it will foster resentment and lead to rows. Try not to compare them, or show you love or esteem one of them more. When they fight or fall out, issue consequences to both if consequences are required – and it doesn't really matter who started it, because if they're fighting, they're both in the wrong.

What the experts say
The child psychologist

Sibling squabbles are completely normal, but they do tend to get worse when a child, or the whole family, is in the middle of a difficult time. Stress can make everyone more bad-tempered, and conflict just adds to the stress, so it's a bit of a vicious circle. Often, children pick up on tension in the house and will take it out on one another, as it's safer and more satisfying than taking it out on the adults – that's because adults are less likely to be goaded into arguing back, and also, they will be less easy to wallop if you want to!

What parents need to remember is not to get really involved, as they will then become an essential element of the squabble. It helps put squabbles into perspective to think about your own experiences while growing up, and the squabbles *you* had. There *can* be lots of good things about sibling squabbles. They teach a child how to negotiate, and share, and forgive: essential skills for a high emotional IQ, and success in later relationships. They can help a child learn who they are, and how they fit into the world.

Things can change as children grow up, and those that squabbled most can be very close when older. The determining factor is how the parent deals with the squabbling or rivalry and how it is resolved. It's a very positive thing if a child grows up knowing that they can argue with their sibling, but that it can all get sorted out, and that they are easily able to forgive one another.

It's important to recognise the high risk times for squabbles – getting into the car, mealtimes, watching television. When you've found a pattern, think about how you can avoid the conflicts. Establish turns for the front seat or the television schedule, and make sure bedtimes and other routines and house rules are very clear. When a squabble does emerge, leave them to get it out of their system if possible. Once a parent gets involved in the heat of the moment, trying to separate them or find out who did what can escalate a situation rather than defuse it. It's good to get involved afterwards, when they've calmed down. Ask what happened and what could be done differently next time. Schools are opting to take this approach rather than find blame or issue punishments to students caught up in a conflict situation – it's called 'restorative justice' (see the factfile, p. 121).

Some siblings are so different that they don't get on. Trying to find something that they do like doing together is useful. Otherwise, talking openly with them about how they can get on with each other may help. If they're not getting on, remember that it may be a symptom of some other stress, such as problems at school, or tension between their parents, and that the phase will more than likely pass. The most important thing in a child's life is to feel loved and accepted unconditionally by their parents. If they feel that this is being compromised by their siblings, they will start to resent them, but as long as there is no obvious leaning towards one sibling, and away from another, then it should be OK.

Dr Angharad Rudkin

The family therapist

The balancing act that parents with more than one child have is amazing. It's not a case of loving each child equally, and dividing your attention equally. Children need different things at different times, and what may seem 'equal and fair' to a parent is so often, quite rightly, not seen as such by a child. There are no easy ways of working it out. Listening to them carefully can help.

Pre-empting squabbles is a good idea, but only some of the time. You also need to encourage them to sort it out for themselves – it's good training for life. And try to set the right example. I've had parents seeking help over fighting and shouting siblings, and often it's been no surprise to learn that they were copying their parents' behaviour.

Often siblings fall out around adolescence, because it's a time when we tend to form our characters. The comforting thing is that they often become great friends later. However, sibling rivalry does go on into adulthood, in more subtle ways – I see it every Sunday lunch time! It's just a fact of life and one that you may have to accept.
Jill Curtis, www.Family2000.org.uk

The Problem Summarised

- Hard as it is to deal with, remember that sibling conflict is normal. Positive, even.
- Leave them to deal with it alone where possible – unless someone's about to be hurt!
- There will probably be periods when they don't get on, and periods when they don't.
- Their relationship now won't necessarily be the template for their relationship as adults.
- Siblings can be very different people, and won't necessarily get on. You may just have to accept that.
- Pre-empt flashpoints whenever you can.
- Love and treat them equally. Don't give them cause to resent one another.

Factfile: Restorative justice

A practice increasingly employed in schools today, restorative justice focuses on repairing harm done to relationships by conflict, rather than laying blame and issuing punishments. But it can be a useful philosophy to draw on in the home, too. Key elements are listening to all perspectives when conflict arises; encouraging children to think about the impact of their actions and make amends, to show listening skills, and to vocalise their feelings; and to allow them to find their own resolutions to difficult situations.

You do need to be in a calm frame of mind, though, if you're going to instigate it successfully – so take a deep breath first! And bear in mind it's not much use for pre-schoolers who won't have sufficient grasp of the necessary skills.

Here's how to do it. Gently separate warring siblings and ask if they would like your help to resolve things. Then invite them to sit down either side of you. Alternate some simple questions to each in turn, such as: 'What's happened?' 'How are you feeling?' 'How could this be put right?' Then, as each makes a suggestion about what they could do, consult the other. They may even be able to negotiate without you. If they manage to reach a resolution between themselves, thank them and round things off by asking how they each feel now, and what they might do next time they fall out.

Find out where you can find out more about restorative justice in the Appendix, p. 387.

Senior moments: How to have a good relationship with their grandparents

The Problem

I have a father-in-law who's a pain in the backside. He's always interfering in our lives. On the other hand, my own dad couldn't care less about me or the girls – he's only seen them a handful of times. Thankfully my mother-in-law (who's separated from my father-in-law) is lovely and is a great support to us all.

Lara from Hastings, mum to Ellie, four and Lola, one

The generation game

When we make parents of ourselves, we automatically make grandparents of our own mums and dads. In an ideal world, Nana and Pops would be over the moon about their special role. They would adore each of their grandchildren, passionately and equally, and always be relied upon to bring just the right gifts, at just the right time. They would be on hand to give enthusiastic help whenever it's needed, yet never be hurt when they're *not* required. And of course, they would be happy to pass on the benefits of their wisdom – but *only* when their opinion is actually sought.

Meanwhile, back on Earth, life's not much like that. Relationships between different generations can be complicated, and require effort to maintain. But in most cases, it's well worth it if you can. Research has shown that there is often a 'special' bond between old and young generation[1] that modern grandparents are more likely than ever to be considered 'fun companions' by their grandchildren[2], and that they commonly provide crucial support in times of crisis[3].

Good granny, bad granny

Grandparents can be a mine of good advice, a huge practical help and a useful extra source of love and attention for your children. Happily, there are millions of grandparents around who play a positive role of one sort or another in their grandchildren's lives. If you are lucky enough to be in this position, rejoice: supportive grandparents are one of the great bonuses of extended family life. Be sure to love and appreciate them – and to show that love and appreciation, too. For one reason or another, not all grandparents are a source of unceasing support. They may be absent altogether, or rarely around – perhaps because of a rift, or because they have exciting lives of their own. Some are critical or intrusive, to an annoying extent.

It's the way things go in families.

The Problem Shared

What the Netmums say

I have a mother-in-law who didn't bother with my eldest, her first grandchild, until she was two and a half. When I told her I was pregnant,

1. Weissvourd, B., *There will always be lullabies: enduring connections between grandparents and young children*, 1996.
2. Anderson, Tunaley and Walker, *Relatively speaking: communication in families*, 2000.
3. Thompson, P., *The role of grandparents when parents part or die*, 1999.

she said: 'As long as you think you're doing the right thing.' Later when she refused to babysit, we got: 'Well, I've brought up my kids, I've done my bit'.

On Mollie's first birthday they were too busy to come over, which made me sad. I think it's very important that children and grandparents are involved with each other. My daughter calls her 'grandma lady' because she isn't completely sure who she is.

She has another grandma, my mum, who she sees every week. Mum sometimes tries to tell me how to bring up my children, but I refuse to accept it when she does. It's a case of my kids, my rules.
Mary from Bristol, mum to Mollie, five and Connie, two

I was still living at home when I had Tiyana so my mum helped out loads, maybe a little *too* much in the beginning. Now that we live further away from her, Tiyana spends every other weekend with her, from Friday to Sunday – this is their time together and I know they both look forward to it and enjoy it. If she can't do it for some reason, it's not an issue. But if anything, she asks to have her more often.
Cherri from Thetford, mum to Tiyana, three and Tidus, two weeks

I don't doubt that my in-laws love my younger son, but he's just not treated the same as my elder son – the first grandchild, and to their mind, 'Golden Balls'! I don't know whether they're conscious of it, but it's definitely noticed by us and other members of the family – and, as he's growing older, my younger son. It's not just presents, it's also their time. It's a difficult subject to broach with them, particularly as they're unaware of it, or at least, they seem to be.
Louise from Cambridge, mum to David, seven and Jonathan, four

Despite working full time in a very demanding job, my mum often has Oliver to stay at the weekend. She does all the stuff nanas are supposed to – lets him stay up late, have chicken dippers for supper, and drink chocolate milk before bed. She's also an avid computer game player which my son loves: they spend hours together on her PlayStation! She always has time for us no matter how tired she is, which she is a lot, as she suffers from Lupus, an

exhausting medical condition. I'm crying as I write – maybe I should tell her all this myself!
Lucinda from Bolton, mum to Oliver, five and Lyla Rose, one

We live with my mother and she's a great help, like an unpaid nanny. The only problem is that living with her means we can never actually send him away for the weekend! Apart from that, it's brilliant. I couldn't work, or live the way I do, without her.
Hollie from Trowbridge, mum to Caleb, two

My in-laws are more like outlaws. They kindly informed us last year, via e-mail, that our son is suffering from malnutrition and has severe behavioural issues requiring some kind of counselling.

They did this just after we all returned from a week in a Spanish villa, during which time they made no mention of these two huge problems. As a result, they have yet to meet their new granddaughter. They did send a grovelling letter full of apologies and I've encouraged my other half to arrange to meet them somewhere for a meal to try and reconcile, but I'm adamant that if we get any more of their poisonous nonsense it will result in them not seeing either of my children again. I do think grandparents are important (especially as both my parents have passed away) but not at the expense of my children's happiness and security.

By the way, my son is perfectly healthy!
Karen from Southampton, mum to Harry, three and Mia, three months

When we announced that I was pregnant my mother-in-law went into a rage as she didn't want to be a grandma. Then everything changed and suddenly she was hugging me every five minutes! Once I'd given birth, she went pretty much back to normal. My parents lived 200 miles from where we were, but my mum was down practically every weekend helping me with the baby. My mother-in-law rarely came over and it always had to be a big event when she did. If I called to ask her over or to ask her to babysit for a couple of hours she was usually busy.

We've moved closer to my parents now and we don't regret it at all. They have him at least twice a week so I can work, and often overnight. It's been difficult to adapt to seeing my own parents so often, and sometimes we disagree over child rearing. But then, they spoil him too. We still see the in-laws. My mother-in-law and I have got into the habit of holding our tongues!

Claire from Worksop, mum to Luke, three

My mother-in-law was the best. She moved to Spain when Bethany was five months old, but she was always at the end of the phone. When I had to go into hospital for a fortnight she came over to help look after our children. She and Bethany would go out for hours, shopping, to the park, to museums. She always used to tell me that if she'd had a daughter of her own, she'd have liked one like me. She passed away in 2006, and we really do miss her, especially Bethany.

However, *my* mother and father are a complete nightmare. They moan about everything I do and have never taken an interest in the children. We had a big argument recently because my father-in-law's elderly dad came to stay with us for Christmas and my own dad went mad because he thought we should be visiting them. I've not heard from my parents since and I don't intend to contact them. I know it sounds bad, but my in-laws were more like parents to me than they are.

Emma from Swindon, mum to Bethany, seven, Robbie, two and stepmum to Owen, 18

My kids have only one surviving grandparent, my mother. Sadly, my childhood was unhappy and she and I have never had a proper relationship. As I got older, our relationship became more and more strained and nowadays we no longer communicate. She's never been the doting grandma, never even came to the last two christenings. She never asks how the children are. Never comes to see them. Never came and helped look after them, even when I was looking after my seriously ill father and had begged for help.

It's such a shame. My children have never experienced having a granny around. They don't know what it's like to bake cakes with granny, or go for walks with granny, or take part in the school plays with granny proudly watching. All they have is mum, dad, and distant aunts and uncles, who live at the other end of the country. A lot has to be said for the old days . . . families stuck together through thick and thin. Grannies were always there for worn-out daughters, willing to lend a hand or give them a well-earned break.

I envy the mums at school, the ones whose parents or in-laws are taking an active role in their grandchildren's welfare. I wonder if they realise just how lucky they are, or do they take them for granted?
Christine from Kettering, mum to Holly, 12, Chloe, ten and Jack, eight

My parents are great with my kids. Although they're getting older and really struggling to keep up with them, they do get stuck in. Hugs are endless, and my kids can talk to them about anything and feel comfortable about it. They gave us all endless support when my youngest was born (she has cerebral palsy). They still put myself and my sister, as well as our kids, before themselves. Good grandparents are magical, they put a twinkle in kids' eyes and they are another role model. Pity they can't be bottled so everyone can experience it when they need that extra cuddle.
Janet from Wisbech, mum to Lianne, 15, Jamie, nine and Rhiannon, four

The Problem Solved

Have their own lives? How dare they!

It's not unreasonable to hope for parents or in-laws who will make an active contribution to their grandchildren's lives. After all, in years gone by, it was the accepted view that families only coped when everyone pitched in – grans, aunties and other relatives included.

Times have changed, though, and the support of grandparents is no longer guaranteed. Families don't necessarily live in the same town any more, much less the same street. And the older generation are healthier and fitter: they may have money to spend and interesting things to do with their own lives, regardless of the fact that they're knocking on a bit.

It's hard accepting that your children's grandparents are too busy, too far away, or too old to be much help, or that they are disinclined to get involved because they've already 'done their bit'. And it doesn't help when you look around and see so many willing and eager grandparents doing their bit for other families you know. Try to see things from their point of view, and do your utmost not to let it become a cause for resentment. Accept whatever input you do get from them graciously. Never let the kids see that you feel cross about it – make an effort for their sake, if nothing else. Encourage your children to forge the best relationships they can with their grandparents and remember, as with any family relationship, it's very much a two-way street: do *they* ever put in a phone call, or drop them a line once in a while? If your children's grandparents are completely disinterested in them and it's no fault of yours, then that is a very sad situation. But it's their loss. Don't be bitter, or at least show you are so. And be prepared to show forgiveness if at some point they change their minds, which is always possible. Of course, a grandparent who swoops in and out of their lives and shows erratic interest can cause a lot of hurt – in that case, you may need to ask them to choose whether they want contact or not. Meanwhile, remain neutral when your child is around and don't criticise unreliable relatives within earshot of the children.

If the children are fortunate enough to have other, more loving grandparents or relatives in their lives, emphasise those relationships. And if there are none, consider 'adopting' a willing family friend or neighbour.

Whose kids are they, anyway?

Almost everyone finds that, sometimes, grandparents can cross the delicate line between welcome support and intrusion. Opinionated grandparents need to be taken with a pinch of salt and a large dose of patience. Modern society is a very different place to the world they grew up in, and the business of parenting, in many ways, is a different game now. Modern parents, for instance, may be more relaxed about discipline and routine. There's a tendency these days to 'overparent' our children – i.e., we fuss over our offspring in a way that the previous generation did not. Obviously, they are going to have some very different opinions on childrearing. Most grandparents who want to have their say will do so with the best of intentions – after all, they probably see their role as important and their opinion as highly significant. Do allow them to at least contribute their feelings, even if you don't actually agree with them. It's only fair, especially if you are already benefiting from their practical help. And often, hard as it can be to admit it when you've disagreed, they turn out to be right!

If they are interfering in a negative or spiteful way and it's causing you genuine distress, you are within your rights to speak up about it. You may have to tread carefully if you're to avoid a potential bust-up during these sorts of negotiations. Try to keep your tone light and don't end the conversation on a negative note: follow it straight up with an invitation to lunch or ask when you'll be seeing them next. Many grandparents are conscious of *not* being intrusive: some may just need a little gentle steering.

If they are persistently nosy or annoying, rise above it. Ignore their behaviour – but don't ignore them, if you can help it. These things can descend all too easily into a full-blown rift.

Dealing with rifts

Making right a serious rift can seem almost impossible and will invariably involve one party swallowing pride, sticking their neck out, and making a concerted effort to smooth things over. If it's you, you can feel justly proud of yourself. Forgiveness is a great skill to pass on to your children.

Occasionally, a serious rift is irreparable. If your family is affected by one, you'll have to explain as truthfully as you can to your child about what's gone wrong – keeping them informed will help them understand the situation and may even help them learn a useful lesson, i.e., that in life, there aren't always roses round the door. Strive to be neutral, though, and try to avoid showing them you are angry or bitter, which won't be a helpful example to set them.

If a child is sad about a lack of contact with a relative, help them to focus on the positive by thinking about the other people in their lives, who love them.

Credit where credit is due

If you and your children regularly benefit from the love, time or generosity of one or more grandparents, make sure they know you appreciate them. Remind yourself that they won't always be there.

It's estimated that around £6.8 billion worth of daycare per annum is provided by grandparents,* and anyone who makes use of such an arrangement will know how wonderful it can be not only in financial terms but knowing that your children are with relatives who care for them. But it's possible that grandparents who contribute so significantly can feel taken for granted. Even if they don't want to be paid, offer them payment – if not financial, then with an exchange of 'services'. The odd bunch of flowers or bottle of wine will probably not go amiss. And remembering to say 'thank you' to them is a good start.

What the experts say

The family therapist

The great thing about having an extended family around is that there are different role models for the kids – there's a sense of safety about having loving grandparents (or aunties or cousins) around – and family rituals such as meals together, holidays and celebrations, give a rich meaning to family bonds. In bad times, they will hopefully be there to offer support.

Of course, things can go wrong and a certain amount of sensitivity is needed, as in all relationships. It's generally better to be honest than to store up resentment and anger. So if it gets under your skin when Grandma and Grandad pop in uninvited, tactfully suggest they call first or plan visits.

If relationships do become strained, try to talk things over before it gets set in stone. Some families who 'don't talk' can't even remember how it first started. Yes, there are many grandparents too busy today to look after their grandkids, and so be it. Tough! There are others who are only too keen to take on the daily care of their grandchildren. You have to play the cards you're given.

There can be a very special bond between the older and younger generations. After all, it's easier to be totally involved with a child who will be going home later. Grandparents have, in the main, learned that time passes very quickly and so are more inclined to linger in the park, and to take time over a hobby or reading to a child.

Jill Curtis, www.Family2000.com

*Source: Skipton Building Society.

The mums' life coach

You don't have to go very far to hear stories about nightmare mothers-in-law and interfering parents. Parenting forums are full of people complaining that their parents and in-laws disapprove of their childcare methods, ignore their routines or rules, or make frequent, unannounced visits. When views diverge, it doesn't take long for tensions to arise, as the issues matter so profoundly to everyone. This can lead to misunderstanding and needless conflict. What is intended as helpful advice is interpreted as interfering.

But at their best, grandparents can be a fantastic source of knowledge, reassurance, support and babysitting. They can mother you when you feel vulnerable and be a much-needed shoulder to cry on when it all gets too much.

It's so easy to get into the habit of endlessly criticising a member of your family. Take a deep breath and ask how your own behaviour stands up. Most of us can't claim to be beyond reproach in our family relations. This isn't a question of who started it, but looking calmly at how you've acted and responded. Have you been snappy? Have you allowed situations to arise that could have been avoided? Have you failed to set boundaries clearly enough or let things pass when you could have spoken out? Being aware of your own behaviour, and addressing your own issues and motivation can make a huge difference to how you get on with family members. Identify the flashpoints – times when conflicts are likely to arise – and plan ahead. Common triggers for tension include Christmas, weddings, funerals and children's birthday parties. If you can work out strategies for avoiding conflict, you'll save yourself a lot of headaches.

Make it clear what your plans are: where you're going for Christmas Day, who's invited to the party – and then everyone knows what to expect. Avoid arguments by meeting on neutral territory, anything to take the sting out of things. The time may come when you have to confront a family member about an issue you have with them. Think about the best place to talk. Work out what you want to achieve from the conversation beforehand, and aim to avoid being provocative in what you say, and the way you say it. 'I'd prefer the children to stick to their usual bedtime' is more constructive than 'You always let them stay up too late!'

Finally, remember that no family is perfect. If things are bad, comfort yourself with the knowledge that you're teaching your children about real life. If they can see you handling conflict confidently, and doing your best to make your relationships the best they can be, they'll be learning a lesson for life.

Patricia Carswell

The grandparents' representative

All children thrive on time and loving attention; grandparents are experienced in raising children and will usually love to spend time with them, so there's no doubt it *can* be a mutually beneficial relationship. For grandparents, the experience of being involved in helping a new generation grow up is all the more thrilling, as they're able to hand the children back to their parents at the end of the day.

Remember that grandparents are also parents themselves, and may find it difficult not to comment on the way that their grandchildren are being raised by their adult children. This may be in part because advice on childcare changes with each generation – and of course they will be naturally concerned about and interested in their children and grandchildren's lives. Communication and a non-judgemental approach is the key. It's up to grandparents to respect the younger generation's decisions about their family, but likewise, it's great if they can be involved too, sometimes. Listen to them, even if you don't agree or have no intention of taking their advice. And if you've done something they don't 'approve' of, help them to understand what you did by explaining it.

It's helpful to grandparents – and parents, too – if it's very clear what the expectations are, on all sides. Every family is different, but lucky families are able to depend on family members to help out in a crisis, babysit, share holidays and most of all enjoy being in each other's company. But help needs appreciation, reciprocating love and affection – make sure they know you value them. It's about give, as well as take.

If children have developed a relationship with any significant member of the family it's hard for them if the relationship is severed. Families are important to children and many children enjoy the relationship with the grandparent. Mediation services can be helpful to develop an understanding when things have got really bad. And it's worth remembering that, even if you don't get on with your mother or mother-in-law, your children might.

Caroline Needham, The Grandparents Association

The Problem Summarised

- ◆ Relationships between older and younger generations can be tricky, and require work!
- ◆ When things are good, grandparents can be a source of great joy and support.
- ◆ Show your appreciation to grandparents who are loving and helpful.
- ◆ Encourage your child to have a good relationship with their grandparents, even if you don't.
- ◆ Plenty of grandparents have their own lives to lead. It's their choice!
- ◆ Try not to be upset by criticism and offended by opinions – they almost certainly mean well.

Talking points: How to communicate with them . . . and help them communicate with you

The Problem

> Because of work and a busy life it's very rare I get to talk much with Joshua. I always make sure we have at least one family meal a week just me, him and his sister and we talk about things like school and what's bothering him if anything. Also, if I sense anything's wrong I'll make a special effort at bedtime to make him feel secure and able to talk.
>
> *Kimmie from Newhaven, mum to Joshua, four and Chelsea-Lou, two*

Why talking is important . . .

Good communication is the key to a great many issues in family life. If you can talk to your children – regularly, openly and appropriately – and they can also talk to you, then you're already halfway to solving all sorts of parenting problems. And talking and listening to little ones is particularly vital as it will help them to develop their own language and communications abilities and go on to learn, read, write and socialise better.

It sounds easy enough: talking and listening, two basic skills. And yet these things don't always come easily where kids are concerned. For one thing, we've usually got too much else on our plate. Children can take an awfully long time to get a sentence out – and you can guarantee they'll choose the moment that you're pulling dinner out of the oven or colouring your hair to engage you in conversation. For another, an awful lot of 'communicating' in families is done during flashpoints. These are the moments when we're supposed to be talking things through in a calm, rational way, but in fact what comes out of our mouths is a load of loud, cross words which we don't even mean.

. . . and so is listening

If you want your kids to talk, you have to be able to listen. It may sound obvious, but if we're honest, few of us do so all the time. Watch yourself next time your child has something to say: are you 'all ears', or are you tuning in with half a mind, while the rest concentrates on whatever else you're doing? It's easily done – we're all busy. But finding the time where it counts will make a real difference to their self-esteem and self-confidence. Kids need to know they are being listened to, that they are interesting, and clever, and funny, and able to say whatever they need to without fear of being ignored, humoured or contradicted.

The Problem Shared

What the Netmums say

I talk to my sons all the time and have a very open relationship with both of them. They've been through a lot in their little lives and talking and being able to express themselves to me has helped them enormously. My eldest son initially doesn't open up when something bad happens and I allow this so he can get his thoughts straight in his mind, then he comes to me, or I go to him and we cuddle and discuss what's on his mind and ways to deal with it. It's taken a few years of hard work to get to this point though.

My youngest is very open, sensitive and thoughtful, but sometimes doesn't like to discuss certain things. We got stuck in a lift a while ago and he got upset about it and blamed me for taking them into the lift. Once he'd calmed down he apologised and we talked about it. Now though, he won't talk about it at all, other than to say he doesn't want to go in a lift again.

If they've achieved something then it's like they're bursting to tell me about it as soon as it happens. Sometimes I make them take it in turns or they talk all over each other. Whatever they want to talk about, I will talk about with them.
Debra from Wolverhampton, mum to Joe, nine and Sam, seven

I've found the best way to talk with my son is at bedtime, when he's clean and relaxed, with a full tummy, and sitting in his bed. We'll look at books for a bit, and I'll ask questions about his day, or bring up something that happened earlier. We can have quite long and meaningful conversations then, where he'll tell me what's happened in school, or, more importantly, if something has made him unhappy, in which case we try talking about what we can do to make it better.
Sissel from London, mum to Alexander, five

I think the key to good communication is starting from a young age. If it's normal within your family to natter about your day, how you're feeling and what's troubling you, then your children should grow up thinking it's normal to talk about how they feel. I grew up in a very open house and my family were so laid back about talking to each other I'm able to tell others exactly how I feel.

I really feel it's important to talk honestly with your children from as early as possible – in an age-appropriate way, obviously – so they feel they can share too and don't learn to bottle things up. Dinner time is always a good time for us. We sit round the table and have a natter about the day. It helps my son to process everything that's happened and is very revealing. I'm always amazed to see the day through the eyes of a three year old!
Shelley from Bushey, mum to Callum, three

With both of the kids I sit and chat with them at anytime. We have family meals together every day with no television or other distractions. They each have their own special hour, at least three times a week, where we do 'their' stuff, be it reading or puzzles, and they know they can talk to me then if they have any problems. The phone is switched off in these hours so they have my undivided attention. I'd never ask them to divulge more than they wanted to and they both know I'm here all the time and even if they only want to give half the story, they know they can. We have a system in place where we can 'chat' even if we don't want to 'talk' – we all have special notepads and we leave little notes under the pillow in Toby's room and under my bedroom door so if he wants me to know something he writes it and sends it to me. It helps break the ice for when he does want to chat. We also have a washable chart in the kitchen on the door, so the kids can write nice phrases if they don't want to actually say them. When it's been read it gets a smiley face or a kiss next to it. It's a good way for the kids to show they care. We adults also use it! My advice is to always be honest and open yourself. I'm not embarrassed easily and can have any conversation with any child, or adult for that matter. Kids will pick up if you're uncomfortable talking about a certain subject, so don't let your facial expressions show if you're upset or disgusted at what they're saying.

Leigh from Manchester, mum to Jack, four and foster mum to Toby, 12

We've found our children open up when we're least expecting it, such as in the bath, or driving in the car. I think they prefer to talk in a relaxed environment. Just to be sure that we find out what they've been up to, we introduced a good thing/bad thing at the table. Basically, as we sit down to our evening meal everyone, including the adults, goes round the table and says one or two good or bad things that have happened during the day. That's when I find out about upsetting stuff at school or that they've got extra marks for good work or whatever! The boys love it and can't wait to start, and even Madeleine joins in now. It's a chance for us to share worries or happy events as a family, and it's made us feel closer to each other somehow.

Julie from Southend, mum to Jude, eight, Leon, five and Madeleine, two

My kids and I chat all the time, about everything and anything really. We talk about nursery or school, what we're going to have for tea, what we're going to do at the weekend, what they've been doing with their friends and what I've been doing with my day. I really hope this will carry on when they grow older as well. I think it helps that children have someone other than their parents that they can talk to. No matter how close they are with their parents, there will be certain things that they just won't want to discuss with them. Recently, Declan was being bullied at nursery, but he didn't want to talk to me about it. However, he is very close to his aunties (my sisters), and on this occasion he did open up to one of them. She then told me what the problem was, although I made a point of not bringing it up until he'd confided in me himself, so he didn't feel that his auntie had broken his confidence.

Lorna from Glasgow, mum to Carla, five and Declan, three

At the end of every day, I ask Liam, 'What was your worst bit of today?' It gives him the chance to talk about anything he isn't happy with, or has been upset by. It *really* helps. If something horrible has happened at school, or if he wasn't happy with how we dealt with something, it usually comes out then. I always ask him what his favourite bit of the day was afterwards, just so that he has something nice to think about while drifting off to sleep.

Kath from Berkeley, mum to Liam, seven and Bernard, one

I find that my daughter opens up better through drawing. If I think something's bothering her I get out the crayons and paper and have a chat whilst we both draw. I think it's the lack of eye contact that helps her feel comfortable and it seems natural to gossip whilst we both doodle. It also produces some interesting pictures. A friend's hamster dying produced a slightly gory picture but it got it all out of her system!

Kelly from Swindon, mum to Holly, six, George, four and Mitchell, two

The Problem Solved

Tips for talking

Households where chatter and conversation are the norm are the sort of places where difficulties are thrashed out more easily. Start up a talkative culture in your home early on, and you'll reap the benefits later. Even when they're teenagers, and they lose the power of normal speech altogether, you'll have a fighting chance of getting information out of them if they feel comfortable about talking in general – and hopefully, the 'serious' subjects like sex and drugs won't be so painful. Try to talk in the most natural circumstances possible – alongside another quiet activity, for example, such as drawing, or as an aside, while reading aloud. Or set apart a very specific period that they can recognise as talking time: just before bed, for example, or over dinner. In fact, round the table is a great place to talk as a family – yet another good reason for eating together!

Don't interrogate them, or insist on heavy subjects: just pass the time of day with one another. It's all talk, so it all counts. And when you do ask questions, make them open-ended, to give them a chance to wax lyrical if they wish. 'Tell me about your day', for example, not: 'Was your day OK?'

Even if you're not a natural communicator, it pays to get to grips with the basics. At the very least, be able to tell them you love them, ask them how their day went and give praise when praise is due.

How to be 'all ears'

There's a very definite skill to listening to children. Stop what you are doing, give them your full attention, make eye contact (and other physical contact, perhaps touching them on the shoulder) and get down to their level. Interject (but don't interrupt) with comment, so they know you're taking it in – 'Really?' 'Gosh, that's amazing' and 'Did you?' Use their name, so they know you are definitely talking to them, and just to them. And give them plenty of time to get it all out: young children can take a while finding the right words, and it may require patience to get to the end of a complicated story! Never brush them off or play down what they tell you – what they're saying may seem trite, but it matters to them. And if you don't agree with what they're saying, don't jump straight in with a contradiction or shout them down. Take their point, and then make yours.

Help to boost those 'emotional literacy' skills by encouraging them to talk about their feelings. For instance, if it's obvious they are cross or scared about something, help them find the words to express those emotions. You'll be teaching them a useful lesson for life.

If you really *don't* have time to talk because there's something else going on, ask them to hold their thoughts until you can give them your full attention. But don't forget about it!

Talking without words

Communicating isn't just about talking and listening. What you do with your face and body counts too: non-verbal gestures such as waves, squeezes, smiles, funny faces and 'thumbs-ups' can speak volumes to a child. And don't forget the written word: once they are able to, children often like to express their thoughts in writing, so make sure they have the materials and encouragement they need to do so. (You'll treasure their first written communications to you for ever!) And don't dismiss text or email. For older kids who know their way round a mobile phone or a computer, they can be a useful way of getting a message to them – or for them to let you know something they might find difficult to say face to face.

What the experts say
The child psychologist

Communication is essential for successful relationships and the driving force for well being. Having clear communication that takes into account that adult and child brains are so very different is paramount for the child to understand the adult, and vice versa. Because children are also developing their social skills, they need a little bit more help and explicit guidance, so effective communication is important for this too. It's never too early to start having conversations with your children, even when they're tiny babies, because they'll be taking in all those non-verbal cues, and learning about social interactions just by watching.

Interestingly, the majority of communication between humans is non-verbal. So when you're talking to kids, you should get to their level, keep your tone of voice calm and your posture open: if you do all that, the child is more likely to listen, and talk back.

Modelling good communication as adults is important, as well as chances to chat together as a family in a non-judgemental, intrusive context: over dinner, for example, whilst hanging the washing out, or driving them to football.

Kids are good at giving us clues if they want to talk or not. We just need to get good at picking up on them. If a child doesn't want to talk, don't force them as that will increase their anxiety. Reassure them that you are there for them whenever they want, and bring it up again gently a couple of days later.

Dr Angharad Rudkin

The mums' life coach

As a parent, you know your child better than anyone else and are best placed to understand him. Communication is vital to both of you. It's important for you, so that you understand what's going on in your child's life (however young he may be) and respond appropriately. And it's essential for your child to learn to communicate what's on his mind; it enables him to handle his experiences and emotions and to have an outlet for them.

If talking to your children about their lives is something you do as a matter of course when they're young, it makes it easier when they enter the teenage vortex. They may only grunt at you, but they know you're interested, and that matters just as much as getting meaningful conversation from them.

Anything that promotes regular conversation as part of family life is helpful. If you can't manage a family meal round a table during the week, you might be able to make up for it at weekends. Discussion and debate as a regular part of your family routine makes it less of a big deal when there's an important issue to discuss. Many mums find that the best time to talk to their children about sensitive topics is when they're doing an activity together, however humdrum. Children are often more inclined to open up when they're walking (which makes walking to and from school so great), tidying or cooking.

And don't forget that it's not just about talking. Non-verbal cues can be just as important. What they don't say can speak volumes, as can their body language – the shrug, the brave smile, the clenched fist. And it works both ways. Sometimes there's nothing you can say to change things, but a hug or a smile or even just a squeeze of the shoulder can let them know you care.
Patricia Carswell

The Problem Summarised

♦ Good communication is absolutely key in happy families. Helping your children to learn 'emotional literacy' skills will stand them in good stead for life.
♦ Kids need to know they can always speak to you, and will be heard – so always find the time to listen.
♦ Try and be a 'talkative' family. Chat together when and wherever you can.
♦ Never force a child to talk, but give them the opportunities to if they want to.
♦ Non-verbal 'talking' counts too. Drop them a line once in a while!

Birds and the bees: What, how and when to tell them about sex and sexuality

The Problem

Benjamin has recently started playing with himself a lot. I tend to ask him to stop doing it and so far he has. When he does want to carry on, I'll ask him to go to his room. He came in the bathroom yesterday when I was showering and later asked why I had a hairy bottom! I explained it wasn't my bottom, it was my front and that most grown-up people have hair there. We've never refused to tell him things if he asks, but so far we've not had to go into too much detail. It's been on a need-to-know basis and what we've told him has satisfied his curiosity, for the moment.

Jenny from Canterbury, mum to Benjamin, three and James, one

Let's talk about sex, baby

Difficult though it may be, sex is one of those things you have to be open about with your children. Kids learn about sex from all sorts of sources – at school, from their peers, from books and magazines, and from television – so they're going to find out one way or another. But with so many different versions, they may end up with a rather confused view. Schools offer a certain amount of sex education (some more than others, as policies about sex education differ), but it's probably fair to say that the best person to tell a child about sex is a parent; the best place for them to do so is in the home; and the best time to start is as soon as they're old enough to understand you.

Why sex talk is important talk

Talking easily and naturally about sex is considered vital by the experts. They believe children from families who are confident talking about sex are more likely to make happier, healthier choices in their own sex lives, when the time comes. That time may seem light years away if your children are still very young. But nevertheless, your best bet is to lay the foundations for openness, right from the start.

The Problem Shared

What the Netmums say

My four year old has been masturbating since she was about two. She really goes for it, and we've found it embarrassing. She used to sit in her car seat and rub herself against the strap. We told her to stop but she refused because it was 'nice'. We didn't want her to have a complex, so we told her if she wanted to do it, she could do it in her bedroom. I do worry sometimes that, at four, she's a bit young, but like I say, I don't want her to be embarrassed by sex. She's asked when I've bought sanitary stuff what it's for and I've told her straight, it's for my period. When she asked what a period was, I told her.
Helen from Folkestone, mum to Rebekah-Eve, four and Amy-Jayne, one

Explaining about the birds and the bees just came naturally with my children. They've always asked questions and I've always told them the truth. (No babies from under the gooseberry bush in our house . . . !)

Holly's friend was given a book to read by her mum, which explained all about periods, sex, pregnancy, but she was too embarrassed to read it. Holly then asked her friend if she could read it, seeing as she wasn't going to. She read it from cover to cover and then told her friend everything that the book said.

My son has the odd phase where he's obsessed with his willy, usually at bathtime, when the movement of the water gives him an erection. He'll yell at the top of his voice to 'come and have a look' and Chloe then runs to see his pointing penis! As for telling the children about the birds and the bees, their school has sex education lessons one week out of the year. But as a parent of three you know that, as soon as one child learns something new, they inevitably pass it on to the others. I think my son was five when he was 'informed' how babies grow and where they come out! That's sisters for you.

Christine from Kettering, mum to Holly, 12, Chloe, ten and Jack, eight

I haven't got around to discussing the birds and the bees with my boys. They haven't shown an interest yet. However, they do know two adults have sex who love each other but don't know what it is other than kissing. They also know about gay relationships.

They call their willies 'wee wees'. My younger son asked me what his 'little bottom' was called though. Trying to keep a straight face, I told him they were his testicles, and he was fine with that. He also sometimes 'fiddles' and shows me how big it is, very proudly. Going to be a typical fella, I think. They are nine and seven and have no problem with running around the house naked. However, the older one does bath himself and has done for the last year. They see me in my underwear quite a lot and sometimes see my boobs. I'm not embarrassed, but I think now they're getting older I should be more careful about how I behave around them.

Debra from Wolverhampton, mum to Joe, nine and Sam, seven

My boys are five, three, and one. The elder two have asked about periods as I have no privacy in the bathroom (which is OK). Having to explain a mooncup [a reusable menstrual cup] was interesting! I've answered any questions as and when they are asked, and they know about sex and where babies come from, but we haven't yet had to go into detail. Nudity is fine in this house, and the boys usually bath or shower with either of us. Willies are called willies, but we don't really have a name for women's 'bits', probably because they've only ever seen the hair on mine, so they just think it's hair.

Shadow from Kettering, mum to Nayan, five, Tallin, three and Ocean, one

My six-year-old son shocked me recently. We were just sat chatting, and he said 'Mum, when I see a sexy lady on telly my willy gets big and hard.' I nearly died! He said it so flippantly, then he changed the subject instantly. He's said before that he likes ladies' boobies and he's always played with his sisters' Barbies quite a bit, topless!

If the children ask us a question we will answer it honestly and age appropriately. They all know what being gay is, and accept it. We've not had to explain lovemaking yet but I don't think it will be long. I have a book waiting for when they ask.

Andrea from Derby, mum to Emily-Rose, nine, Lucy Mae, eight, Korben, six and Tyeran, four

Both my girls like to play with themselves. I ask them not to, as they can get sore. Their daddy once told her it was dirty so I had a word with him and asked him not to say that. He just wasn't really thinking, although it does make him a bit uncomfortable.

Lucy is really interested in Caitlin's bits. When she's naked she follows her around, poking her. I think it's because she can't see her own! We have to get Caitlin to wear knickers, or she'd never get any peace. I don't have my 'boobies out' often, as Lucy's also fascinated by them and wants to bounce and squish them. They don't really know about boys' bits yet, although Caitlin has looked at Daddy in the bath, clearly puzzled. She didn't ask, so we left it. We'll cross that bridge when she's ready.

Donna from Manchester, mum to Caitlin, three and Lucy, two

I told my son the facts of life just before we started trying for a baby, when he was seven or eight.

They were learning at school about caring relationships and about themselves as babies. It seemed a positive way to let him know how he was made. I had a book, so we went through it, looking at the diagrams.

My daughter was told the facts just before Andrew was born last year. We were planning a homebirth and I wanted the kids there, so she'd been watching lots of birthing programmes with me.

Knowing how babies come out prompted the inevitable question about how they got in there, so I had the same conversation with her that I'd had with her older brother a few months earlier.

She was fascinated. I also explained briefly that sex needed to be with someone special.

In our house a willy is a willy or a penis. I don't have any nicknames for girl parts so it's a vagina, although it isn't a word I use a great deal with my daughter just yet. My wee man found his willy a few weeks ago. That look of surprise and confusion when their hand finds it . . . then they spend the rest of their lives with the same expression!
Cassandra from Motherwell, mum to Aiden, eight, Anya, six and Andrew, eight months

My daughter knows that men have seeds that they put in a woman's tummy and that babies come out of a woman's bits. Thankfully she's been content with this explanation and hasn't required any further details. My eldest boy has been enthralled by his willy for as long as I can remember. He's especially proud of it when it goes hard and enjoys displaying this to close family members. We all try to look unimpressed and vague and he seems to get the idea that we don't really want to engage in a full-scale celebration each time he gets a stiffy!
Kelly from Swindon, mum to Holly, six, George, four and Mitchell, two

The Problem Solved

Too much, too young?

There's no lower age limit when it comes to talking about sex with children. In the early years, you don't need to volunteer information before they bring the subject up themselves. But even little ones will inevitably have questions about bodies and biology, and when they ask, you need to be ready with the most honest answer you think they'll understand. As they get older and exposed to more snippets of information about sex, they'll probably require more detail. Let them have it!

Seeds of truth

Be brief and as honest as you can, adapting the language according to their age. There aren't really any hard and fast rules on quite what to tell them and when: only you can decide what feels right. If you're unsure, give them truthful answers to whatever they ask, and you won't go far wrong.

When it comes to their bodies, explain what everything's for and what it's called. Sex education experts say we should use proper names for body parts, and although most parents find the words 'penis' and 'vagina' just don't trip off the tongue that naturally and tend to use more informal terms, it's a good idea to make sure they know what the proper words are, too.

Tips for talking sex

Never brush them off if they ask questions, or appear to want information. Even if it feels awkward and embarrassing, always respond if they bring the subject up, or they may be put off doing so in the future.

Talk about it while you're doing something else to take the pressure off. Use a book or a leaflet as a prop if it helps. Don't take it too seriously. Laugh about it if it helps. If you're not sure of an answer – and when it comes to it, it's amazing how many adults aren't that well up on the full facts of life themselves – suggest you look it up together.

Don't make a song and dance about 'telling them' – wait for them to ask. Using something they've seen on telly or read about in a magazine as a springboard for discussion can be helpful.

Body talk

It's completely normal for kids to touch or play with their genitals, from a very early age. Early on, this is more about comfort than sexual pleasure. And although even very young boys can get an erection, it doesn't necessarily indicate sexual arousal and in the early years is more likely to be a source of fascination or amusement than anything else. Even so, it's perfectly normal to feel a little freaked out by these things. As a parent, it's hard to think of your little boy or girl as a potentially sexual person. But it's absolutely vital not to make them feel bad or 'dirty' about it. Clearly, there's a time and a place for everything, and to avoid embarrassment you may want to gently suggest it's something they do privately. Girls sometimes reach the beginnings of puberty these days as early as eight or nine, and boys generally enter it from ten or eleven onwards. It's important they know what these amazing changes to their bodies mean, well in advance. They'll get the basics in their science lessons, but depending on their school's Sex and Relationship Education policy (see the factfile, p. 154), it may not tell them everything they need to know. In any case, a teacher's words can never be as reassuring as a mum's or dad's. Of course, it's not easy coming to terms with your 'little' girl growing boobs, or the thought of your son ejaculating. But these things are facts of life: if they hear them from you and can talk about them with you, they'll be more likely to cope with an awkward phase of their young lives.

Love, etc

It's really important to talk about sex in its wider context, too, helping them to get their head round feelings and emotions, and the idea of different sorts of relationships. Openness is also a good rule of thumb when it comes to discussing issues such as gay partnerships – if they come to you with questions, then answer them as well as you can. Remember that children will make up information if it's not given to them – and something we do know is that prejudice is fuelled by ignorance.

What the experts say
The sex education forum co-ordinator

Of course it isn't always easy for us to talk to our children about sex. We may feel embarrassed, and we may not be sure of the facts ourselves. But it's critical that we do, because children who have good sex education at home and school tend to start sex later, and are less likely to have an unplanned pregnancy or to get a sexually transmitted infection. These things may seem irrelevant if your children are not even out of primary school yet, but the fact is that the earlier you start talking to your children about relationships, feelings and sex the easier it will be to carry on talking to them when they come under pressure as teenagers.

It's important to talk to children in a way that's appropriate to their age, but very young children are curious and ask questions, and there's no right age to start. Make sure you're honest, and use straightforward language. And try to bring things up in the context of everyday life, for instance chatting about their bodies while they're in the bath, or while you're changing a baby brother or sister's nappy. It's good for children to be able to use the proper name for body parts: even if you do find the right terms awkward, try and make sure you use them alongside whatever other words you use so your children can be understood when they are at school or outside the family.

Talking about body parts and 'making babies' needn't be complicated. Be sure to mention love and nice feelings – after all, sex is one of the ways in which two grown-ups show they love each other. Also sex education in schools tends to focus on the negative consequences of sex, so if or when older teenagers decide to have sex, they are often taken by surprise by the strong feelings involved. This can make them completely forget about the responsibilities which go with sex, such as making sure it's mutual and safe rather than forced or a cause of regret.

Children see and hear things about sex from a young age. By talking to them and answering their questions, you are giving them the building blocks they need to start to make sense of the adult world. You're also sending a powerful message about sex being an accepted and pleasurable part of adult life and not something furtive, dirty or shameful, which could help your children to seek help if anything unpleasant or unsafe happens to them. And if your faith or culture means that you have particular beliefs and values about sex and relationships which you want your children to understand and respect, talking to them at home is an excellent way of getting these across.

Gill Mullinar, Sex Education Forum

The child psychologist

Children are very good at filling in the gaps themselves. If adults don't tell them what's really going on they'll make it up themselves, usually pieced together from things they've heard, which can lead to misleading beliefs about pretty important things. So being open with children about sex is important – but, as they'll show different levels of interest, you do need to be guided by *them*.

It can seem awkward talking about sex with our kids, because it's still a hugely taboo subject. Also, it's the kind of thing that kids can't bear the thoughts of their parents doing, and parents can't bear the thought of their children doing! Adults may fear saying the wrong thing, or that they'll be putting ideas in their heads. But parents are the most important role models for children, and the people they have the most intimate relationship with, so the way parents talk about and feel about sex is really important for the child.

It's difficult to say what sort of language to use when talking about sex, as each child's understanding and emotional development can be so different. There are lots of books that can offer guidance on this. Another way of working out what sort of language to use is to look at the kinds of books they're reading themselves. They'll soon let you know if they understand, so you need to be alert to their signals. Girls are best warned about periods, although there's a fine balance between giving them enough information to know what is happening when they start theirs, without scaring them so much that they dread the prospect. In reality, most girls will already have had chats about it with their friends so there's probably not much a parent can do other than let them know where the things are if they need them, be there for them on the day, and let them know that they understand.

As for the matter of children touching their genitals, they do so because they are pure pleasure zones and touching them makes them feel good, in the same way as sucking their thumb! The sense of 'naughtiness' comes when people tell them to stop! Even open-minded adults can find it hard to watch as their child has a good old grope in the bath. Once they get to school and realise that boys and girls are different they'll probably go through a different phase of exploring – 'you show me yours, and I'll show you mine'. So it's very natural to touch these areas; it doesn't mean that they're perverts, it just feels nice. How this is responded to over time will contribute to a person's feelings – guilt or not – about masturbation and sex. Of course, it's normal to be a little bothered by it because as adults we associate playing with our bits as sexual. I would advise just to let the child get on with it! If they're doing it to the degree that really concerns you, then distracting them rather than saying 'stop' would be the best way forward.

Dr Angharad Rudkin

The Problem Summarised

- ◆ It's vital to talk about sex with your kids: if you don't, someone else will!
- ◆ Be as honest and open as possible. Let them lead the way with questions.
- ◆ They're never too young to start talking about sex.
- ◆ Don't rely on their teachers to tell them everything. It may not be enough.
- ◆ Use a book or something they've seen on television as a starting point, if it helps.
- ◆ Give them plenty of warning about puberty.
- ◆ Don't forget to talk about love, and other important relationship issues, too.

Factfile: What will they learn at school about sex?

Sex and Relationship Education (SRE) is taught in all schools as part of the National Curriculum for science. Under guidance from the Department for Children, Schools and Families, schools are expected to teach children at Key Stage 1 (ages five to seven) that all animals including humans reproduce, and to recognise and name the main external parts of the human body; and at Key Stage 2 (ages seven to 11) the basic facts of human life processes, including reproduction.

Many schools also look at the subject beyond basic biology, as part of the non-compulsory Personal, Social and Health Education (PSHE). At Key Stage 2, this means exploring subjects such as different types of relationship, and how puberty can cause changes in their feelings. Some experts would like to see PSHE become a compulsory part of the National Curriculum so that all children can benefit from these lessons.

All schools must draw up a sex education policy, and must by law make available a written statement for parents, explaining what will be taught and when. Parents have the right to withdraw their children from all or parts of SRE, except for those required by the statutory curriculum – though in fact, very few do!

Buddy talk: How to help them make friends, and stay friends

The Problem

My daughter had a terrible time with her so-called 'best friend', whose behaviour became increasingly spiteful and often caused her to come home in tears. Try as you may as a mum, you can't choose your child's friends. All I could do was try to help her see why someone else may be a better choice of 'best friend' and to teach her what true friendship is about.

Louisa from Wimbourne, mum to Marla, aged seven

Why friends are good for you . . .

Friends are a great asset at any time of life, but when you're a child and you're still finding your way in the world, they're particularly good to have around. For a child, friends can be a great source of support, comfort and security, particularly during those tricky early days and weeks in a new group or class. Friends can help a child develop their own personality and self-esteem, and the business of making and keeping friends is more or less essential practice for a child if they're going to find a place in society.

And of course, friends are fun, too. The world would be a sad place without them.

. . . and why they are bad

The flipside to all these good things is that friends and friendships can also cause quite a bit of heartache. As a general rule children are sociable creatures, just like adults. But it's not always easy making friends, especially for those of a shy disposition. And even when they've got friends, children fall out with them, regularly – it's par for the course. Sometimes they make up, and sometimes they don't. Either way, they'll go on to make new ones. It's hard as a mum not to worry about your kid's friends, or lack of them. But the basic truth is that children, by and large, are resilient little humans who can probably weather their social storms better than we realise.

The Problem Shared

What the Netmums say

My son has a best friend that he met at nursery and is now at school with. According to their teacher they are always there for each other and help each other out with school work. However, when playing together they're like an old married couple, bickering constantly! I'm sure this means they will be friends for life.
Lucinda from Bolton, mum to Oliver, five and Lyla Rose, ten months

I almost cried when Amy came home from school recently and told me that her friend Emily hadn't wanted to play with her that day. Why do little girls do that to each other? I remember quite clearly having the same experience when I was a girl – and doing it to others, too. I felt like going up to Emily at school the next day and saying: 'Oi. Be nice to my daughter!' Of course, they were best buddies again straight away. I guess it's just the way life goes.
Lorna from Winchester, mum to Amy, five and Izzie, two

My eldest is due to go to senior school soon. She has a small circle of four friends, and I so wish I could wave a magic wand to help her make more. I have got her going to the local Youth Theatre, where no one else from her school goes, and that's helped. She also goes to Guides. The senior school she's going to has several after-school clubs which I'll encourage her to join, and she'll meet lots of other kids there. I have also been to see her teacher to ask her to arrange work groups in such a way that she's not always with her four main friends, so she has to try to get along with others.

Sharon from Chester, mum to Becky, ten, Sean, eight and Charlotte, five

Sometimes my boys squabble with their friends, but I don't intervene, I just allow them to make friends again at their own pace, which always happens. If the boys are upset about it then we talk through it so they can see both sides of the argument. They both make new friends very easily. I think this is because they have each other and that's a confidence boost. When my daughters were teenagers I had some nightmare times though. All their fallings out ended with bullying and resentment and bad feelings all the way round.

Debra from Wolverhampton, mum to Joe, nine and Sam, seven

My daughter is a drama queen and since she was two I've been regaled with tales of her making and breaking friendships – more complex and entertaining than *EastEnders*! Moving to a new home 500 miles away, where we knew no one else with kids, has been an interesting experiment. Whereas my daughter has had friendships with my own friends' children from birth, my eldest son has not had this due to the move, and he went to nursery knowing no one. He's made his own friends and it's been fascinating to see him choose people because they share similar interests (mainly dinosaurs) or are compatible in personality – and not just boys, he has a favourite friend who's a girl. They play very detailed games such as pirates and have never argued, whereas my daughter with her 'pre-destined' pals clashed on a regular basis.

With this experience under my belt, I plan to do the same with my youngest son, in the hope that he will make his own friendships naturally at nursery, rather than be coerced into them at toddler group by his well-meaning mummy!

Kelly from Swindon, mum to Holly, six, George, four and Mitchell, two

When my eldest child started pre-school she found it really hard to make friends because they all seemed to know each other and had their own little groups. It really did break my heart.

Personally I think that's half the problem: everywhere you go, people form cliques and if you don't fit, neither does your child. Anyway, we persevered and we managed to get through the rough period. Then, of course, she encountered the 'you're not my friend any more' phase, which made her really upset. If and when she does fall out with a friend, we sit and talk about it. I ask if perhaps the other child was upset or sad. Then I tell her: 'Tomorrow is another day.'

Mary from Bristol, mum to Mollie, five and Connie, two

Recently my son started reception class at a school outside our parish, where he knew nobody. It was a terrible few months for him while he was trying to find his feet and make friends. It broke my heart when he told me he was sad because he had no friends to play with. I think communication was key to helping him through it. We talked about his days, and the children in his class, then he started to tell me about some of the boys he did like and I was able to start arranging play dates. He's now made some good friends and he's a happy and confident little boy.

Sissel from London, mum to Alexander, four

My younger daughter has difficulty in making and keeping friends due to behavioural issues. But to try and help her with the social aspect of things we've enrolled her in many different groups, such as Girls Brigade and Rainbows [the youngest group in the Girl Guides]. This has been great for her as it means she gets to interact with other children of her age and can see how she's supposed to behave – she now has a number of little friends she runs off to play with when she gets there. My eldest doesn't have one particular friend, but has a large group of them. She's a sociable child and often plays the role of peacemaker within her group. I've found from my own experience

that unless there is violence or severe bullying involved then it is best to let them get on with the business of sorting their own disagreements out, otherwise how do they learn to cope with difficult people in later life. After all, they're not going to get on with everybody, are they?
Alex from Telford, mum to Raechel, ten and Hayley, six

As a pre-schooler, Noah was very confident about making friends. We'd go to the park and he'd look around and then go over to someone and start playing or talking to them. But since starting school, he's really struggled. He doesn't play football so that rules out a large proportion of the boys in his class, and the rest he just doesn't gel with. He's bright but can be silly, and he gets called 'weirdo' although I can't work out why. He gets on well with some of the girls, but he's grown out of playing mums and dads with them. I've tried to help him with any friendships that do start up by inviting the friend for tea but he hardly ever gets invited back and then they just seem to drift apart.

I hate wishing his life away but I'm looking forward to him going to high school. Maybe he'll meet some boys more like himself.
Laura from Cheltenham, mum to Noah, eight

The Problem Solved

Helping them make friends from the start

It's a good idea to help your little one make friends well before starting school. They'll have enough on their plate coping with that momentous life event, so if they've already got a well-honed ability to socialise, it'll be one less thing to worry about.

The simplest way to find friends for your children before school is for *you* to find friends, with kids of their own. You may well have long-standing friends who happened to have procreated around the same time as you and live within spitting distance. Or you may need to make some: ante-natal classes, mother and toddler groups, or just the good old park are all likely meeting grounds, not to mention online communities like Netmums.

In most towns there'll be a complex social network of parents, and once you've met a few, it usually leads to meeting more.

It's true that 'cliques' of people sometimes dominate these groups. Be bold: penetrate them by introducing yourself. If that doesn't work, start your own. And if people are really sniffy, they're not worth bothering with – try a new group, somewhere else. On the other hand, if your child is managing to make friends perfectly well on his own, let him.

Once they've played with another child on public territory and they seem to get on, you can invite them round for a 'play date' or suggest meet-ups elsewhere. When they're little, these will probably involve their parent or carer coming, too, so make sure that's a scenario that suits you. Then a friendship may blossom, or it may not. Before school, friendships are pretty casual affairs and should be taken as such. Don't be upset if some go by the wayside. There'll be lots more round the corner.

Some grown-up friends find to their disappointment that their offspring don't get on. If that happens, don't force them to endure each other's company. Try and establish the things they do have in common and the things they both like doing. Otherwise, you may have to accept they'll never be pals and agree to meet in the evening, instead.

When friendships mean more

If they don't have any friends once they've started school, they soon will. After this point, friendships will usually become more enduring, or significant to them. They may also be more upset if things go wrong, but all you can really do is take a back seat and let them feel their own way through. Of course, if a friendship sours to the extent that bullying is involved, it's time to take action. (See p. 332 for more on this.) You can help them be as prepared as possible for the ups and downs of friendships by nurturing the skills they'll need – sharing, good manners, and communicating among them. And for when things go pear-shaped: negotiation, compromise and empathy.

Good friend, bad friend

Most mums worry about the friends their kids keep, although it's unlikely to be a source of major problems before they hit their teens. Their peers do have huge influence over children: it's a fact of life, and even from an early age, it may be a cause for concern.

Trying to force them apart from 'bad' friends won't help, and it may even make the friendship stronger. Keep a close eye on things if you can – invite the friend in question to play, and make it your business to meet their parents: you may find they are perfectly nice people. Otherwise, try not to fret. Emphasise your own family values, and keep providing clear boundaries at home. There's every chance that the friendship will fizzle out with time as their shared interests and attitudes wane.

A word about imaginary friends

Imaginary friends are perfectly normal. They can help a child feel less lonely and more in control, and help them learn how to be with others. Humouring children with imaginary friends is fine, but you'll need to let them know that other people might not be so understanding, for example, teachers might not make a space for their friend at the table, even if you do so at home.

If they're very dependent on an imaginary friend, it may be a sign that they're struggling to fit in and find real life pals. You may need to gently encourage them towards a bit of real social interaction.

What the experts say
The child psychologist

Friendships are an important way for children to learn about essential life skills such as sharing, negotiation, and forgiveness. We all want to be liked, and popular children have higher self-esteem and a greater belief in their abilities. And the experiences we have in early life friendships pave the way for our adult ones. As adults we put great store by our friends and measure our success by the number and quality of friends we have. We then transfer this to our children, believing that the more friends they have the 'better' they are.

Some children do have less sociable temperaments – often because they have anxious or shy parents – and they'll be less confident in socialising. Providing structure for friendships initially, inviting friends over for tea, for example, or taking them places where there'll be other kids around will help naturally shy children learn to be with friends without having to find the confidence themselves.

We're also very protective of our children, and watching them go through the ups and downs of friendships can be heartbreaking. But allowing children to go through this on their own is giving them a valuable lesson. If they do fall out with friends, it's better to guide them as they sort it out independently, rather than jump in immediately. This is far easier said than done, of course, and does depend on the child's ability and age. It's horrible, but nonetheless normal, when children form cliques and then exclude members from time to time. There's a real pressure within groups to identify who's in and who's out. If a child learns to tolerate this and rise above it then they'll learn how to deal with similar difficulties later on in life. But there is a fine line between this and actual bullying – in general, keeping clear and open communication lines between you and your child and between you and school offers a great safety net for the child, should they experience any difficulties. Children who find it easier to make friends are those that are confident, sociable, resilient and have good self-esteem. Those that find it difficult are children who are over-controlling and so want to dominate every time they are with their friends, and those who are shy and insecure. Helping your child to learn different ways of being with friends by letting them see how *you* form and keep social connections, or supervising their play for a little while should help. In the end, most children find their niche.
Dr Angharad Rudkin

The mums' life coach

'Nobody likes me' are the words no mother wants to hear. We all want our children to have the security and the warmth of a solid group of friends, and agonise if they can't make any or if they fall out with them. Friends can make the difference between surviving and thriving, which is why this subject is such a crucial one.

For many mothers, the issue is a charged one, for it brings back memories of their own experiences of childhood. Who can forget the taunts of the jealous classmate? But it's important not to let these memories unduly influence your reaction to your child's experiences. Your child may respond entirely differently from you, so seeing it through your own eyes, though it may help you to empathise, may not always be helpful.

You can make the path a lot smoother by encouraging your child to socialise from a young age, going to playgroups or mother and toddler groups. And you can teach them skills to handle conflict.

Ultimately, though, this is an area of your child's life where you can't be too controlling. Try as you might, you can't make your child like Max next door, just because you think he's a suitable friend, any more than you can stop him from being drawn to the gang of children you'd cross the street to avoid. What you can do is be there to guide, advise, comfort and encourage.

And don't forget that if it's tough for your child now, the chances are that it'll get better. If you look round your group of friends as an adult, you've probably met many of them at a later stage in your life.
Patricia Carswell

The Problem Summarised

- Overall, friends are a very positive part of childhood. Children want them and need them as much as adults do.
- Kids can be very good at making their own friends, but they'll need some help when they're very young.
- It's absolutely normal for children to fall in and out of friendships. Hard as it is, it's better to step back and let them do so alone.
- Help them make and keep friends by passing on the social skills they need to do so.

Beating Lego loathing: How to enjoy spending time with your children

The Problem

Honestly? Really, truly, honestly? I find Karli incredibly boring at times. How on earth can someone be content to do the same thing over and over again for hours at a time? There are exceptions, of course. I love lying on the sofa with her, reading books. We can draw together for hours, as well, and enjoy long, bubbly baths together. But I hate any other form of crafts. And she'll ask me numerous times to dress and undress the same dolly, over and over. Luckily Daddy is on hand for hours of Lego building, so I just cherish doing the things with her that we both love.

Ellie from Cheltenham, mum to Karli, three and Alexander, two months

Am I a bad mother if I don't like play?

Terrible as it may seem to admit, there are large numbers of mums who find being with their children is no picnic. It's completely and utterly normal to feel this way. Kids are hard work and the truth is that they, or at least the things that they like to do, are often boring when you're an adult. It's not exactly surprising: they are usually at least two decades younger than us, with different interests. They commonly have small concentration spans, and they tend to make a large amount of mess.

The extent to which we mums can enthuse over their preferred choice of activities is variable. But if you're on the bottom end of this scale because you're underwhelmed by potato printing, or cannot summon any interest in play dough, don't fret. It doesn't make you a bad mother. It just means you are a grown-up.

Do they really *need* me to play with them?

It varies hugely but, at some point, kids reach an age or a state of mind where they're able to play alone, or with friends or siblings, without the constant participation of a grown-up. Until then (and even afterwards, to an extent) the truth is that they need a certain amount of your time and attention to thrive – socially, emotionally and developmentally. So, one way or another, it's a problem that requires a happy compromise.

The Problem Shared

What the Netmums say

I've always been very honest about the fact that I've found parenting boring at times. However, I've stuck at it, tried my best and have never shown my feelings. I just made sure I did other stuff like evening classes, or nights out here and there, to remind myself I was once a human with a brain!

I've often wondered why I chose to stay at home rather than go back to work, but I know my kids need me. Yes, the park – *again* – can be tedious. But this time is short and if I can't invest a bit of self-lessness and be with the kids now, then when can I? Sometimes I want to beat my head against the wall playing snakes and ladders, but other times when we have a fantastic day out, or do something new and different, I love it. Whenever I get down about my life at home, I think back to full-time work and how boring *that* was, and remind myself the grass isn't always greener!

Julie from Southend, mum to Jude, eight, Leon, five and Madeleine, two

Being with children can be incredibly dull! But it can also be the funniest, sweetest, most precious of times. It's so hard when you have to read the same story over and over. And playing peekaboo is great, for the first five times (not the million you have to force a smile through!) I sometimes find myself gazing into space, then come to, beating myself up because I'm supposed to be entertaining the poor little man.

Kath from Berkeley, mum to Liam, seven and Bernard, one

Yes, I do find being with my daughter boring sometimes. There are times when I just don't *want* to sit at the table playing with play dough or drawing and painting, and sometimes I long for an adult conversation. And some days, when my daughter says: 'Mummy, will you do a jigsaw with me?' I want to scream! But most days, it's OK.

Helen from Brighouse, mum to Delaney, three

I have days when I'm so frustrated that I can't do what I need to do, housework for example, that it can make me rather impatient. And I do find it very hard to keep three children all occupied for more than five minutes, particularly when they all have such different personalities. What tends to happen is that the boys will busy themselves, perhaps making a den, and my youngest stays with me and we'll read or play while they get on with it. I have to say, parenting is hard work. Sometimes it's very hard not to just plonk them down in front of the television.

Anna from Bristol, mum to Josh, seven, Max, three and Isabella, 18 months

Being with kids can be mind-numbingly boring. Luckily both Jack and Toby play well together and I can leave them to it, but when Toby's not around, Jack tends to get bored easily. He enjoys reading, writing, puzzles, board games and the computer, among other things, but usually only for short bursts. To liven things up, we do some whacky stuff, too: for example, using different ingredients in the house to 'design' a new food stuff; making a 'maze' out of old wallpaper; penning a play, where we have to make up characters/stories/costumes (although these plays can get pretty confusing, especially with a four-year-old as the director/producer/scriptwriter!).

And when we really can't find anything to do we just lie on the sofa and make up stories by using an egg timer so when the sand runs out it's the next person's turn to carry on the story.

Leigh from Manchester, mum to Jack, four and foster mum to Toby, 12

I'm going to admit it as well . . . being around a small child constantly can be extremely dull. My daughter always wants to read the same books again and again, and play with the same toys (usually bloomin' play dough), over and over. She's quite content to do this – I, on the other hand, am not! We usually go out somewhere every day, even if we just walk to the shops for a paper, or a play on the swings. It protects my sanity, and makes me a better, more patient mum in the long run. I work part-time, too, and I find this helps me be 'Lucie' not just 'Mummy'. Netmums is a life-saver during those moments when Freya is asleep, the housework is done, and I'm stuck inside. Other mums (and the occasional dad) to chat to . . . and some (usually!) grown-up conversation.

Lucie from Sheffield, mum to Freya-Grace, two

God, I hate it! It wouldn't be so bad, but my little one doesn't have any attention span. By the time I've got all the painting gear out he'll splodge a bit around the paper and he's done. Or we'll set a game up, and two minutes later, it's over. He does enjoy pretend fighting or role play stuff, but I usually only manage to stay focused on that myself for about ten minutes. He loves cooking, but it drives me crazy! Slopping flour and eggs all over the place, trying to actually make something out of the blinking mess he's producing, and then two hours to clean it all up. But he likes it, so *occasionally* we do it. He also likes to help, which I've actually got down to a fine art now – I give him a mini spray bottle and a cloth and ask him to clean the floor. I have to inspect each bit he does which means I can wash a cup . . . inspect floor . . . wash a plate . . . inspect floor. This is the sum total of his independent play and it's the best way to get my dishes done! Then there's the tablecloth tent, draped over a couple of chairs. I have to knock on the door every five minutes with a 'pizza delivery' or some post. I can generally get a broken 15 minutes out of that one.

It was different when my older one was small. He used to play for hours on his own with figures and books. If I even spoke to him, I felt like I was intruding!

Anita from Sunderland, mum to Gary, 14 and Harry, four

I often find myself switching off when Alex is doing something, or I get impatient, especially when he is 'mam mam mam'-ing at me incessantly! Also, as his speech is rather limited, conversation tends to be a bit one sided! In honesty, to try and combat the boredom of it just being the two of us I try to make sure we spend plenty of time out and about. We are out more than we are at home.

My grandparents seem to have endless patience with him – they'll sit and look at the same books over and over, or play with the same six building blocks for hours. I wish I knew their secret!

Sometimes I try to get him absorbed in doing something on his own, so that I can do something else – even if it's just watching TV!

Tracey from Teesside, mum to Alexander, two

My daughter loved this one book so much, that I read it repeatedly for days on end and ended up hating it. I knew it off by heart and had begun reading it in a monotone voice, at 100 mph! Also, I admit I find some of my boys' games really, really dull. I have no interest in Power Rangers and find I can only stand them for five minutes before my interest starts to pale. I encourage them to take their favourite Power Ranger out to the garden so I can get on with other things – we've even had Power Rangers help with the housework!

Whenever I have one of those 'Oh God, this is so dull!' moments, I just remind myself that in four hours' time they'll be in bed and I will be in a bubble bath up to my eyeballs. Or that come Saturday, they'll all be at Granny's and I will be out for a meal with my other half trying to find something other than the kids to talk about!

Kelly from Swindon, mum to Holly, six, George, four and Mitchell, two

I have to admit that being with the kids often drives me loopy. I hate board games, I hate dollies, I hate being in the park. I also get really stressed out during craft or cookery sessions, although this isn't boredom so much as fear of the mess! For me, the simple solution has been to work part-time. If I had to be a mum five days a week, I don't think I could cope – and knowing I don't have to means I can throw myself into my days at home, and really enjoy them. I also make an effort to set up play dates and get-togethers with other mum friends and their kids. It's nice for Izzie, and it's nice for me, too.

Lorna from Winchester, mum to Amy, five and Izzie, two

The Problem Solved

Variety is the spice of life

It's easy to slip into a rut when it comes to spending time with your children. Kids are creatures of habit, and they know what they like: you bring out the same old books, toys and activities that you know they'll enjoy rather than introducing something new – even if you're sick of them. However, variety is the spice of life, so make it a point to try something different every day. It's not a question of getting in new stuff – let's face it, most kids have a huge number of things they've never actually played with. Dig out every item that's languishing at the back of the cupboard or festering in the bottom of a storage box, and give it a whirl. Or forget the props, and make your own fun. OK, we're not all blessed with fervent imaginations, but you can pick up a book from your local library (there are some suggestions for recommended reading in the back of the book), log on to Netmums or get Googling for some ideas.

It's kid's play

To truly enjoy time with your children you need to be in the right mindset. Cast aside adulthood for a while, with all its excess baggage, and join them (sometimes literally) on their level. It's easy to tell yourself that this game or that activity is boring. But if you've really got nothing else on your mind but having fun with your kids, you might just find yourself doing so.

Often, the weight of other, adult responsibilities on your mind can prevent unfettered play. Where possible, let them join in *your* activities (or at least, think that they are): cooking, cleaning, shopping and all manner of general admin can be successfully (if a little haphazardly) undertaken with a little bit of help. They'll love it, and you might even get something useful done in the process.

Some parents feel a little embarrassed about playing with their kids, especially if it involves imaginary games or making a bit of a fool of themselves. If that's you, just remember: no one's watching. And if they are, don't worry. They're probably just thinking how much fun you're having!

Get by with a little help from your friends

If you find the four walls pressing in on you when it's just you and the kids at home, the obvious solution is to multiply the possibilities by increasing the numbers. Having a pool of mum friends you can call upon when the going gets tough can be a life-saver, as a get-together can serve as the perfect antidote to boredom – for kids *and* their mums. Be sure to organise dates well in advance, as most mums' social diaries get booked up early. If you and your child have struck up a really good friendship or you're part of a group that really gels, make it a regular thing: if you know you've got a guaranteed gathering on Friday morning to look forward to, it'll put a spring in your step on Thursday.

On the other hand, it's always worth making a spontaneous telephone call. You may find someone who's also being driven up the wall and is equally in need of company and a cuppa!

Let's get *outta* here!

Weather permitting, life is almost always more interesting outside the home. Sometimes it can seem like a lot of effort to get the troops rallied, bags packed and plans made for a trip beyond the garden gate, but even if you gain nothing more than a breath of calming fresh air, the effort usually pays off. Keep it simple and cheap. Explore a park or green space you've never been to before, hang out at the local library, check out your nearest swimming pool, soft play, or child-friendly café. And if you've exhausted the possibilities of your locality already, try the same things, only further afield. If you don't have a car at your disposal, a bus or a train is even better fun, anyway.

Mother and toddler groups, and other parent and child gatherings are wonderful. With a vast selection of interesting toys and activities and a host of potential playmates, they're usually seventh heaven for little ones. You don't have to clear up afterwards. And there'll always be at least one other adult in the room that you can pass the time of day with. There may even be tea and a biscuit thrown in, which makes your average session a few quid well spent!

If you're not sure what's on and where in your town, investigate at your local library or council – or better still, ask the other mums you know. You could also check out the local boards, which have comprehensive listings of what's on and where in your area, on Netmums.com.

Know your limitations

Maybe there are things that your kids like doing but you can't abide. Perhaps crafts bring you out in a rash, or puzzles make you want to poke your eyes out. As much as possible, focus on the things you *do* enjoy. Make the dreaded ones bearable by promising yourself something enjoyable afterwards: half an hour's telly or a trip to the nearest café for a cup of hot chocolate. Where possible, set them up and let them get on with it: remember, it's good for children to play independently. They don't *need* activities on tap – there *is* such a thing as overstimulation, and doing nothing very much at all together can be quite a lot of fun.

Time for you, too

You can enjoy time with your children much more if you know that, sooner or later, you're going to get a break from it. Every mum, whether she's at home full-time or juggling family life with paid work, needs and deserves a certain amount of time to herself (or time with a partner or her friends, if that's what she prefers). Whilst a daily professional massage and a European mini-break every other weekend may be pushing it, regular bouts of 'me-time' help to offer an incentive which will get you through the more mundane bits of motherhood – whether it's an evening out with the girls once a month, or an hour to yourself in a bubble bath every night. You may have to negotiate for these moments, perhaps even trade some favours. But you shouldn't have to fight for them. It's the least you deserve!

Don't feel bad about it

Many mums find that being with their children all the time isn't do-able. It's an issue that's opened up a million debates over the years and one that there isn't room here to explore. Suffice it to say that if it's how *you* feel, you are not alone, and you shouldn't feel guilty about it. Working mums don't love their children any less than full-time mums. But resentful ones might.

What the experts say
The mums' life coach

So you don't enjoy jigsaws and you find arts and crafts intolerable. Relax. You don't have to enjoy the same activities as your three-year-old to be an involved, caring parent. There's a reason why the Tweenies aren't screened at 9 p.m. – what thrills the toddler just doesn't do it for the rest of us.

The obvious advice would be to find something you do enjoy doing with your children and stick to that. But the reality is that the one activity they'll pester you to do is the very one that you can't stand. Some mums find that setting clear limits is the best sanity-saver. Agree to the dreaded game, but for a strictly limited time – set the kitchen timer if they can't read the clock – and then do something different. That way you're not always saying no, but won't lose your mind.

Remember, too, that you're not expected to be a qualified play assistant with the enthusiasm of a kids' television presenter. Children love their parents to play with them, but it's also important for them to learn to occupy themselves, to develop their imagination and independence.

Getting together with other mums and children is another great tip; the children will generally be happy to play with each other and you can have a break and some adult conversation.

And finally, forget about what other mothers say and do. Yes, many mums genuinely do enjoy repeated games of Pop-up Pirate and are happy to read Owl Babies for the 99th time. There are even some who get pleasure from *Balamory*. But if that's not you, don't beat yourself up. Parenthood isn't a club based round a set of activities you're expected to enjoy. It's a relationship as unique as any other, so do it your way.

Patricia Carswell

The Problem Summarised

+ You're not weird if playing with your kids leaves you frustrated or bored.
+ They do, however, need you to play with them *sometimes*, especially when they're little, to aid their social and emotional development.
+ Try and keep playtimes varied. Don't get stuck in a rut.
+ Company is a great boredom-buster, so get your friends round.
+ Get out and about when possible: four walls can add to the frustration.
+ They don't need attention all the time: let them play on their own when they will.

In it together: How to be partners, as well as parents

The Problem

I lost my confidence a lot as a woman and as a person after having two children. Before I was a mum, I could cope with my emotions, and could distance myself from the things or people that affected me in a negative way. But afterwards, I couldn't do that so well.

I found losing my figure a huge shock, as well as the 24/7 pace of life. There seemed so little time left over at the end of the day for me, let alone enough for my hubby, too. Our relationship has evolved, but it's been a struggle.

Rosie from London, mum to Sean, 11 and Owen, eight

A change of life

Once you've had children, life is never the same again – and neither is your relationship with your other half. Sharing parenthood can strengthen the bond between a couple in fantastic ways – what greater project could two people collaborate on than making a family? But the truth is, it can also cause a good many stresses and strains.

It's hardly surprising that bringing up children together puts pressure on a couple. Wonderful as they are, kids sap your spare time, income and energy. And they change your identity forever: once parenthood becomes your primary role in life, it affects your whole outlook, as well as the way you see your partner.

Sex lives usually diminish once kids come along – for a while, they might even disappear altogether. So does precious time together as an adult twosome, sidelined by the relentless demands of family life. And sometimes, the exhausting and constantly challenging business of parenting causes rows between couples as they suffer sleep deprivation, disagree over domestic issues, and resent one another's differing attitudes to family life.

It's easy to think that relationship issues have nothing to do with our kids, or with our ability to be good parents. But children need stability at home, wherever possible. So striving for a good relationship with your other half is one of the best things you can do for them

The Problem Shared

What the Netmums say

I never realised how much having Jack would affect my relationship with Alan. I went from being sexy lover to mum overnight and it's been hard to overcome the feeling of 'mumsiness'.

For the first two years of Jack's life I was only concentrating on his needs, not Alan's. Our sex life went from earth-shattering to mundane, mainly because of the tiredness, but also because my feelings towards Alan had changed. We went for about five months without sex before we talked about why, and how it could be resolved. It was awkward, but we managed it. We also 'spiced up' our sex life again by trying a few new things, so the physical side came back as strong as ever. The emotional side was harder to overcome. We chatted for ages about how we saw each other's roles now, and how the parent role came first. We decided to start having 'date nights' to get back a bit of mystery, and it worked.

I used to let Jack get away with a lot more than Alan and this can cause tiffs. I'm not as bad now and we work as a team, but at first he wasn't allowed to tell *my* baby off. If I think Alan is too strict then I have to bite my tongue in front of Jack, but once we're alone I'll tell him if I think the situation could have been handled better. We keep a book of tips that we each write in when a situation arises which we can refer back to, so we're working from the same hymn sheet.

Leigh from Manchester, mum to Jack, four and foster mum to Toby, 12

We used to go out lots in the evening before we had children and I think it came as a shock when we had to stay home every night. At first we got quite bored, but in the end it probably made our relationship better because we overcame that by playing board games and cards, which meant we were getting a lot of 'us time' during the evenings.

We didn't go out together until our first was a year old, and for about 15 months after the second was born. We do enjoy a night out occasionally, but now it's become the other way around we find it difficult because we're so used to being home. Neither of us feel we've missed out on 'us time' since being parents, though. On a Saturday night we have a nice meal, curl up on the sofa, and watch a film together. We perhaps don't have as much time for just us, but what we do have is much better quality. Last year we had our first night away from the children and it was fantastic to do what we wanted when we wanted, but we agreed the time we have together at home is just as special.

Zoe from Kings Lynn, mum to Shannon, five and Kacey, three

Well, I can honestly say that our relationship has changed hugely since the arrival of our first daughter. Although my hubby does help out around the house, his attitude has changed dramatically. Once very caring and loving, he's changed into a grumpy, miserable, demanding man. When we do get the odd five minutes to talk, all I get from him is: 'I'm tired'.

Amy-Jayne has severe reflux, so no one in this house gets much sleep and I understand when he says he is tired, because I am, too. The chances of us getting to talk are slim because we go to bed straight after dinner, and when we get there, the only thing on my mind is sleep. And anyway, after having my two girls jumping on me like a trampoline for 14 hours a day, the last thing I feel like is hubby jumping on me. I just want to be me, and not be poked and prodded for a while. I've explained this to him, but I'm not sure he's convinced. We've never had a night away from the girls as we don't have relatives near to us and haven't been out on our own as a couple in years.

I'm hoping that when the girls grow older that things between us will improve, and that more sleep and their increased independence will give us a chance to be us for a bit, instead of just Mummy and Daddy. I know that we will come through this because we do love each other very much. It's just at this moment our kids need us more. They're worth the sacrifice.

Helen from Folkstone, mum to Rebekah-Eve, four and Amy-Jayne, one

From the word go we both discussed our roles and what we would expect from each other – who would do what chores, and how we'd raise the children. Everything we discussed still stands today, and we still do our fair share. (And secretly we all know who's boss – me!) We never let the children play us off against each other and we always discuss things together, which I think is very important. There are times when we disagree on things and sometimes it happens in front of the children, in which case we always make a point of making up in front of them too.

We make time for each other, which I think is highly important otherwise you're just two people living in a cocoon, and when the children have grown up you'll wonder who you both are. The children are all in bed by 7.30 p.m. and that's our time to talk, listen to music, play card games, watch telly, have a drink, or whatever takes our fancy (if you know what I mean!) We don't have the opportunity to go out that often together due to lack of babysitters, so we make up for it by cooking each other romantic meals at the weekend when the kids are in bed. We still have our own lives as well. I think everyone needs their own space. He plays rugby, I go running, and we both go out separately sometimes.

We put effort into our relationship – you have to. We fall out, we make up. The key thing is talking. If you don't talk, no one knows what you're feeling. And you have to listen, too.

Frances from Halifax, mum to Sophie, seven, Emily, two and Jacob, one

Our first daughter had severe reflux and has never slept through the night – at her worst, she woke every hour in pain. How did it affect our relationship? Well, I can honestly say we didn't really have one for a long time. The sleep deprivation alone caused arguments and our sex life became non-existent. For roughly 18 months my husband slept mainly in the spare room, because he needed sleep so he could work the next day. In this situation, you do become resentful of the child. All we did was care for her. You lose sight of your love for each other: you just function as Mummy and Daddy.

Things have improved. A strict routine in getting the kids to bed has given us a bit of time to get things back on track. It gives us a chance to catch up on our days, talk about our worries, and have a cuddle. I do think a cuddle a day is important. Mollie has a fear of the dark and tends to spend a lot of time in and out of our room in the night, so we have to be in bed by 9 p.m. to get any kind of sex life.

We've been together 15 years and I think after that time, love moves on to a different level. Sometimes I do think people forget to love each other. We haven't, and it's what's kept us together.

Mary from Bristol, mum to Mollie, five and Connie, two

We've bickered so much since I had Callum, mainly because I feel he doesn't respect the job I do. I'm sure he resents the fact that I'm home all day while he's working – but I feel that my day is harder than his! When he comes in, he's often in a bad mood, doesn't want to engage, and makes comments if the house is a mess. We don't have a babysitter at the moment and have tried to talk things through, but always seem to end up arguing. I don't really know what to do to make this situation better.

Jeanette from Northampton, mum to Callum, three

My hubby works silly hours and my youngest son doesn't sleep through so when we get any time together, we're both shattered and have no energy for anything. We've even stopped hugging and kissing, apart from saying goodbye at the door. Although I know I want to sort this out, I just don't have the inclination to make the effort lately. My hubby is fantastic with the kids and I get time off in the day to do my own thing, but he works such long hours, and he doesn't get enough sleep either. I really don't see how we get round this. I've already let the housework go, and we don't have a television so it's not as though we could cut down our viewing. There just aren't enough hours in the day for everything.

Nina from Warwick, mum to Luke, seven, James, five and Rowan, two

Having a child dramatically changed our relationship. We'd been married for 14 months when Madeline was born, and until then it was a very good relationship. We hardly argued and got on very well most of the time. I had PND, which didn't help, and since then things have been a bit up and down. Mainly we row about money, which had been scarce as we both made the decision for me to stay at home for a bit, which I did and enjoyed. But it meant we had hardly any spare cash and we'd been used to being comfortably off. The worry contributed to lots of our arguments.

I've gone back to work part-time and now things are better. We have more money to do things as a family and we're trying for another baby. It feels as if things are getting back to the way they were before Madeline was born. I know that it will be difficult again money-wise if we do have another, but I am sure we can get through it now. There were times when I wanted to leave, but we love each other too much to just let go. When I said 'till death us do part', I meant it.

Victoria from Basingstoke, mum to Madeline, three

The Problem Solved

Finding time for each other

It's easier said than done, of course, but it's vital to spend at least some time alone together, so you don't lose sight of each other in your non-parenting roles of spouse or partner.

If your kids are small and you get evenings to yourselves when they're in bed, use the opportunity to talk, touch, and just to be with one another, whenever you can. Inevitably, evenings offer the only chance to do all the chores there's no time for in the day. And if you *do* get free, a long day with children, at work, or both, can render you so tired that silently slumping in front of the television is as much as you can manage. But even if you can only get your heads together once a week, you should. If you don't sit at the table to eat as a couple – perhaps because you have tea as a family or because it's so much easier to have a tray on your lap – make a conscious effort to share a meal, and a chat, at least occasionally. It doesn't matter if your conversations centre on the minutiae of life: just passing the time of day together can bring you closer. It's important to talk about things other than the children, too.

Try to get out on a 'date' every so often. It's easy not to bother – after all, staying in is easy and comfortable, and reliable babysitters can be hard to find (and expensive). But a drink in the pub, a meal in a restaurant, or a trip to the movies will help remind you that you're partners, and not just parents. If you're in the fortunate position of having someone who'll take on the kids for an 'overnighter', make the most of it and indulge in a weekend away when you can. It may seem like the least of your priorities, especially if money's short. But getting out of the house altogether is a wonderful way of leaving the day-to-day domestics aside for a while.

If you can't get out for a date, then stay in. Light some candles, cook up something special, and have an early night.

No sex please, we're parents

Sex can be a bit of a sore point for parents. Even when you're long past the baby stage and the various barriers to an active sex life that implies, things can remain a little creaky. But a sex life of some sort is pretty much vital in a loving adult relationship. Sex is a great way to relax and relieve tension, helps forge intimacy and communication with a partner, and serves as the perfect reminder that there's more to life than just being someone's parent.

All parents lead busy lives, which means that exhaustion is still a common issue, even when your nights are no longer disturbed by nocturnal children. If you're too tired for sex, go to bed an hour earlier. Leave the dishes in the sink, if necessary, or tape the programme you really can't bear to miss. Or trade in some babysitting credits and make an appointment to do it during the day, one weekend. Having sex is a bit like going to the gym – sometimes you really have to force yourself to get there, but once you've had a good work-out, you're glad you made the effort.

Sometimes, mums just lose sight of themselves as sexual beings, which is not that surprising – where once our main relationship involved being someone's partner and lover, motherhood gives us a very different identity, and one that can seem at odds with an active sex life. The answer is to put the kids out of the equation temporarily: if you haven't got a reliable baby-sitter, you need to find one. And make sure, when you do get together, that the kids aren't the only thing you talk about!

Body image, too, can take a bit of a battering post-kids and that can impact on the way mums feel about sex. Drooping boobs, extra pounds and stretchmarks are all normal souvenirs of childbirth, but not everyone is able to wear them with pride. Chances are, your other half loves you just the way you are. But some soft lighting and a pretty nightie can go a long way to easing insecurities.

If you're going through a very long period without sex for a good reason, perhaps because of ongoing sleep problems, you may just have to accept it as a temporary drought. In the meantime, it's vital to keep on cuddling, kissing and talking about it if you're unhappy with it.

Good sex lives can and do come back to life at some point after the dawn of parenthood, but it's worth bearing in mind that they're rarely the same again. You may only have sex once a week or once a month (perhaps even less), and you may be forced to trade in those long, lingering sessions of yore for a 'quickie' whenever you can get it. As long as it's good when you *do* get around to it, and both parties are content with that arrangement, then you're doing OK.

Not in front of the children

Few things raise the hackles quite so much as someone questioning your skills, judgement or commitment as a parent. It's not surprising, then, that couples can find themselves at loggerheads over family matters.

If you have different opinions where the kids are concerned, you need to thrash them out when you're alone and decide on a consistent policy, compromising if necessary. Unless you're wildly opposed to their methods, it's only fair to back your partner up if they're in the middle of a 'situation', even if you would have dealt with it differently yourself. Ask him to do the same for you. Don't argue about children in front of them. If they see they've caused a ruckus between their mum and dad, they'll be confused. They may even exploit it.

More generally speaking, it's no bad thing to have moderate rows in front of children as long as you let them see you resolve the situation and make up afterwards. It's a good lesson for life.

Why talking is so important

As with so many other problems, communication is key. If frustrations or anger have no outlets, it will lead to resentment. It can be hard making yourself heard when children are around: all the more reason to set aside time without them, when you can have a conversation in peace.

It's generalising (and of course, it can work the other way), but men and women often have the same sort of reasons for resentment. Lots of mums get cross with dads for 'not doing things properly'; many dads get fed up with mums being fusspots. Mums complain their partners don't pull their weight enough; dads frequently feel pushed out because the kids get priority.

Empathy is everything – on both sides. Whatever the issues in your house, make sure you understand each other's point of view. If you don't think your partner appreciates what you do or understands the things that are important to you where the children are concerned, tell him so – not in anger, but calmly, when you're both in a good mood. (And if he's never spent a whole day alone in charge of the kids, make sure he gets the chance.) Help him to understand your point of view by expressing it. And return the favour by taking into account his side of things, too. Maybe he worries the kids love you more. Perhaps the constant tidying does his head in. He may feel under pressure if he's the sole breadwinner. The only way to flush out the things that come between you is to talk them through.

If any of the issues in this section are affecting one or both of you to a serious extent, consider seeking some relationship counselling together. Details for Relate are included in the back of the book.

What the experts say

The family and relationships researcher

Once you've become parents, the sheer quantity of things you need to do and the demands on your time means you look for support from those around you. We know from research* that levels of conflict rise when partners become parents, and it's usually associated with feelings of being unsupported, which can trigger a lot of anger and hostile behaviour.

Modern parents have stressful lives. They may be struggling with the demands of work, paying the mortgage and feeding the kids, and underneath things are building up. All that juggling comes at a cost. You need to feel you've got a pretty seamless system in place, and that's not easy, so there are bound to be clashes. It's a common pattern. You can end up wondering: 'How did we go from being people who get on, to people who shout at each other all the time?'

Sometimes it's easy to assume you're in a bad relationship when in fact, you're having a bad time. It's sad when that happens, and people lose confidence in the fact that it's *not* actually a bad relationship, just a bad time, and things can change. Hard as it is when you're caught in the midst of money worries or screaming children, it's important to pay attention to expressing your feelings, in a non-accusatory way. But even more important than being able to talk is being able to listen, and to listen actively – not just sitting there but processing and trying to understand what's being said, and reflecting back on it. If you need to say something but aren't sure how to, it can help to talk to someone else you trust first, someone who you know will listen, to get your head round what you want to say to your partner. If things don't feel right, then that's the time to start talking about it. Leave it, and you'll start disliking each other.

Yes, you should spend some time together if possible. It doesn't have to be the perfect setting – in fact, sometimes organising a

*Cowan & Cowan, *When partners become parents. The big life change for couples*, Lawrence Erlbaum Associates, 2002.

babysitter and a night in a restaurant can be so stressful you don't enjoy it. Find whatever little moment you have and make the most of it to focus on each other, even if it's just walking to the bottom of the garden together, once the children are asleep.

Children know if things are OK or not OK, because of the emotional temperature of the house. If you are cross or miserable, the best thing you can do for your child is to try and address it because they want their parents to be happy. If you can get on with each other, it will bring huge benefits to your kids.

Penny Mansfield, One Plus One

The mums' life coach

Children can bring huge joy and happiness to your relationship, and some couples find that parenthood brings them closer, but this is not everyone's experience. The arrival of a baby can put a lot of strain on a relationship, which may not be resolved as your children grow.

It's hardly surprising if becoming a parent brings tension to a relationship. You're having to cope with exhaustion like you've never known before, and at the same time you're trying to forge a relationship with a new little person. Add to this the fact that you're both getting used to a new identity and added responsibilities, and it's small wonder if your relationship is under pressure. And as your children get older, it's easy for your relationship to be more of a practical partnership than a love affair.

Making time for each other is essential. You may not have the freedom and the spontaneity you once had – no more spur of the moment visits to the cinema – but this doesn't mean you should allow yourselves to neglect one another. Whether you have babies or teenagers, it's important to let each other know that you're still emotionally connected and to feel like you still have an adult relationship. Honesty and humour are the keys to a good sex life after you have children. Talking candidly about how you feel can dispel any misunderstandings. And a sense of humour will be essential: you may need to become wily opportunists, and a refusal to take things too seriously will make this much easier.

Patricia Carswell

The Problem Summarised

◆ Life is never the same again after children. You need to accept certain changes.

◆ Finding time for each other, whenever you can, is essential.

◆ Talking is vital. And listening even more so.

◆ Sort out your sex life! You may not be hanging from the rafters any more but it's still an important part of a loving adult relationship.

◆ Kids know when things aren't right. You owe it to them to make sure it is.

Ditching the dummy: How to help them give up their comfort habits

The Problem

> I've never liked dummies but I understand that some kids really take to them, as my second daughter has. Nyah didn't, instead she became a thumb-sucker. It didn't bother me but I did worry it would be difficult to break the habit if it went on too long. After all, you can't take their thumb away can you? Hers became sore, so I put Vaseline on it which helped. She only really sucked her thumb when she was tired and was going off to sleep, but when she was 18 months old I suddenly noticed she wasn't sucking it any more – she'd 'cured' herself of the habit all by herself.
>
> *Rebecca from Croydon, mum to Nyah, two and Willow, four months*

Dummies for dummies?

For such a small item, the dummy sparks some strong views. Experts hold varying opinions about them, but in the main, they disapprove of dummy-sucking by kids past their first birthday. And the general public can be rather sniffy, too. There's a feeling that walking, talking dummy-suckers just look a bit daft.

Dummy-sucking is pure comfort-seeking. So is thumb-sucking, hair-twiddling or nose-tickling with the frayed edge of a favoured blanket. A child who comes to associate a particular item or activity with comfort, relaxation and security, may naturally get very attached to it. For many, it will be the thing that helps them get to sleep at night, or the way that they can feel better when they are miserable. Chances are, a child with a comfort habit will dump it eventually of their own accord. But that may be long after you really want them to, if you're concerned about the possible implications, or by the looks they're getting. The fact is, the dummy has to go at some point. And the sooner you try to lose it, the easier it is.

What's the damage?

Official advice varies, and even the experts cannot come to a united conclusion on the rights and wrongs of dummies. Dentists generally warn that too much dummy use, or thumb-sucking, *could* have a detrimental effect, but only on the secondary or adult teeth. These don't start appearing until after a child is five, by which time, hopefully, most sucking habits will either have stopped altogether or been dramatically reduced. If they're still sucking *to a large extent* after then, it may well have an impact on their smiles later on.

Communication experts hold firmer views than that. They say that dummies may affect speech and language development, as they restrict tongue movement, and because the simple fact of having an object in the mouth limits the opportunities to practise talking. They recommend that dummies should be dispensed with, especially during the day when they're interacting with other people, by the time a child is one. However, they are generally not as disapproving of thumb-sucking, because a child needs their hand to do other things and is therefore less likely to be sucking for long periods.

There's some evidence that dummy-users are more likely to suffer from inner ear infections, as they're dropped on the floor an awful lot, and bacteria can pass back through the throat.

Seeking comfort in a prop such as a blanket is extremely common and basically harmless. Unless they use them in conjunction with thumb-sucking, there's really no reason to fret about it. In truth, many children have these for needy moments, well into childhood.

The Problem Shared

What the Netmums say

Joshua had his dummy from birth. A midwife gave it to him in hospital because he wanted to suckle so much, but for medical reasons, I wasn't able to breastfeed. Later we tried everything to take them away, including hiding them, and 'posting them' to other babies who needed them more! By the time he was three he still had it, and I was concerned it might affect his speech or his teeth. Also, there's definitely a stigma attached to them: people seem to look down on you if your child has a dummy, and you get the odd negative comment. Around the same time, he started a pre-school playgroup. No other child there had a dummy and I didn't want him to be 'different'. So we explained to Joshua that the 'dummy fairy' would come, collect his old dummies, and leave him a present. One night, we left all his dummies in a bowl on the kitchen table, and in the morning he found a wrapped present. His face was a picture! For the next week or so, he asked for them occasionally, but we didn't give in, and he remained dummy free.

Candice from Bedford, mum to Joshua, five and Amelia, two

Jack never had a dummy, but he had and still does have his 'pillows' – four little square cushions with tassels on the corners that he likes to rub between his fingers at night. When he was little, we couldn't leave the house without one. Now he just has them at bedtime – he plays with the tassels until he's asleep. I say, let kids have comforters if they want them. They're obviously doing a job nobody else can do and until the child's ready to let go of it themselves, it's something that can be worked round.

Leigh from Manchester, mum to Jack, four and foster mum to Toby, 12

My children have both had comfort blankets since they were babies. They didn't take to dummies, and they liked to snuggle their blankets to get to sleep, or to soothe themselves when they were upset or ill. My elder daughter also sucked her thumb from birth. We tried cutting back on the use of 'blankies' once they started nursery, and stopped taking them out of the house. Once they started school, blankies were confined to their bedroom! They still have them now, aged five and eight, in bed with them at night. So long as they're not taking them to school, or getting teased about it, I don't see a problem in it. The main thing to me is that they sleep at night! Imogen has cut down on her thumb-sucking on her own (with a few gentle reminders). She now just sucks it if she is upset or tired – and she has lovely straight teeth, so they haven't been affected.

Lisa from Wolverhampton, mum to Eloise, eight and Imogen, five

As an ex-thumb-sucker myself, I think the best way to stop them is to ignore it. Everyone tried for years to get me to stop, but the more they pushed it, the more attached I became. I actually stopped when I was 18 – and I still do it sometimes. My teeth were pushed forward but I'm not convinced it was anything to do with the thumb-sucking because my son's teeth are similar and he has never sucked his. I feel the same about comfort blankets. My elder two daughters got rid of theirs through choice, with no pushing from me, at the ages of two and three. My youngest is two and slowly breaking the habit herself. At the end of the day, she needs it for a reason, although what that is I'm not sure. But when she has it, she feels safer.

Sally from Birkenhead, mum to Connor, nine, Phyllippa, five, Jessica, four and Natasha, two

I think a dummy can be taken away at any time – it's the parents that need to be prepared to stand by the decision. When my daughter was two, we took her to the dentist because her teeth were sticking out a bit at the front, and he told me it may have been caused by her dummy-sucking. I told her that the 'poorly babies' needed to have her dummies back, and that they'd send her a present if she did. She was happy to send them off, and loved the gift she got in return. After three nights, she stopped asking for it. Then, when she was nearly three, she was poorly with a series of infections. Because I still had a new pair of dummies hidden in the cupboard for emergencies, I stupidly gave her them. Two nights later, she was hooked again! I hated it. She spoke less and, when she did, all I could hear was this horrible sucking noise. She had it for about a month, and then when she wasn't looking, I hid it. Later when she asked for it, I told her they must've gone back to the poorly babies. I felt so mean! Cue tears and a tantrum. We tried to give her a present, but she told us to take it back, as she wanted the dummies instead. I stood firm and although it took a bit longer, she eventually stopped asking for it.

I still have all of her dummies upstairs in my drawer because I can't bear to throw them away. My son hasn't bothered at all, which I am relieved about, because I can't afford all the gifts!
Sarah from Scarborough, mum to Hermione, three and Locksley, one

I was really dreading getting rid of Sammie-Jo's dummy. My sister told me that she'd got her three girls to put theirs in their stocking for Santa to take to a new baby, so that was what I did too. We tried taking Charlie's at the same time, but at 15 months she was too young to understand, so we did it the following Christmas instead. George was really attached to his until recently, when I insisted he started to leave it on his bed when he got up in the morning. It broke his heart the first time, but he's used to it now and he shall be putting his in his stocking come Christmas, too. I was concerned about speech. George has really started to talk now, but when he's got his dummy in his mouth it's harder to understand him. But also, I don't really like seeing kids walking around with dummies in their mouths.
Teresa from Heywood, mum to Sammie-Jo, five, Charlie, three and George, two

Once Arren was a year old I stopped letting him have a dummy in the day – to keep his mind off it, I entertained him constantly. After a while he didn't want it at all in the day, just at night. Eventually I took it away from him at night too and by the time he was 19 months old he wasn't that bothered and he dropped it completely.
Sarah from Essex, mum to Arren, five, Sky, two and Harmany, one

I let the whole dummy thing happen naturally with my eldest. As soon as they became worn out, I threw them in the bin and didn't replace them. At night, rather than have his dummy, he was allowed a DVD on for half an hour instead. His sister still has one though and the little toad's constantly stealing hers. So every time he does, I take a train away. It seems to be working so far, and he's helping *her* get off them. He reads her a story at night (OK, he looks at the pictures and makes a story up!) which settles her, so she doesn't need it.
Kimmie from Newhaven, mum to Josh, four and Chelsea-Lou, two

Both of mine had dummies from birth. When Rhys was almost four, I was getting a lot of nasty comments from my mother-in-law. She went on about it constantly, saying that it looked awful, was bad for their teeth, that they were too old for a dummy. I was also getting funny looks in the streets now and then. I thought I'd better do something about it. So we gave all our dummies to the baby reindeer on Christmas Eve. Even thought Rain is younger, it was Rhys that missed them most. He whined about it for about a week, but we didn't give in, so that was that.

Personally, I didn't have a problem with them and would have let them grow out of them naturally. But the comments got to me. My daughter also used to carry around an old sock and rub it on her nose – you can imagine the looks we got with that! But eventually she just lost interest, and I'm sure it would have been the same with the dummies.
Kim from Manchester, mum to Rhys, seven and Rain, six

The Problem Solved

How to ditch the dummy

Most children will quite naturally put their dummies aside more and more once they're toddling and are distracted by other things. If they're still very attached to their dummy and spend significant chunks of time sucking on one, aim to limit those periods. Try hiding it altogether during the day (sometimes when you can't see something, you don't want it), and encourage them to think of it as something that only comes out when they're very tired or in need of the comfort. Don't let them have one as a matter of course if they haven't actually asked for it.

When it comes to ditching it permanently, most parents find the 'cold turkey' approach most effective. Always be upfront about your intentions, before getting rid of something a child relies on for comfort: if you try and do away with them in secret, you won't be very popular. Better to get them involved and grant them the responsibility of abandoning their dummies – if they believe it was entirely their choice and a decision they made because they are a 'big' boy or girl, they're far more likely to accept it.

Some children get satisfaction from throwing their dummies in the bin. And asking Santa, the 'dummy fairy', or some other public-spirited fantasy figure to take dummies away to other children in need is a well-used technique. (It's quite usual for them to bring a small token of thanks, in response!)

Prepare yourself for several difficult days. There may be a fair bit of whinging to overcome – although many parents are pleasantly surprised at how easily they *will* give them up. Bedtimes in particular can be tough, especially if they rely on a dummy to soothe themselves to sleep. Be prepared for difficulty in settling them for a while. Distract them with lots of cuddles, or their favourite games, stories or DVDs. Once you've done the deed, don't go back. Throw the dummy away rather than stashing it in a hiding place 'just in case'. That way, you can't give it back to them even if you're tempted to.

All right for thumb?

Thumb-sucking is a harder habit to break because a thumb's permanently attached and you can't very well get rid of it. So it's likely to be a more enduring habit than dummy-sucking. In general, it's probably best ignored. If it really worries you, you could try implementing a reward system to help motivate them to stop. But the majority of thumb-suckers – influenced by peer pressure or distracted by other interests – will stop of their own accord. They may secretly carry on in private, but undertaken in such restricted bouts, it's unlikely to cause any harm. Once they're old enough to understand the possible implications for their teeth, you can explain what they are, and gently encourage them to stop. Pushing or criticising will probably have the opposite effect.

What the experts say

The dentist

My views on thumb-sucking changed after I had children of my own, as my youngest daughter sucked hers. Thumb-sucking is not abnormal and parents shouldn't be made to feel guilty about it, or make their children feel guilty about it. My advice to parents has always been, don't worry about it. They'll usually stop of their own accord, anyway – up to 90 per cent of children have given up sucking their thumbs by the age of five, and the small percentage who carry on beyond that are usually the ones who were badgered about stopping, which can have the opposite effect.

Adult teeth usually start to come through at the age of five or six, and as long as they've stopped by then, it won't cause them any damage. If they're still sucking their thumb excessively once they've got their permanent teeth that *could* cause orthodontic problems – although it's by no means universal.

Dummies are a bit different. I personally don't see the point of introducing one, because that's almost condoning something you'll eventually want them to stop. But the argument in their favour is that they're easier to 'lose' than thumbs. You can buy 'orthodontic' versions these days, but, again, there's no evidence that sucking a dummy in the first five years can damage their teeth anyway and presumably they're unlikely to be in use beyond that. If your child does have one, my main advice would be to get one you can put in the dishwasher, for reasons of hygiene.

Gordon Watkins, British Dental Association

The speech and language therapist

We would say that a dummy gets in the way of developing the strength and fine movement that children need in their mouths in order to be able to articulate different sounds, prevents normal mouth movement, gets in the way of making speech sounds, and distorts the resting position of the mouth and tongue. If you've got something stuck in your mouth for any part of the day, then developing those abilities is going to be hard. And also, it will reduce a child's opportunities for talking, commenting on what they see or copying the sounds that people around them make.

If your child is talkative, has clear speech sounds and good oral development, then it may be seen that the benefits of having a dummy at night outweigh the risks, but on balance, my advice would be that it's best not to use one at all after the age of 12 months. *Kate Freeman, Professional Advisor for I CAN, the children's communication charity*

The developmental psychologist

I take a relaxed approach, and my feeling is that children who have an attachment to their dummy should be allowed to have them as long as they want within reason, certainly at night-time. Some children like to suck on something because they get comfort from it. I don't see the harm in it. They're only children for a few years and I don't think we should be pushing them to grow up.

Most children will give up their dummies on their own, often when they start nursery or school and they don't want to be different from their friends – they know dummies are really for 'babies' so they'll ditch theirs eventually. After all, you don't see any 16-year-olds with one in their mouths, do you? It's actually quite rare to see a three- or four-year-old with a dummy in its mouth because most children of that age don't want to be sucking them in the day.

I'm not saying dummy-use should be *encouraged* at that sort of age. You wouldn't actually give one to them before they've asked, and you wouldn't let them walk around all day long, or go to nursery or school with one in their mouths. You should make it clear that their dummy is only for certain times. Having one at night is fine. They only suck it for a while anyway, and then it falls out. Or, if they want it in the day because they're tired or upset, let them have it. It really won't hurt for short periods of time.

Thumb-sucking tends to go on for longer, and if they're still doing it when their adult teeth come through they could be affected (and in fact thumbs, too, can end up misshapen). With a thumb-sucker, wait until they're old enough to understand why and then you can reason with them, by saying: 'You know, that might push your teeth forward'.

As with so many aspects of parenting, the pressure to do one thing or another is intense and you feel you have to keep up with it. But there are a lot of homes where 'secret' activities like dummy-sucking goes on. Perhaps we should all just stop feeling so guilty about it.

Dr Janine Spencer, Brunel University

The Problem Summarised

- It's a common and very natural instinct for children to seek comfort from sucking.
- Most children will probably stop a comfort habit on their own, eventually.
- However, you may want to help them stop before then, as there are some dental, medical and developmental implications linked to dummy use.
- The majority of experts say they are not a great idea for children aged more than a year.
- If they do have a dummy, try and restrict its use. Don't let them have permanent access to one, and keep them for the moments they're needed most, such as bedtime.
- Some experts think thumb-sucking is less likely to cause harm than dummy-sucking. However, it may well go on for longer!

Potty time: How to get them out of nappies and into knickers

The Problem

It's a bit embarrassing, but I've successfully trained all my children to use the loo or a potty by performing the 'peepee in the potty' dance when they do the business in the right place! This is done to the 'Come on and do the Conga' tune and is always a hit. A couple of weeks into it, they've got used to the potty and don't need the song.

Kelly from Swindon, mum to Holly, six, George, four and Mitchell, two

Nappy days no longer

At some time or other, there comes a point when small children are ready to leave their nappy days behind them. Achieving control of their bladder and bowels, and learning how to use a potty or loo, is a normal physical and social developmental stage, which they all get to eventually. But they usually need a little help with it. Which is where the fun starts.

Ready? Steady? Go!

Previous generations of mums had their children out of nappies much earlier than is normal these days, no doubt driven by the misery of soaking, washing and hanging a load of dirty terry towelling nappies every day. These days, it's widely recognised that children will only be in full control of their toilet habits when they're physically, verbally and emotionally ready, which is generally later than assumed in the past, and extremely variable, but commonly somewhere between two and four. Unfortunately, a certain amount of social pressure lingers – much of it from the aforementioned previous generations – which means that a lot of mums are tempted to try too early, or worry if it's taking longer than they thought. But potty training is not a race, and a successfully potty trained child is no more advanced or intelligent than one who isn't. Wait until they're ready – whenever that may be – and you'll be halfway there.

The Problem Shared

What the Netmums say

When my daughter got to around 18 months we put her in pull-ups and started encouraging her to use a potty. But because I'd just given birth to her brother, I didn't really support her enough and soon she was just 'going' in her pull-ups! Then we had a really stressful period when we lost our house, followed by a succession of illnesses, so potty training went totally out of the window. During this time she was becoming aware of going to the toilet, was talking more about it, and became fascinated about us going! So, just after she turned three, I took her shopping for pants.

I put them on her when we got home and from that moment, other than one wee accident, she was fine. I'm glad I waited because she was able to understand everything and also went straight to the toilet, so there was no emptying potties, and she wipes her own bottom and washes her own hands, too. For us, waiting that little bit longer made it so easy. My son is 20 months old now, but I'm in no hurry to potty train him. I'll wait another year yet.

Sarah from Scarborough, mum to Hermione, three and Locksley, one

I used sticker charts, and within the week Mitchell was going to the toilet by himself. Night-time dryness came quite quickly afterwards. But then he got very bunged up and found it hurt trying to have a poo. Since then, he's screamed blue murder every time I tried to take him into the toilet. I've tried the sticker chart again with no luck, nothing would encourage him to sit. He even got to the point of peeing in the garden, because he was too scared to go near the loo. We've been taking it slowly, encouraging him into the toilet with us, and rewarding him, even if he's just put his foot over the door. It's been a long process and we still have a good way to go as he's only just starting to pee in the toilet again. He actually sat on it for the first time today without being terrified, so it's a start.

Allison from Shotts, mum to Mitchell, three and Alyssa, ten months

I don't go in for all this training lark myself. From about two years three months, it was apparent that Rebekah-Eve was aware when she needed the loo, but when you asked her if she wanted the potty, she'd say no. She just would not wee unless her nappy was on. Anyway, one day we put her on the loo and she did a wee, we made a fuss of her, and from that day on she's been dry, both day and night. When it comes to Amy-Jayne's turn, I plan to wait until she's actually asking me for the loo, before I start chasing her around with a potty.

Helen from Folkestone, Mum to Rebekah-Eve, four and Amy-Jayne, one

I potty trained both Charlotte and Alex at the age of three with the help of sticker charts, although we had had much pressure from the in-laws to do it from the age of 18 months. I wasn't ready to potty train them then, and the children wouldn't have been willing, either. It's important to wait for the right time or it won't work – don't let friends or relatives push you into it. They both only took a week or two to go from nappies to being completely dry, at night, too. If they do have the occasional accident, I don't make an issue out of it. I just say, 'Never mind, we'll make it to the loo next time.' I may try to potty train

Rosie a little earlier, as she learns so quickly from the older two, but certainly won't push her to, until she's ready. I think the key thing to remember when potty training is to have patience, it won't happen overnight. Also, expect accidents, and be prepared for them.

Berni from Stoke on Trent, mum to Charlotte, four, Alex, three and Rosie, one

The best advice I was ever given about daytime potty training was to wait as long as possible, and to do it over a two-week period at home. If your little one isn't ready, just forget about it, and choose another two weeks later on. A child who's ready to train can do it in two weeks.

Then after two weeks, if you think they've 'got it', start venturing out. Don't bother with pull-ups, as these seem to confuse the child. But make sure they have a wee before you go out, when you get there, while you're there, before you set off, and when you return. If you can continue this for another couple of weeks (with periods on the loo while you're at home, accompanied by reading and singing, for a poo) you should have it pretty much cracked! Everyone I know who has tried this way had a pretty painless experience of potty training.

Rosie from London, mum to Sean, 11 and Owen, eight

I waited until mine were just over two to start potty training, and both of them had it sussed in just over a week. I chose a week when I didn't have much to do, and stayed at home with them and gave them my full attention. They went round the house with no nappy on, a couple of potties dotted about, and whenever they had an accident, I said, 'Uh-oh, missed this time', and made it fun. We also sang the 'pee pee in the potty' song whenever they did one in there. By the end of the second week they were completely trained both day and night. However, my youngest contracted a urinary tract infection a few months later, and that set us way back. It took us over a year to train her again, because she couldn't really tell when she needed to go. I didn't put her back in nappies, just carried around spare clothes everywhere I went. She could go days with no problems and then have another few days with accidents.

It wasn't until she turned five that it all seemed to come together again.

Alex from Telford, mum to Raechel, ten and Hayley, six

I tried to potty train my daughter when she was 18 months old, because she'd started to show an interest in sitting on the potty I'd bought. It seemed a big step, as, until then, she'd been using it to put toys in! I managed to keep her dry for two days, but realised that it was only because I was lucky and had been asking at the right times and caught her in time. I gave up, but let her sit on the potty every morning before breakfast and every night before bed and if she managed to do anything in it I made a big deal out of how clever she was.

I decided that I'd try again in the summer, as I have the school holidays off. So one day I put her in knickers and we spent three days confined to the house and garden where I frequently asked her if she needed to go. By day four we'd ventured out in the car and the pram using a disposable changing mat as a protector. By day seven she was dry through the day and two weeks later I ditched the nappies for bed because I found that in the mornings I was throwing them away dry.

Victoria from Liverpool, mum to Katie, three and Daniel, six months

Don't waste time with pull-ups, go straight to pants or knickers – anything else is just confusing for a child. Set aside a week where you can stay in and tell your child what you're going to do. We tried twice with Callum. The first time he was just not ready (accidents everywhere, even after two days, and not one successful trip to the potty), so we left it a couple of weeks. We then gave him a few days' warning that he'd no longer be wearing nappies but pants, and agreed a reward system with him, so he knew what to expect and what he'd get if he got it right. He doesn't get sweets very often, so he asked for a lollypop if he went all day without an accident and a jelly bean each time he did a wee or poo in the potty. On Monday he got three jelly beans (only one accident), four on Tuesday (one accident) and by Wednesday, he had his lollypop! Yes, I know in most cases bribing your child with sweets is a bad thing but when you're faced with toilet training a two-and-a-half year-old, believe me, it's worth bending the rules a little.

Shelley from Bushey, mum to Callum, three

I think I was probably a bit mean when potty training my son. I knew he was ready because we'd tried for ages at home and he would use the potty if he was naked, he just had a real problem with pants. Eventually I just decided to go for it anyway. I put him in pants and took both children to a drop-in nursery every day for a week. For the first few days he peed within minutes of leaving the house, but he had to stand on the buggy board wet and cold for another 15 minutes until we got there. After three days, he realised that it wasn't very nice standing in wet pants, and just stopped doing it. My daughter trained herself by copying her brother before I was even ready to start trying.

Kim from Manchester, mum to Rhys, seven and Rain, five

The Problem Solved

Right time, right place

If you attempt to potty train too early, you'll almost certainly fail. The pressure could make them anxious and they may take much longer, or they may succeed only to regress a bit further down the line. If it does become obvious they're not ready, because they don't seem willing or are having lots of accidents, the thing to do is to stop, relax, go back to nappies and to try again later.

There are likely to be a number of indicators that your child is growing ready to swap her nappies for knickers. They'll become increasingly aware of when they're pooing or weeing, or when they are wet or dirty (and may not like it), and will then begin to understand the physical cues leading up to a wee or poo. Their bladder capacity naturally grows, so they'll be able to go for several hours in between wees, and their bowel movements may become more regular. They may also show interest in watching an adult or sibling use the loo, and begin to ask questions or become keen to try it themselves.

Regardless of these things, there are also times when it's not a good idea to embark on potty training: it's better to avoid a period of upheaval in their normal routine or environment – the arrival of a new baby, a house move, settling in to a new nursery or during a stressful period at home, for example. Sometimes, a child who regresses after successfully potty training, or who persistently fails to master toilet skills, may do so because of an underlying anxiety in their life so they may require extra help and patience.

Generally speaking, the later you leave it, the quicker it's likely to be. Beware of leaving it too late, though. Older children can be less compliant because they're growing independent minds and testing boundaries – if they decide to dig their heels in, they just might!

Different ways of doing

There are a number of approaches to potty training: which one you take will depend on which best suits you and your child – and that may not be obvious without some trial and error. Loads of mums swear by the intensive method, which involves setting aside a period, of at least a couple of days, when you're able to stay at home as much as possible and focus entirely on the task of training. It involves some serious commitment and concentration, but the advantage is that – if they're ready – it can be cracked relatively quickly. You need to be prepared to put them on the loo or potty regularly, nudge them frequently and respond like lightning when they make the relevant noises.

Others prefer a more natural approach, with a longer timescale. If you're in no hurry, and you're prepared for any amount of wet pants and puddles, easing them into dry days over a gradual period of a month or more may be a more relaxed alternative. Some children don't need any potty training at all, as such, and work out how to do it for themselves – usually when they've got older siblings or friends around to provide an example. In which case, make sure they've always got a potty or a childsize toilet seat to hand, and let them get on with it.

The golden rules

Whichever way you go about potty training, there are some rules that always apply. Never put pressure on them to use the loo or potty – chances are, they'll become anxious or even rebel. It needs to be a task they feel happy and relaxed about. Some people swear by reading a story to them, singing a song, or letting them play with a favourite toy while they're 'on the job'.

Ask them regularly whether they need to go, and encourage them to sit on the loo or potty regardless, after meals and at regular intervals in between.

It's vital to be relaxed when things go awry, and they almost certainly will. Be well prepared for accidents – have carpet cleaner to hand at home, and plenty of changes of clothing in your bag when you're out. Never get cross if they wet or soil themselves, miss, forget or generally fail to rise to the challenge. Just say 'Never mind, you'll get there next time' and quietly clean up. Reinforcing success with praise is just as important: make a big deal out of it when they do manage to do a wee or a poo in the loo or potty. Lots of mums find a reward system such as a sticker chart can be a really useful aid (see the factfile, p. 208).

As with most things, they learn by example, so let them see you using the loo and encourage your partner and their siblings to do so, too. Make life easier for them by making sure they have their potty around – have one on each floor of the house if it helps. Take them shopping so they can pick their own.

Fear of toilets is very common: they may worry they will fall in, or off, or even be flushed away, so a small toilet seat which can be slotted over the big one and a small stool are good ideas. Dress them in easily removed clothing for the period. Making a big deal of their new pants will help them feel very grown up and can seem like a reward in themselves, especially if they have their favourite cartoon character on them.

Finally, have patience. It can take a while, and even when you've got there, remember that accidents can and do happen.

Girls v boys

Girls commonly potty train before boys. It's not completely clear why, but they tend to be physiologically and developmentally ready sooner. Boys also have the added complication of a penis, which they must be careful to tuck in if they're to avoid spillage, and later on, of learning how to wee standing up!

If it's proving a strain

Constipation can be a relevant factor when it comes to encouraging a young child to poo because, if they begin to associate pain with a bowel movement, they may stop wanting to go. Then the problem becomes compounded, because the longer they hold it in, the more constipated they'll become. An increase in fibre and fluid is the obvious first step, so make sure they get extra fruit and vegetables, and plenty to drink, ideally water. Keeping active can be helpful, too. If the problem continues, always seek medical help: a GP may want to rule out other possible causes, and can prescribe laxatives if necessary.

What the experts say
The developmental psychologist

I think that generally speaking, two is a good age to start introducing the idea of a potty. Have one around so they get used to the idea, and let it take as long as it takes. Most mums, especially if they work, just don't have a whole week spare to spend on the intensive method.

The most important thing is to keep calm when you're potty training because there's no point in getting stressed about it and if you're anxious it might rub off on them. The fact is, there are going to be accidents, possibly lots of them!

Take your time about it, and take it easy. Never tell them off, but always praise them. Even if they've made a mess all over the sofa, pick them up, put them on the potty, and then praise them for doing that.

Make it fun, exciting even. One idea is to use the potty or loo as the 'reading seat'. It's all about making them feel comfortable and happy about sitting down to do their business. But don't bother with those potties that sing because they always stop working after a while!

One thing I would say is, once you've got them out of nappies, don't go back (unless it becomes obvious they really aren't ready). Even if it's tempting at tricky times like car journeys, don't! You only have to put them back in nappies just once for them to be confused. A better solution in a car is to put one of those absorbent bed mats on their car seat, and to stop frequently. And I don't think pull-ups are much help. To a child, they're still nappies. When it comes to night training, bear in mind that they're not usually ready for this until quite a bit later – up to a year after they're dry in the day.

Occasionally, they can be completely potty trained and then go back if there's some sort of upset in their lives such as a new sibling. They won't be doing it on purpose, it's just that they're not thinking straight and even though they're potty trained, that doesn't mean their bladder or bowel control is as good as ours. In that situation you would probably have to go back to the basics, lavishing them with praise every time they get it right.

Dr Janine Spencer, Brunel University

The Problem Summarised

- ◆ Potty training's easier and quicker if they're ready. This is unlikely to be much before they're two (and it may be quite a bit later). Ignore anyone who tells you to do it sooner!
- ◆ Have a potty permanently on standby. A small toilet seat is also useful.
- ◆ Accidents will happen. Always keep your cool . . . and plenty of spare, dry clothing.
- ◆ Praise them like mad when they do get it right. A reward system can work wonders.
- ◆ If they don't seem ready, stop and try again later. These things take time.

Factfile: Reward systems

A reward system is a great aid to the business of positive parenting, which is all about focusing on the good things children do, rather than the bad. They can be useful in a more general context, encouraging good behaviour over a long period of time, and are also helpful in tackling a specific challenge, such as potty training. If you've got a clear aim in mind, it's worth actually writing (or illustrating) it on the chart, as a reminder to the child of what you're expecting of them.

Most parents run a system in which their kids earn a tangible prize after reaching a certain goal – five stickers on a star chart earns them one treat, for example. Keep rewards simple and inexpensive though: don't start a costly precedent by making big promises. If you choose to offer them cold hard cash, for example, make the denominations small – otherwise overachievers may clean you out!

Reward systems are most useful for children over three, when they can properly start to grasp the concept of rewards for good behaviour. But children as young as two can also benefit – they'll get satisfaction from choosing a sticker and putting it in the appropriate place, and when combined with lots of praise in an enthusiastic voice, they'll soon start to equate positive behaviour with another space filled. Be sensitive to younger children who may feel put out if a brother or sister is rewarded – although a bit of sibling rivalry is no bad thing, and may even be inspirational. Set little ones their own challenges and help them work towards their own rewards.

Try to be consistent with reward systems. Enthusiasm and commitment for them can easily wane, so you need to keep them going if they're to help in the long term. Keep your promises – you can't expect them to influence a child's behaviour if they don't always get what they're owed! And never make the goals too difficult: empty spaces are demoralising, and children need to earn a regular reward to stay motivated. Many experts feel you shouldn't take away rewards they've already earned – certainly not if they've failed to rise to a challenge, such as weeing in a potty. Generally speaking, reward systems are not about persuasion or punishment, but about celebrating the positive. Give praise and hugs alongside the rewards. In theory, as time goes on, children will stop needing a sticker for their achievements and will do stuff because they know you'll be proud of them!

You can buy star charts in the shops. But it's more fun, and helps the child to feel involved and interested, if you design and make a reward system yourself. Here are some ideas you might like to try (courtesy of the Netmums):

- Create a chart with the chance to earn stickers as they work towards a greater goal – and a special reward. Try drawing round 10p pieces, and mark achievements by filling in each circle with a tick or a sticker – ten ticks, and they've earned a pound.
- Instead of offering a tangible item as a reward, try offering an activity such as a trip to the cinema or leisure centre.
- Put marbles, pennies, or small balls in a special jar.
- To encourage a bit of healthy sibling rivalry, get them to write their name on a piece of paper and put it in a jar when they've done well at something. The child with the most 'behaviour merits' in the jar at the end of each week or month earns a reward (it's motivating because the more pieces of paper you have in the jar, the more likely your name is to be pulled out).
- Design and print a 'certificate of good behaviour' with a blank to fill in their name when they've earned one. Display prominently.
- Decorate a shoe box and fill it with inexpensive treats – stickers, pencils, hair clips, note pads. Whistle it out when they've been well behaved and let them take their pick.
- Let computer-savvy older kids design their own 'behaviour spreadsheet'. Award them a coin for positive behaviour, and let them do the calculations as the pennies and pounds add up!

High and dry: What to do if they wet the bed

The Problem

Encouraging your child not to worry about still being in a nappy or pyjama pants is important – they feel babyish if they hear that their friends are dry. I did stop the drinks but this made no difference, he could still wet the bed even twice a night. I set my alarm to lift him but just got more stressed by doing this as well as tired and cranky, so I put the pyjama pants back on, and relaxed. If the pants were dry in the morning I gave praise, if it was wet I acted as if nothing had happened, and it worked a treat. It gave my son confidence, and the time he obviously needed, and by five and a half, he was dry. I think I felt pressure from other parents, whose children had been dry much earlier. But every child is different. As parents we need to step back and stop trying to make our children grow up before they're ready. We wish their lives away sometimes.

Jenny from Johnstone, mum to James, six

Why there's no shame in soggy sheets

Some children lose their night-time nappies when they become dry in the day, but more usually it takes a while, up to a year, before they're ready to sleep through without one. As with just about every other developmental stage of childhood, there's pressure to get them out of nappies at night, as though doing so were some great parental achievement! But other than the cost of the nappies (and the environmental implications) there's no real reason for it to be a concern in the early years – in most cases, they'll get there by the time they are three or four. However, a significant number will still be in need of a nappy, pull-ups, or pyjama pants [absorbent night-time underwear] to get through the night dry beyond that.

No one seems certain why some children take longer than others to acquire 24-hour control of their bladders, but it's only rarely linked to an actual medical problem, such as a bladder infection, and like day-time potty training, it has absolutely nothing to do with aptitude.

Experts believe it's due to one or more of the following factors: the body's system of slowing down urine production at night (triggered by the release of a hormone called vasopressin) isn't working; the bladder may hold smaller than usual amounts of urine, or be overactive; and/or the brain's signal to the bladder to 'hold on' isn't getting its message through. Sometimes anxiety can either delay dry nights, or trigger recurrent bedwetting, later on. And frequently, there's a family link: many children who wet the bed have a parent who did so, too.

More than a wee worry

Bedwetting beyond the age of five, or 'nocturnal enuresis' to use its technical term, is actually far more common than you might imagine: more than half a million children aged between five and 16 – and some adults, too – are thought to be affected. It's not the worst problem a family might have to cope with. But it can cause significant distress, not least because having to get up in the middle of the night to deal with soggy sheets, whilst remaining calm and positive, is an exhausting business. And, after a certain age, it can become a cause for social embarrassment, spoiling holidays, school trips and sleepovers and chipping away at a child's self-esteem.

The Problem Shared

What the Netmums say

My eldest girl still wets some nights, maybe if she's stressed at school or if I've let her have a drink past a certain time. I've never made an issue out of the accidents and when we go on holidays I always take a small supply of night-time knickers. She has no problem putting them on, and we generally have dry ones all through the holiday. In fact when her sister has a giggle at her in 'nappies', she just smiles and says: 'Well I can't help it, and we don't want to ruin the beds do we?'

At home she has waterproof covers on her mattress, pillow and quilt. When she's wet she just strips the sheets off the bed and puts them in the wash leaving the bed to dry out and air for the day and makes it again later that day. When we're out she has to know where the public toilets are and goes regularly. I wet the bed until I was 17. I think that having suffered from it yourself makes it easier to cope with when your child does too. As for the cause, I've always felt that the signal that's supposed to tell me my bladder's full doesn't work, so I don't wake up. I think it's the same with Ceara, who sleeps heavily.

I really feel for mothers who just don't know how to cope with this, but there really isn't a lot you can do, other than be sympathetic, and don't make an issue out of it.

Jo from East London, mum to Ceara, ten and Zarah, eight

Some advice from personal experience, don't belittle your bed-wetting child! It's humiliating enough as it is. I wet the bed as a child. I'd often dream that I'd got up and gone into the bathroom. I could feel the toilet seat beneath me, but alas, I was still soundly sleeping in my bed. I was told I must be lazy and was then taunted by my sisters (I still am, occasionally). Countless mornings I would get up early after an accident, strip my bed and change my clothes to try to hide it (of course it didn't take long for Mom to find out, as she had to wash the sheets). I think the torment I felt caused me to suffer with the problem longer, rather than help cure it. Kami's been dry at night for a long time now and has had few accidents. If it ever was a problem though, I'd do whatever I could to ease her embarrassment.

Kearsten from Dudley, mum to Kami, three

As a child I wet the bed until I was 14. I had a hormone deficiency – my mother and her five siblings had it, and so did my brother and sister. For holidays we were given a nasal spray which stopped it from happening, but couldn't be used continuously. Now it seems my eldest son, six, has the same problem. We've taken him to be assessed at an enuresis clinic, and they said he seems to have the same problem I had. They gave him some tablets that could control it, to take before bed each night. They didn't work! So he wears 'pyjama pants' each night and he's got used to it. I remember not being able to do sleepovers or go away on school trips, and I wish he didn't have this. But he has, and so we're dealing with it as best we can.

Claire from Darlington, mum to Liam, six and Kristian, two

I had problems with my eldest son bedwetting and I wet the bed myself, well into my teens. One of the main things with bedwetting is being discreet about it – never tell people in front of your child about it. I used to cringe, and get very upset, when my mum did that to me. Also, never ever tell a child off for wetting the bed. It's the worst thing you could do, as the child thinks it's their fault, which it isn't, as it's beyond their control. I could never have people to stay at my house and I could never go to theirs. You worry about whether you smell. All this was heartbreaking to me and has stayed with me ever since. My mum never really told me off for it, and she really did try to help by taking me to the doctor, which I hated.

Things are easier these days. My son could always stay over at friends' houses as I would pack him some night pants. I'd let the other parent know, but ask them not to mention it. He also had problems with wetting himself in the day. It all caused him so much pain it was heartbreaking. He'd hide his underwear from me, no matter how much I tried to reassure him it was OK.

After months of fighting I finally got a referral to a special clinic. He's been given some help and medication and he's a changed boy. He's not wet the bed once since he started there.

Me, well I eventually grew out of it in my very late teens. My younger son is fully potty trained and although we haven't tried him without a nappy on at night yet, I'm just keeping my fingers crossed that he won't take after me, too.
Tracy from Sheffield, mum to Luke, nine and Bailey, three

I'm mother to eight-year-old twin girls, one of whom still has 'accidents'. When I realised it was starting to affect her self-confidence I took her to a paediatrician, and I wish now that I'd done that years before. She advised me to help increase the capacity of her bladder by encouraging her to drink large quantities of liquid during the day, and then to stop her drinking an hour before bed-time (if they're thirsty, you can let them suck on an ice cube or a piece of juicy fruit.) She has also been prescribed some medication, which she takes when she has sleepovers and overnight school excursions.

Having followed this advice we've gone from 'accidents' every night to only once a week or so and I'm hopeful the problem will right itself naturally. It's not perfect but it seems to be working and the mixture of the medication and the timed regime seems to give my daughter a feeling of control that has helped to improve her confidence no end.

My advice to other mothers? Don't wait until it affects their self-esteem. If you think that your child has a problem, see the doctor and don't let yourself get fobbed off with petty responses.
Miranda from north London, mum to Ellie and Liv, eight

The Problem Solved

Losing the night-time nappies

Making the leap from wet to dry nights is usually a simple case of time and patience. As with day-time potty training, wait until they're ready or it won't work – you'll get a good idea how close they are by how dry their nappies are in the morning. Help prepare them for nappy-free nights by encouraging them to go for a wee first thing in the morning and last thing at night. Ask them to use the loo in the middle of the night if they do wake up –

leave a night-light on so they can get to the toilet if necessary, or make sure they have a potty nearby. And talk the idea through with them first, so they know what's happening. Washable waterproof bedding protection over the mattress will inevitably prove a sensible precaution.

Consistently dry nights can take a while to achieve. The extra laundry's no fun, but it's essential not to show them you're cross about it when they do wet the bed. Praise and reward the achievements they do make. If they're under five and still repeatedly wet, they may need more time – you might decide to put them back in pull-ups or pyjama pants (don't refer to them as nappies: it may make them feel a failure), and try again a few months later.

Lifestyle changes that can help

If they're still not dry at night once they're at an age when a night-time nappy or absorbent pants are not emotionally or socially ideal, there are lots of things you can do to help them. Cutting back on drinks is *not* the answer. In fact, although it may seem contradictory, it's vital that they drink plenty of liquid, six to eight glasses, at regular intervals throughout the day, as it will help their bladder stretch to hold more urine, and aid them in recognising when they need to go. (Water, milk, squash and juice all count, but fizzy or caffeinated drinks should be avoided as they can increase the kidneys' production of urine.) Assuming they're getting plenty of fluid in the day, it makes sense not to give them a drink too close to bedtime and to make sure they've emptied their bladder before bed. Some parents find it's useful to 'lift' a child who bedwets – gently waking them and putting them on the toilet during the night. It may reduce the number of wet sheets, but as a long-term solution it's not much use, as it won't help them to be dry of their own accord.

Praise and reward can work wonders, so it's a good idea to get a sticker chart or some other reward system up and running (see the reward systems factfile, p. 208). However, you need to be sure that the goals they're rewarded for are achievable otherwise you run the risk of demoralising, rather than motivating them. Don't reward them for dry nights, especially if they're few and far between. Give them a sticker (or whatever incentive you use) for other positive steps taken, too, such as having their recommended six to eight drinks, letting you know when they've wet the bed, or helping you with the wet bedding.

And keeping your cool is vital: if they feel stressed and under pressure, it may make things worse. Encourage openness and keep them talking about the subject, in case anxiety is exacerbating the situation. Remind them that bedwetting is nothing to be ashamed of, and, once they're old enough, help them to feel positive about taking control of the situation themselves.

When you've tried all you can at home

A child who's still regularly wetting the bed as they approach their seventh birthday will need some professional help. A health visitor or GP can make a referral for more specialised support from staff at the nearest Enuresis Clinic. Established treatments include the use of enuresis alarms and in some cases medication. You can also get details of these clinics (along with a vast amount of other helpful advice) from ERIC, the Enuresis support organisation. You'll find their details at the back of the book.

What the experts say
The helpline worker and clinical advisor

Bedwetting can certainly be a stressful issue for families. Children who wet the bed can start to feel different, they may feel babyish or belittled, and it can have far-reaching effects on their confidence. Parents too may feel there's a stigma attached if their child is still wetting the bed, because of some of the old myths that remain – that children who wet the bed must be developmentally slow, or that their parents have somehow failed to 'train' them in the right way. We know when children are bedwetting that one or more physical factors are against them – it's not a simple case of training them to hold on, or wake up, it's more complex than that. There's also the common assumption that they must be unhappy about something. But although we know that worry and anxiety can be a factor – particularly in the case of secondary bedwetting, when they've previously been dry, but some sort of upheaval in their life triggers it again – it's only ever part of the picture.

There's also the stress of the various practical implications – broken nights; all that extra laundry — which are not to be underestimated. Sometimes the stress shows, however much a parent tries to stay calm.

That can cause worry for a child because they want to please their parents, which can of course make the situation worse. It's important to stay positive when you're dealing with bedwetting but at the same time, you need to find a balance. Although it's true that in many cases, nature does eventually kick in and children 'grow out of it', they can usually be helped to overcome the situation before then, and we believe it's better to intervene once they've reached an age where it's a problem. If you're too casual about it, and the child is wrapped up in a 'comfort zone', they won't feel motivated to change the situation. They need to be encouraged to do that in a calm, positive, nurturing way: yes, reassure them that it's nothing to be ashamed of and that lots of boys and girls do it, but let them know it does matter. Ask them how they think *they* would benefit from dry nights, and gently encourage them to take charge of the situation themselves, by becoming 'boss of their bladder'. These may be psychological measures but they're still worthwhile: the crux of it is that we don't completely understand what triggers the physical elements that cause bedwetting, and awareness and motivation may well play a part in successful treatment.

If they've reached the age of seven and are still regularly bedwetting in spite of your attempts to help, then we would recommend seeking medical help. Individual assessment is vital, because every child, and every family, will be in a different situation. *Anne Weaver, Education and Resources for Improving Childhood Continence (ERIC)*

The Problem Summarised

- Some children take longer to get dry at night than others: it's a fact of life.
- As many as half a million children between the ages of five and 16 wet the bed.
- Expert opinion, from current research, seems to be that the cause is probably down to one or more physical factors.
- Bedwetting often runs in families. Anxiety may trigger it, or make it worse.
- Never scold or punish a child for a wet bed. Keep calm and positive.
- Many children grow out of it. Those who show no signs of doing so should be helped to overcome it.

Tell me about it: What to do if you're worried about their speech and language skills

The Problem

It became clear early on that Ciaran had speech problems, but when I mentioned it to his nursery and health visitor they told me he was still young. Then, a week before his second birthday, they decided they *were* worried about his lack of speech. Tests showed he was on a par with an eight-month-old in speaking and language. I'm on a waiting list to see a speech therapist at the local hospital, although I've been told I might be able to jump the queue because his results were so poor. It's frustrating trying to teach him to talk. He understands a lot but just won't say anything. It's awful not knowing what he wants, and he has tantrums because he can't tell me. It's very hard.

Kerry from Plymouth, mum to Ciaran, two

When words don't come easy

Talking and understanding are fundamentally important skills, for all human beings. Speech and language develops at very different rates in different children, but as a general rule, most little ones will be speaking their first words by at least 18 months, and will be joining words together by two. At three they should be forming proper sentences and by four they should be getting to grips with basic grammar and making themselves understood by most people.

For any proud parent, those early words and phrases are among the most important milestones of the early years. But for a very significant number of children – an estimated one in ten in the UK – these skills don't come easily for one reason or another, and they may have what the experts call a communication difficulty. This umbrella term covers a massive range of more specific problems, from the very minor, to the highly significant. Little ones who appear to be delayed in their language, speech or communication may be taking longer than is normal to enter this developmental stage, or it may be an indication of a more serious issue such as a hearing problem, a language disorder – or a learning difficulty. Either way, it can be a major worry for concerned parents and it's not always obvious what to do in response, and when. Concern can be compounded by feelings of guilt: wondering if it was something you did or didn't do that's to blame. And on top of that, there's often unsolicited advice and unwanted comments from well-meaning friends, relatives and even strangers to deal with.

Why communication matters so much

It's impossible to over-emphasise the importance of effective communication in childhood, because children who struggle to communicate can suffer educationally, socially, emotionally and behaviourally. Experts are increasingly concerned about the problem and they estimate that as many as half of children these days enter school without the speech and language skills they need to thrive, with as many as one in ten in every classroom with a recognised communication disability.

Fortunately, there's a great deal of help and support available, even if getting it isn't always plain sailing. If you believe your child may be affected by a speech and language difficulty, you will need to seek further, specialised help. This section offers only a brief summary of the main issues involved.

The Problem Shared

What the Netmums say

I didn't feel that there was anything 'wrong' with Dane at first, but I did begin to wonder when he passed his second birthday and his peers at his nursery were chatting away. Dane was saying lots of single words but not making clear sentences. It's been a lonely road for us. I even stopped meeting people, so I wouldn't get questions about why he wasn't speaking 'normally'. We've had review after review at speech and language therapy. We've also completed a six-week 'Talking Fun' course, which teaches you how you can help your child and was a fantastic help. With this course, together with the tremendous support of Dane's nursery, his SENCO and our family not only did Dane's speech come on but my own personal confidence came back. At last I didn't feel so alone. We've had to accept that there's no real cause for Dane's language being delayed. It's caused me endless emotional upset as I've blamed myself – what did I do, or not do as his mother? He is talking more and more now. He's a child with his own agenda and he'll do it when he wants to! Recently he said: 'Mummy, I love you,' and it was the best thing ever. I don't care that he's a little way behind, because we *will* get there. We're fortunate that delayed speech is the only thing we have to worry about when there are children out there fighting just to be here.
Tamra from Surrey, mum to Dane, four

My son didn't babble until he was 16 months old and had very bad tantrums, which seemed to be due to frustration. His hearing test was normal, but our GP said he seemed nine months behind in development. He was referred for speech and language therapy and he did this for a year without any progress. Finally, after his second birthday, he said 'yeah', his first word. Three months later, he had six words. He was then referred to a paediatric speech and language therapist, who told us it's hard to give a definite diagnosis at this stage. It was devastating. I don't know anyone else who's been through this, so Netmums has been a lifeline to me.

He's a year ahead in his understanding, and a year behind in his speech, so it's doubly frustrating for him. He's now having speech therapy once a week with a new therapist whom he loves, and has come on in leaps and bounds. He has about 150 words and is starting to put two or three words together. I'm very anxious about how he will get himself understood when he starts pre-school, without me to interpret for him, but the therapist is going to visit the staff there to explain how to communicate with him. It's a big worry for us as he seems a very bright lad. We just hope it doesn't hold him back in the future.

Nina from Winchester, mum to Joseph, three

As the months rolled by people started asking when my little one was going to talk, to which I always replied: 'When he's ready'. But eventually I started to get a little worried myself that he wasn't speaking, and contacted my local Sure Start programme. They set us up with a parent link worker, who visited once a week to do some specific work around language with him. He did make some progress but not as much as I'd hoped for. Later, I contacted our health visitor and asked for a referral to a speech and language development centre. I finally got the appointment, and they agreed his speech was quite delayed. I know he's still quite young, two years eight months, but he's starting nursery in September and I'm glad we've already got the ball rolling.

Deborah from Halifax, mum to Kelsey, nine, Luke, six and Cameron, two

My daughter has a condition called Ocular Motor Apraxia, which is a breakdown in eye movement control, and the fact that her speech is delayed is linked to that. She's now 22 months and apart from a lot of babble the only clear words she can say are 'ma', 'da', 'who's that?', 'whats that?', 'hello' and 'bye'. She makes 'noises' for a lot of words which seem like random sounds; it's not until you realise she uses the same sound for one particular thing that her meaning clicks. At the moment nothing 'official' is being done, but she may need to see a therapist if it's still bad when she is older. So at the moment we just talk to her a lot and try and speak 'properly' and clearly (not easy for a Cockney!)

Rebecca from Croydon, mum to Nyah, 22 months

My son talks in full sentences, has a good vocabulary and sings all the time but his speech in general is not as clear and crisp as it should be for his age. My daughter could talk clearly at an early age, but with my son I always felt there was a problem with his speech, even though everyone around me said: 'He has lazy boy syndrome', or 'second child syndrome', and 'It'll come, he's only young'. I asked my health visitor about it several times and eventually she referred him for speech and language therapy. I then asked her for a hearing test referral, which had never been suggested. He was found to be mildly deaf, and has glue ear, which was what affected his speech. His hearing is a bit like ours would be with our fingers in our ears. We then discussed hearing aids, and surgery for grommets. I felt bad because if I'd been firmer with the health professionals earlier on we might have had time to get it fixed before he starts school. I do worry about him although the staff at his nursery say he's brilliant and that you'd never guess he had hearing problems as he joins in everything and sits still at story time.

His operation to have grommets put in should go ahead soon and he'll then have a few months of decent hearing before he starts school. Poor little man, I'm glad they found a reason for his unclear speech. I've been reassured that it's very common and he should be fully cured when he gets older.

Gina from Lancashire, mum to Amelia, seven and William, three

Joe was born at 27 weeks. He had hearing problems, although thankfully he only has a slight hearing loss now, and because he had a tracheostomy, a surgical procedure that leaves an opening in the windpipe, he couldn't hear his own voice until he was one, so he didn't even attempt to talk.

At one of his hearing tests I raised the point about his speech. He wasn't attempting to communicate; he'd just point to things and get so frustrated if we couldn't understand. Joe was then assessed by a speech and language therapist and they agreed he had a problem – he's about a year behind for his age. She set a programme for us and he's come on loads. She also told us that younger siblings sometimes suffer when an older child says everything for them, so we've told Ben, his brother, that Joe cannot have things until he answers for himself.

It does worry me that he may always have an issue with his speech because I know that people can be cruel. My husband didn't say a word until he was five and he had to go to a special school, which made him feel stigmatised. We've been told that Joe will have to, too, if he doesn't get the adequate support he needs. It's a big worry.

Amanda from Manchester, mum to Ben, five and Joe, three

When my daughter started nursery at the local school she was assessed and I was told she'd need some speech and language therapy. She has problems with her L's, which come out as W's, so instead of 'love' she says 'wove'. Her J's come out as T's, so instead of saying Jessica, it's Tessica.

A year and a half on, she still hasn't had a single session of speech and language therapy. I've asked them to reassess her since, and they said she still needed it, but we're still waiting. What's worrying me is that as she's getting older she's getting more used to the way she talks and it's going to take a lot to change it. It's frustrating. People say that you need *this* or *that* for your child, but there aren't always the facilities. And it's the child who suffers.

Samantha from Rochford, mum to Jessica, five

I got fobbed off repeatedly by my health visitor when I kept telling her my son, then 15 months, wasn't talking and didn't pay attention when you spoke. Finally I went to my GP who referred us on to the ENT department at our local hospital. I was lucky that at the time our GP surgery had a brilliant private speech and language therapist who used to come in on a Saturday morning and work on a one to one basis with children and families. She helped us learn to sign and gave us lots of ideas for games that we could play at home to encourage his speech. Eventually they found he had really bad glue ear and he had his first set of grommets soon after he turned two. He went from communicating with grunts and pointing, to using long sentences in three weeks. He now has a very advanced vocabulary and we're using all the skills we learned to help his brother, too, who at 19 months has very advanced speech.

Mandy from Grimsby, mum to Peter, nine and Samual, one

The Problem Solved

What are communication difficulties, and what causes them?

Not all communication difficulties have an obvious cause but the established ones include hearing loss (either short-term which may be caused by ear infections, or due to a more profound hearing disability); general learning difficulties; physical disorders such as cerebral palsy which may affect the facial muscles, needed to make the movements for different sounds; genetic factors; problems during pregnancy and birth; and recognised syndromes with communication and language difficulties as a known consequence, such as autism.

Communication difficulties are broadly divided into three main areas, and a child may have a problem in some or all of these areas. If a child doesn't appear to know what you're talking about, they may have a difficulty in understanding, or problems with their *receptive skills*. This isn't always easy to spot, because they're often able to pick up on other cues. For example, you might tell them it's time to go and although they don't understand what you're saying, they'll see you pick up the car keys. A good way to test them if you suspect they're not understanding is to look at a book together and ask them to find things within the picture, being careful not to give any non-verbal clues.

They may have a problem with their *expressive skills,* that is, they aren't able to get the words out, or collect them from their heads and put them into the right order. Or they may have a problem with their *speech sounds*, which means they're understanding sentences and using them as they should be, but cannot be understood because their sounds aren't right for some reason. This can cause a great deal of frustration.

Know what's to be expected

There's a great deal of variation in how and when children's speech and language develops, especially between the ages of one and two, and it can be hard to know what's normal and when in terms of speech and language.

This fact isn't always helped by the people around us who can't seem to help but comment. Some view developmental milestones as points on a competitive scale, making you feel bad if your child is taking a little longer with theirs. Others may try and reassure you in a well-meaning way that there's nothing wrong, and that they'll get there in the end, when in fact, they may not actually be right about that.

Arm yourself with a good grasp of what to expect and when. (There's a rough guide in the factfile, p. 228.) That knowledge, combined with your own powerful natural instincts as a parent, should ensure that you can tell for yourself if there seems, at least, to be a problem.

If you have concerns about the speech and language development of your child, bear in mind that it's always best to get these things sorted at the earliest opportunity. So talk to a heath visitor or GP if you're worried. You don't have to have a referral though, you can go direct to wherever your local speech and language therapy services are based, usually in a community clinic or hospital department, and make an appointment yourself.

What the experts say
The speech and language therapist

Communication is vital because it provides the backbone to everything that we do – making friends, learning and thinking, and making our needs known, for example. If those skills aren't in place, the consequences can be hugely significant. Social relationships may be difficult. If you're at school or nursery and you can't understand what's going on, follow instructions or predict what's going to happen next, it could lead to behavioural difficulties, and learning will be hard.

For a parent, having a child with a communication difficulty can be stressful. They may well feel guilty, usually quite unnecessarily. And managing a communication difficulty can be hard. You have to constantly try to make sense of what they're saying, or help other people to understand them. Or you may have to explain their behaviour if they're frustrated and behaving badly as a result. It creates a lot of difficulties, and if you've got other children as well, the whole family can be affected.

Children's communication skills do develop at different ages, and it shouldn't be seen as a competition, but if you're concerned, it's a good idea to look at children of a similar age and ask about what they're doing. And go on your gut instinct. Other people don't necessarily understand communication disabilities. They say things like, don't worry, they'll get there in the end. But actually it's important to get help as early as possible, because the years from birth to four is the time best suited for learning language. That's when you can make the best of a child's capabilities, and after that it's more of a struggle. Also, the length of waiting lists and referral times can be very long. My advice would be that if you're at all worried, get them a referral anyway, or find out where your local speech and language clinic or department is and contact them direct. Better for you to turn up and for the therapist to tell you there's not a problem, than to end up waiting and miss an important chance to help them. There are many ways you can support a child's speech and language development, regardless of whether or not they have a difficulty. Talking in short sentences is one: if they can follow what you're saying, they'll be better able to copy it. Sit with them, spend time with them and allow them to direct whatever activity they're doing. Talk to them as they play, and when you eat.

Life can be so busy. You're getting them to places, trying to make them food, juggling frantically, especially if you've got more than one. Sometime it's easy to forget to sit down and talk to each other, which is what's really important.

Kate Freeman, professional advisor for I CAN, the children's communication charity

The Problem Summarised

- Good communication skills are fundamental to life. Without them, children may suffer in their relationships and in their learning.
- Communication difficulties are widespread and include a range of specific problems.

- Know what's normal in speech and language development, and you'll be able to recognise if your child's development is behind.
- Be vigilant, and get help early if you think your child may need it. They may be late learners, but it may be a more serious problem.
- The best way to boost a child's communication skills is to communicate with them: Keep talking!

Factfile: Speech and language development – what's normal when

At 18 months to two years, most children will:
- Understand a range of words, probably around 100, and simple instructions like 'Get your shoes.'
- Be using up to 50 words themselves, although they may not sound like real words.
- Be starting to put two words together.
- Probably *not* be able to concentrate well enough to play and talk at the same time.

At two to two-and-a-half years, most children will:
- Understand more difficult words such as 'big', 'little', 'on' and 'under'.
- Be able to join two or more words together.
- Be learning new words every day, although they may be unable to use all the adult sounds yet and may get frustrated if they cannot be understood.

At two-and-a-half to three years, most children will:
- Appear to understand most things other people say, although there'll be lots of words they *don't* know.
- Be using sentences with four to six words in them, ask simple questions and talk about what has already happened.

- Probably stumble over their words sometimes, as they have lots to say but can't always say it right.

At three to four years, most children will:
- Be able to understand longer sentences with two parts, like 'put your farm animals in the big box'.
- Be using longer sentences – and may use the word 'why?' a lot!
- Perhaps find some sounds hard still. Tricky ones are 'f', 'l', 'y', 'th', 'r', 's', 'ch' and 'j'.

At four to five years, most children will:
- Understand most things you say to them.
- Probably ask what words mean.
- Join in conversations, argue and tell stories, and enjoy singing, rhymes and songs.
- Probably not get everything right, for example, saying 'runned' instead of 'ran'.
- Not necessarily be able to manage some sounds, such as 'th', 'r', 's', 'ch' and 'scr'.

Too much, too young?
How to slow them down if they're growing up too fast

The Problem

My daughter is seven and I try very hard to keep her as a child. I find a lot of the clothes in shops inappropriate and I worry that if she dresses like a grown-up that's how some people will treat her and I can see that causing problems in a few years. I do let her play computer games, but I want to know what she's doing and that what she's doing is appropriate for her age. Chat rooms are just not allowed.

It's very hard, as children want to do everything that their friends are doing and when other parents don't feel the same way and let their children act like grown-ups, peer pressure soon kicks in.

Lisa from Hull, mum to Jamie, seven

Whatever happened to childhood?

It's traditional for mums and dads to bang on tediously about how things were in their day. But in truth, the world really *is* a different place now to the one that previous generations of children knew. And there's no denying that kids these days are exposed to all sorts of influences that, frankly, don't fit in with our vision of an ideal childhood. Many experts have voiced concern that increasingly 'toxic' childhoods are becoming the norm. They fear the potential consequences of our children hurtling too soon into adult lives.

Naturally, it's a worrying subject for any caring parent. And like all other worrying subjects, one that we need to weigh up carefully, and put into perspective.

Our changing world

Among the perceived 'threats' to childhood are the all-powerful commercial forces which thrust sophisticated products such as cosmetics and sexy clothing at an ever-younger target market; advances in technology and an increasingly influential media, which expose our kids to a whole series of undesirable lures like internet chat rooms and violent computer games; and the high-pressure, competitive lifestyles that parents themselves are caught up in which, inevitably, become the lifestyles their children must have, too. Changing family structures may also be relevant, as kids increasingly have to come to terms with difficult emotional situations such as divorce and step relationships.

The Problem Shared

What the Netmums say

I hate to see children who look like little adults instead of kids. It also makes me worry that maybe mine are immature when in fact they aren't, they just act their age. Sam is still happy to use his imagination and play with his Bob the Builder toys, whereas lots of his friends are bragging about their PlayStations, which they play horrid fighting games on. I really don't like to see young girls dressed in clothes my mum and dad wouldn't even have let me wear as a teenager. It looks fake and cheap and it just makes me sad. Where's the excitement of getting your first bra at twelve if you've had one since you were five? And girls' shoes! When I see a four-year-old in Wellies with heels or delicate silk slip-ons, I can't believe it.

I don't want mine to be so innocent that they're gullible, but I do want them to keep on being kids for as long as possible. As for watching 'adult' TV programmes – no chance! They're both tucked up in bed before they come on.

Donna from Rotherham, mum to Sam, five and Emma, four

Some girls' clothes are just ridiculous. I've seen micro minis, skimpy tops and thongs in junior sizes. Why would a seven-year-old want a thong? Other pet hates are ear piercing and hair gel. Children will have plenty of time to discover those when they are older. Mobiles seem to be a big thing as well, and I think some children have these far too early.

As for PCs and video games, I think you have to be reasonable. My son loves the computer and he's learned a lot from using it. I also allow him the use of his dad's console for limited periods, but only for children's games. With television, he's only allowed to watch children's stuff.

I want my little boy to enjoy his childhood as much as possible and encourage him to have as much fun as possible. We love messy play, and simple things like taking a ball to the park and feeding the ducks.

Jo from Mow Cop, mum to Alex, four

Moderation is key. Both my two have been using computers since nursery and I don't think that's any bad thing but I want to be able to control what they do or say on the computer for a while longer yet. Dan asked for MSN a while ago, and I said no. He's getting to the point where he wants nice trainers and stuff, which I'm happy to go along with to a certain point. Clothes for a girl are different. Luckily Rebecca has a unique fashion sense all of her own, which usually involves lots of layers. I shudder when I see a lot of her friends in cropped tops with inappropriate slogans and more make-up than I would wear in a year. These are eight-year-old girls for heaven's sake, but sadly some parents seem happy to encourage it. My daughter will grow up far too fast anyway and I don't want to do anything that will accelerate it. I try my best to bring them up somewhere approaching the way I was: you can't have everything all the time, and sometimes what you want just isn't suitable for your age. They seem happy enough with that at the moment.

Allison from Cramlington, mum to Dan, 11 and Rebecca, nine

The media are partly to blame for the fact that kids grow up too fast these days. But also, they mature a lot earlier, especially girls. My eldest daughter was asked out by a boy in the year above her when she was just ten! She knows I wouldn't let her have a boyfriend before she's 16, and that's already caused rows between us.

But, as much as I try to keep them as children, I also feel that in today's world the children need to have a bit more knowledge about sex and drink and drugs, so we talk about these things openly in our house. I try and monitor the films and television they watch; the computer games they play and sites they visit; and the clothes my daughters wear, but it's hard to find an even balance. They're not allowed to wear thongs, skimpy tops, or t-shirts with offensive slogans. I've let them wear make-up to parties but I always put it on myself, rather than letting them loose with a make-up bag. I let Jack watch films with a 12 certificate, but make sure I've seen it myself first. If you don't give them a little bit of freedom and say no to almost every request they make, they'll just hanker for it even more.

Maybe I'm old fashioned, but I want my kids to have a relatively innocent childhood. They can spend the next 60 years behaving like adults.

Christine from Kettering, mum to Holly, 12, Chloe, ten and Jack, eight

Yes, kids are growing up too quickly, but I also worry that if they don't keep up with their friends that they'll be left behind or bullied! My son wants his hair cut in different styles, and I let him, and my little girl wants her nails painted, and I let her do that too. I would love to keep them sheltered, but I think you have to let them do things within reason, or they'll just rebel.

Rebecca from Erith, mum to Harry, five and Mia, three

My eldest knows there's stuff on the web I really don't want him seeing. It started innocently enough – he spotted an unusual bird when we were out so he keyed 'black and white bird' into the search engine. You can imagine the sort of search results that came up! He was about to click on 'sexy slutty babes' when I came up behind him and shouted at him to stop. Of course, he wanted to know why and tried sneaky searches after that, so we had to put special blocks on the computer.

I've no problem with him being curious about women's bodies, but there's a big difference between a picture of a topless woman and some of the disgusting stuff on some websites. I don't want him to get the wrong impression about women and sex at his age.

Julie from Southend, mum to Jude, eight, Leon, five and Madeleine, two

I think the rate children grow up is all down to society's influence, and that we as parents have a choice to make regarding how fast this rate progresses. If we allow our children to dress like grown-ups and inhibit their play, and stop them being children at a young age, of course they'll grow up faster than a child who's encouraged to make mud pies, build sand castles or kick a ball in the park. We're causing our kids to grow up too fast. We need to get down to their level and make some mud pies of our own.

Helen from Kent, mum to Rebekah-Eve, four and Amy-Jayne, one

The Problem Solved

We have the technology

There's no doubt that technology has made breathtaking advances in the last couple of decades, the result of which is that our children's generation only know a world where mobile phones and computers are elements of everyday life. All too frequently, we read headlines about the negative aspects of these advances: happy-slapping; cyber-bullying; internet predators; screen violence replayed in real life. And understandably, it scares us. But anything that highlights the horrors of the modern world is good news fodder, and these things are almost certainly not as widespread as we might fear.

When it comes to media consumption and what's appropriate for children, common sense does rule. Obviously some games, websites, programmes and films are not ideal for young kids, others are downright unsuitable. In many cases a certificate rating gives you a solid idea of what's appropriate; else-where you may have to work it out for yourself (and you may prefer to make your own judgement by taking a look beforehand). Some children are more sensitive than others and more likely to be scared, confused or embarrassed by something that's intended for an older age group. And different parents have different views of what they're happy with – it's a subjective thing.

As children become more aware of what their peers are getting up to, they're more likely to put pressure on their parents to watch, play or log on to material you aren't happy about. It's a tough position to be in: you may feel reluctant for them to watch something that you don't feel they're ready for, but neither do you want them to be left out of conversations with their friends or laughed at for missing out. It's a judgement call that a parent must make on their own but if you feel strongly, then stand firm. Where possible, quietly vet their choices beforehand. And if it's a programme or a movie which you know nothing about or you're not that keen on, at the very least, watch it with them and talk about it afterwards. Try to avoid making a song and dance about censoring anything, as you run the risk of making it all the more appealing.

Most experts say it's not a good idea to let a child have a television or a computer in their bedroom, but to keep them in family rooms so you always know what's on their screens. For children under ten, it's probably sound advice. And don't forget, non-stop exposure to television and computer screens isn't a great idea anyway (see Media Matters, p. 287, for more on this). If they're on more than they ought to be in your home, try switching off the computer or TV sometimes and indulge in some old-fashioned fun, instead. There are some ideas on how to do this on pp. 241–2.

Mum versus the marketing men

Walk into any high street shop with a significant children's market, and the mighty commercial forces that all parents are up against are all too obvi-ous. Girls in particular seem to be targets – their love for dressing up and desire to 'look like mum' is exploited to a shocking degree by some manu-facturers. If, like an awful lot of people, you feel strongly that sexy or sophis-ticated underwear, clothing and shoes are inappropriate attire for small girls, then don't buy them. And if you're under pressure from the determined small girl at your side, gently steer her towards something else – it's better *not* to make a big deal about these products and how much you disapprove of them. If 'pester power' is a real problem, don't take her shopping with you. The simple fact is that the way your child dresses (as well as the comics they read and the toys that they play with) is down to you. Peer pressure – passed on to you via your kid – can be intense, but it's probably not nearly as influential as you think. Don't feel bad about putting your foot down. But consider being flexible, if you can: in most cases, some kind of compromise will go a long way to overcoming conflict. On the other hand, some people argue that these sort of things – along with lipgloss, trendy haircuts, pierced ears and expensive trainers – are harmless lifestyle accessories, and that there's no reason why children shouldn't be allowed to indulge in them, just as we adults do. At this stage, there's no clear evidence to the contrary. And one thing is certain: the sort of clothes you let them wear isn't really important compared with the boundaries you set them and the emotional support you provide. If you're happy for them to be lured by the sophisticated trappings of modern market forces, there's probably no harm in it – as long as you keep reinforcing the fact that *inside*, where it counts, they're still a child.

Work less, play more

We live in an increasingly frenetic, competitive society. Adults are working longer hours, aiming to earn enough money to finance expensive lives. Achievement – in all aspects of life – is everything. Mummies have to be 'yummy'; dads have to be 'cool'. Children ought to be immune to all these pressures, but sadly they aren't. If their parents are rushed and under stress, chances are their kids will be, too. If they're intent on keeping up with the Joneses, the whole family will probably be caught up in the competition. Even at school, kids face increasing pressure to compete and perform these days and many people feel this subjects them to the kind of stress that shouldn't be part of childhood.

As individual mums, there's not a lot we can do to counter huge social and cultural changes to the way we live. Neither can we take task against the demands of the school curriculum – it's statutory, after all. But if necessary, perhaps we can look at our home lives and, where possible, take things down a pace or two. If good, old-fashioned fun isn't on the menu much in your home, perhaps you could give it a whirl some time.

How we can help

In the end, there's no avoiding the grown-up world that awaits them – or the fact that it approaches sooner than ever these days (and indeed, it would probably be daft to try). Before very long, they'll hear about it and see for themselves anyway. How can we protect our kids from these things? The answer is that in the main, we can't. They're facts of modern life, for better or worse. In some cases, we can limit or control their exposure to undesirable elements. And if we want, we can encourage our kids to focus on the joys of a traditional childhood as far as we can. Equally though, we need to accept that the world we all live in is a rapidly changing one. It's scary, sometimes. But with love, support and the right information, our kids can face it head on – and will probably cope perfectly well with it all.

What the experts say
The children's campaigner

There can be no doubt that the childhood experienced by today's children is significantly different from that of previous generations. New technology has led to vast changes in communications, where the mobile phone and the internet are now largely taken for granted by children, and continue to evolve at a pace few adults can keep up with. With a sophisticated understanding of communication technology, children and young people interact directly with others in a virtual world that has few boundaries. Another contributing factor is that demographic changes mean that children are growing up in an increasingly diverse society. Changing family structures have also had an impact on childhood in the UK today.

Certainly our young people are continually subjected to pressure to achieve, behave and even consume like adults at an ever-earlier age, and we believe it's crucial that we consider the impact this is having on our children.

It's important for parents to allow their children the time and space to enjoy being a child, rather than focusing too heavily on the skills needed to become a 'successful' adult. Interestingly when we asked

8,000 young people what makes for a good childhood the overwhelming response was friends but when adults were asked the same question the importance of friendship was rarely mentioned. If we're to successfully create a vision of childhood for the twenty-first century we need to view childhood as an exercise in 'well-being' as well as 'well-becoming'.

Bob Reitemeier, Chief Executive of The Children's Society

The mums' life coach

Childhood in this generation certainly involves pressures and influences their parents weren't exposed to. Children do many more exams and activities, and may come across adult material much earlier, through television and the internet. We see young girls dressed like women and hear children listening to lyrics not written for young ears.

Many of us look back on our own childhoods with an element of nostalgia: long hot summers, white ankle socks, endless hours outside, long dresses for parties and Enid Blyton-style picnics and feel that our children are missing out. If you're worried your children are growing up too fast, first of all don't panic. Every generation has these worries. Our grandparents were concerned about the dangers of pop music, not to mention that strange, new-fangled concept of the 'teenager'. The brave new world they're inhabiting may not be as scary as you imagine.

At the same time, don't be afraid to go your own way. If you don't like what other children are doing or wearing, don't feel you have to follow the crowd. If you want to keep your children young and protected, do so. Children can survive quite well into adulthood without the latest bit of gadgetry or fashion.

Use your judgement. You don't want them to be a target for bullies, so listen to them if they complain of being left out or teased. You may find you have to make some compromises, but the important thing is that you're taking control and not just being led by the nose. It's your life; they're your children. Be yourself and encourage your kids to do the same.

Patricia Carswell

The child psychologist

I think it's probably true that kids are being exposed to adult preoccupations far earlier than they have the capacity to deal with. Part of it is because the pressures that parents are under these days are transmitted to their children. They are having to have it all, and be cool and trendy, and rich, which is why we hear now about girls as young as eight having birthday parties with limousines and makeovers! Children become a symbol of how well parents are doing on these factors. This is all determined by fashion and trends (and sadly, someone out there is making an awful lot of money by cashing in on parents' feelings of guilt, because they want to be seen as providing the very best of everything for their children).

Rather than laying down the law if you're not happy about what they want to do, watch or wear, it's a good idea to try and involve them in decision making – talk about why you don't want them to be playing with that game or wearing those clothes (without making veiled threats about horrible men who might want to come and get them), and ask them what their opinion is. And then aim to bridge that yes-no barrier by rationing the desired thing; for example, if they really want a pair of high heels, agree that they can have them but only for very special occasions. Or they can play that computer game, but only for 15 minutes a day.

The most important thing in this sea of change is to help the child develop a robust sense of self so that they can take all these adult influences in their stride and be able to make their own decisions wisely. You can do this by letting your child know that you love them, unconditional on what their achievements are, encouraging them to do whatever it is that they enjoy – not what you as parents think they should be doing – and always offering them your open communication and support.

Dr Angharad Rudkin

The Problem Summarised

◆ The world is a changing place. It's a fact we have to face. But it may not be as frightening as we think.

◆ If you're worried about the way children are exposed to undesirable influences in the media, keep careful tabs on what they watch, listen to, log on to and play.

◆ Don't be bowed by 'pester power'. But agree to a compromise whenever you can.

◆ If you want your child to be a child, treat them like one. Set boundaries – and play games!

◆ Don't push a child to perform, achieve, or be something they're not. No one needs that kind of pressure, and kids certainly don't.

Jumpers for goalposts: Ten ideas for some good old-fashioned fun

◆ **Make a den**: The simplest way to create a hideaway haven is to drape sheets over the dining room table. Pile up cushions, and climb inside with drinks, snacks and some books or colouring. Outdoor versions are even more fun if the weather's OK.

◆ **Dressing up**: Build up a good collection of wacky garments and accessories from charity shops and let them be whatever they want: the weirder the better!

◆ **Hide and seek, sardines or 'Pom Pom 123'**: Get stuck in and play with them – you might be surprised to feel the adrenalin kick in!

◆ **Bubbles**: Ever popular, particularly with little ones. See who can pop the most, or blow the biggest. Best outdoors, or indoors where the floor covering doesn't matter.

- **Doctors and nurses**: Role play boosts the imagination and helps social development. Fantastically good fun, too! (And if you're forced to be the patient, think of it as a chance for a lie-down . . .)
- **Hunt the object**: Hide one or more objects in the room and give them 'hot' and 'cold' clues while they search for them.
- **Shops**: Fill a play till with pretend or real coins, and set up a 'shop' on the dining room table with empty grocery boxes and containers.
- **Teddy bears' tea party**: Spread an old rug on the floor, invite some favourite toys to join in, and serve up mini sandwiches, fruit and goodies on miniature plates.
- **Nature trail**: Wrap up if it's cold and hit the nearest bit of green space or woodland. Take a basket and fill it to the brim with pine cones, leaves, moss and bark. See how many birds, animals and interesting plants you can spot.
- **Puppet show**: If you don't already have what you need, make your own theatre out of a cardboard box, add some fabric curtains, and create puppets out of socks!

Class struggles: How to help them if they're not coping at school

The Problem

During the last year my daughter has become more and more withdrawn. She's always been quiet in her classes, but at the last parents' evening, her teachers said she hardly spoke to them and when she did, it was barely audible. They said it was a serious problem, and that experts might have to be brought in such as a speech therapist (although she has no problem with speech at all at home) or an educational psychologist. She's a bright child but the problem is she lacks confidence. The minute she steps into the playground, she looks sad and lost. She won't speak up in class in case someone laughs at her, and she's scared of being told off if she asks for help. It breaks my heart.

Elise from Colchester, mum to Isla, seven and Jamie, five

School rules, OK

Every parent wants their child to fulfil their educational potential, and, more important still, for them to be happy at school – after all, they spend a large part of their childhood there. But for a range of reasons, a significant number of kids struggle to cope in the classroom at one point or another. They may encounter difficulties in learning, emotional issues, or both, and that can cause a great deal of anxiety. In theory, there's a system in all schools to provide help to those children who need it. And regardless of that, a child who's struggling in the classroom needs a huge amount of support at home, too.

The Problem Shared

What the Netmums say

From the start, Jack was behind in his handwriting and had problems recognising letters. He just couldn't put them together to make the sounds. And he couldn't hold a pencil correctly. Time and again, his teachers told me he was below the usual standard in all subjects. At first they put it down to him being the youngest in the year, then they said he was just a slow learner. I asked whether they thought his problem could be dyslexia, but they didn't think so. I had a gut feeling that something wasn't right, so I made my own flash cards, which we used at home. His reading started to improve, but his handwriting was still all over the place.

I hated the way the teachers kept implying that he was 'slow', when I knew that he was a very bright boy. Finally they admitted he could have a problem, but months passed and there was still no action taken. I went to my GP in desperation and he referred us to a paediatrician who agreed Jack was probably dyslexic. Finally, he came home one day and told me he'd been given a special keypad, so he can keep up with the rest of the class and his teacher can read his work. I was so glad that they'd finally done something constructive. He also has extra help from a classroom assistant. Now his grades have gone from D to A and he actually enjoys going to school and writing stories. But I feel that if I hadn't pushed, Jack might still be classed as the 'slow' child.

Christine from Kettering, mum to Holly, 12, Chloe, ten and Jack, eight

Sam was coming home in a terrible mood, and not wanting to go to school at all. It was out of character and we wondered if he was being bullied. We talked, and I was really surprised when he admitted he didn't like learning. He's a bright kid, and he's always been so eager at school. I pressed a bit more and found he was upset about his handwriting. He said he was messy and couldn't finish anything. I explained that learning wasn't just sitting at a table and writing and he did finally agree that he wasn't stupid. It was heartbreaking to hear my clever little boy put himself down so much. We went in to school to speak to his teacher and she said she believed he might have dyspraxia – I know all about it, because my brothers have it, too. She's now collecting information and keeping a record of Sam's abilities, not just his handwriting but also his physical co-ordination. We've got special work for him to do at home that she does with children in the lowest writing level in class as she didn't want to put him with those children and knock his confidence. It helps already knowing that they're looking out for him and we're lucky that the teacher is so encouraging and approachable, and has told us we can make an appointment to see her any time.

Donna from Rotherham, mum to Samuel, five and Emma, four

My eldest struggled in year one badly, so much so that when he started year two, he went to a tutor for a year. At the time, I think everyone thought I was doing it for the SATS. I wasn't, it didn't even cross my mind, I just wanted him to get the basics under his belt, as I felt he didn't have them. And it's held him in good stead. He does very well now, and I do think that's down to the tutoring.

My younger son really struggles at school, and they're aware of this but seem to give him little help, just easier homework! I'm not sure where that's getting him. I kept going into the school to see his teacher, but we've given up with them. He now has private tutoring twice a week, and his confidence has soared. We struggle to pay for it – my mother-in-law and my nana help out with the cost. But without it, he'd be falling further and further behind. As parents we felt we had no choice if they weren't even getting the basic education they need within the school day.

Rosie from London, mum to Sean, 11 and Owen, eight

I couldn't understand why Freya was having problems because her older sister was bright. The school thought that she must have emotional problems at home and an educational psychologist was brought in, who found that Freya had problems with eye contact, speech, gross motor skills and understanding instructions. I was mortified when her teacher told me that Freya, then six, didn't even know the difference between a triangle and a circle! She didn't have these problems at home. I took her to my GP and she was referred to a paediatrician. He ruled out autism and she was given blood tests, all negative, then she was semi-diagnosed with something called Central Auditory Processing Disorder, and referred for tests.

She has extra maths and is on the school action register, but she receives no other one-to-one help and her confidence is at an all time low. She goes to senior school next year and is at least two years behind the average for her age.

Steph from Burnley, mum to Katie, 14 and Freya, ten

My son had a speech and language delay diagnosed at two. He went to the local mainstream school, where they told me he'd need to be assessed for a statement of special educational needs. The statement process was a nightmare. It took eight months and in the end they could only fund a support teacher for two hours a day, plus 20 minutes' speech therapy a week. I wasn't happy with this and set a tribunal in motion – they came back to me with four hours a day! If I hadn't pushed for it, I would never have got it.

Lara from Bolton, mum to Karl, eight, George, five and Ned, one

Stacey had no problems in her first junior school. But then we moved house and she started a new school. She'd been there about 18 months when I picked her up one day and the teacher mentioned something about her support assistant. Apparently she'd been struggling with her reading and writing for about a year, and had been attending a special group. Nobody had thought to mention this to me! As far as I knew – having no other kids to gauge her learning by – she was at a normal level for her age. I was so furious that they hadn't kept me informed, I pulled her out of that school and got her in to another one, where she soon caught up. They sent her to a scheme run by the local rugby club to improve confidence in reading and writing. Thanks to the support she received there, and from the school and at home, she's now at a normal level again.

Vix from Lymm, mum to Stacey, 14 and Ethan, four months

The Problem Solved

Please sir! We need to talk

The majority of children experiencing a problem in the classroom should be able to get the help they need from within school. And it's mandatory for schools to give that support, so a parent with concerns has every right to express them.

In an ideal world, all educational difficulties would be picked up quickly by a child's teachers, their parents would be kept informed, and any special help required would be immediately forthcoming. But it doesn't always work that way, not least because modern teachers are under pressure, classes are often large, and schools don't always have all the resources they need. Sometimes, a parent will notice there's a problem at school before the school does.

Naturally, the first step to take if you have concerns is to talk to your child's class teacher, who'll know more about them than anyone else at school. Sometimes, a single appointment in which you register your concerns with a teacher can be a hugely positive move, as it may inspire them to be vigilant. Parents' evening is the obvious opportunity to talk, but if it's pressing, you have the right to make an appointment for another time. Do bear in mind that most teachers won't want to chat in the morning, when they're concentrating on preparations. Writing a note is probably the easiest way to make contact.

Their class teacher is a very important person in a child's life and good communication between home and school are vital, particularly when it comes to thrashing out classroom concerns, so it's worth staying on good terms with them. If discussions don't resolve the problem, arrange a meeting with another member of staff. But don't automatically go over their head in an attempt to speak to someone with more seniority – it will cause bad feeling. Make an effort to find out the school's policy on raising concerns and the route you should use – it may be in the prospectus or on the school's website.

Remember that, once they've started school, children can take a year or more to settle in to the business of learning. Unless there seems to be an obvious problem, or they have an emotional issue, which they need your help with, there's no point in fretting while they're still in Reception.

Getting help: the first stage

It's a fact of life that children learn at different rates, and for some that means they come in below average in the learning stakes. Most classroom difficulties can be sorted out swiftly with a bit of extra help from the right people at school. Often, a child may be a bit behind their peers in basic skills and a bit of extra attention is all they need.

Don't panic if you are told that your child needs some 'extra help'. It doesn't necessarily mean they have a recognised 'learning difficulty' or a 'special educational need', just that they need more time and attention to fulfil their potential. It could be that their teacher has to adjust the requirements of the National Curriculum slightly (known as 'differentiating'), or teach in a slightly different way to suit a pupil's needs. Or they may arrange for a child to have some extra help with a classroom or learning support assistant, individually or in a group, or provide some specialist equipment, such as a computer. And 'extra help' will most likely be a short-term measure, so think of it as a positive move forward: just because they need some at one point, it doesn't mean they'll need it throughout their entire time at school.

Special Educational Needs

When a more significant learning difficulty is identified, a child is said to have Special Educational Needs (SEN). Although this seems a rather dramatic label and can be alarming for parents, it refers to a wide spectrum of issues and won't necessarily mean a more serious disorder or disability such as dyspraxia or ADHD. Once a special need has been identified, the child's parents, their teacher, and the school's special education needs coordinator (SENCO) will meet to discuss what their needs are and how they're going to get them. Usually, an individual education plan (IEP) will be drawn up, setting out a series of targets and how they can be helped to meet them. This support is part of a process called School Action. If, after a while, it seems obvious that help is still needed, the school may arrange for someone from outside school to come in and assess the situation: for example, an educational psychologist (EP), or a speech and language therapist. This is known as School Action Plus.

Occasionally, if their needs are serious enough, a parent, or the school, or the combined forces of both, can ask the local education authority (LEA) to assess them for a statement of special educational needs – a legally enforceable document setting out their precise needs and the financial provision that will be made for them. If they agree to an assessment, the 'statementing' process that follows can be long, complicated and bureaucratic, and a significant number of applications are unsuccessful.

Getting help from elsewhere

Sometimes, parents find they are not in agreement with the staff at their child's school or are unhappy with the sort of support they are giving. In that situation, you might try writing to the school's Chair of Governors asking for further investigation. You could seek advice from ACE, the Advisory Centre for Education or from IPSEA, the Independent Panel for Special Educational Advice. Or you could try your local Parent Partnership Association: this organisation exists to provide impartial advice and information to parents of children with special educational needs. If you can afford it, you might consider seeking the services of an independent specialist.

How you can help them at home

If the system's working, a child who needs extra help will get it at school. But they'll also need backing from home, too. And whether or not your child needs extra help or has a special educational need, it will be massively beneficial to them if their parents take an active interest in their learning.

Read to them and listen to them reading, talk about their lessons with them, if they're willing to, and answer their questions if you can – don't be afraid to admit you don't know the answer. Offer to help look it up with them, instead. Never force learning down their throats. Always remember that children usually come home from school feeling tired, and they need to think about something other than work.

Homework's a fact of school life, although in the early years there shouldn't be more than an hour or two a week, and it may well come disguised as fun. Help them rise to the challenge by having an upbeat attitude towards it yourself, encouraging a routine and providing a peaceful place where they can concentrate, and giving a bit of guidance where needed. Don't be tempted to help too much, though – teachers need to know if a student is struggling with the homework they've set. If they're not coping with it, it can be a useful indicator that something else is wrong. And don't be afraid to consult their teacher if you feel it's too much, or too hard for them.

Whatever the reason or the extent of their class struggles, they'll need extra emotional support just as much as practical help. It's all too easy for a child who can't keep up to feel they are 'stupid' and the result can be anger, frustration and shattered self-esteem. More than ever, they'll need to know how much you care.

What the experts say

The educational psychologist

It's fair to say that the majority of children will have some difficulty, at some time, at school, whether emotional or with their learning. A special educational needs code of practice exists so that if a child isn't making reasonable progress, the school's SENCO should be picking it up and dealing with it in the classroom. Often in state schools there are so many in the class that only the obvious ones will stand out and get picked up, and sadly, some do slip through the net. A vigilant parent may notice a problem first. And sometimes specific learning difficulties like dyslexia and dyspraxia aren't identified because they're mistaken for bad behaviour.

When a child struggles at school it doesn't necessarily equate to a special educational need, it may just mean that some intervention is needed. It could turn out that they have a mild learning difficulty, that is, their ability is below average, or a specific learning disability, such as dyslexia.

Children learn at different rates and that rate depends on so many things, including the support they have at home. It may be that they're just not 'getting it' – particularly in the early years – or that they're not particularly suited to the learning style in their class. Education in many schools is geared to auditory learning and some children find it harder to concentrate on talking and listening. For some, school is harder work than for others! Sometimes, it will just be a blip, like a difficult period in their life, which can really throw them.

A parent's role is vital when it comes to helping a child who's struggling at school. The SEN code of practice says that schools work in partnership with parents and often educational psychologists like myself will make recommendations for a school to work very closely with a child's parents.

It can be traumatic as a parent when you find out your child needs extra help of some kind because they're not keeping up with their class. But actually, it's often a great relief for parents to hear because at least they know there's definitely a problem and that, hopefully, something's going to be done about it. Once it's on the table, they feel a lot better.

As a parent in this situation you need to reassure the child that you will sort it out and get them whatever help they need. Liaise with the school, find out what's happening while they're there.

Help them with their work outside school hours, but if they don't want to do it, don't push it. Boost their esteem by picking out whatever their strengths are and praise them for those. Hopefully, their teacher will be doing the same thing in the classroom, too.

Janet Frodsham, www.jfeducationalpsychologist.co.uk

The Problem Summarised

- A vast number of children will experience some form of difficulty – educational, emotional or both – at some point during their years at school.
- All schools have a system in place that – in theory – means that children who need extra help will get it. Some kids do slip through the safety net, and their parents' input will be vital.

- If you're worried about anything, talk to their teacher. Make an appointment rather than trying to pin them down at a difficult moment.
- Remember, all children learn at different rates.
- If your child has Special Educational Needs identified, stay positive. Once a problem's been pinpointed, it can be tackled.
- Children struggling at school for some reason will need lots of love, support and self-esteem boosting at home, too.

Job done: How to get your kids to do the things they don't want to

The Problem

My daughter has a naturally strong will, an internal sense of order, and a healthy interest in testing the limits. Many times we're at odds and I have to resort to the 'two choices' or 'natural consequences' methods of persuasion. Incidentally, the 'two choices' method is an old cross-examining lawyer's trick, and can work well on husbands too!

There is another option, which is to give up on the stuff that doesn't really matter. I had to learn this when my daughter decided she would wear only one particular shirt and dress for six months. I liked choosing her clothes and it took a lot of arguments for me to realise that she needed that independence. (I've been informed by my own mom that as a child, I only wore a red and white cowgirl outfit for many, many months.) In the end, it was a phase. She gradually increased her repertoire to two dresses, and then many. But I still let her choose. And why not? It's a short window in your life where you can go grocery shopping dressed in pink sequins and fairy wings and get away with it!

Alicia from Ipswich, mum to Lola, four and Eve, seven months

Why won't you do as you're told?

Wouldn't life be easier if our children did everything we told them to do, the first time we told them to do it? How much less time would be wasted, and how much anger avoided, if only each instruction was cheerfully responded to in a positive manner instead of being unheard, ignored or downright disobeyed. Of course, you might as well wish money grew on trees or that chocolate was calorie-free. Kids can be disinclined to do as they're told, and you can't really blame them. Imagine how you'd feel in their shoes. If you're enjoying yourself watching the telly, naturally you'd object if someone told you to turn it off. If you've spread your things out over the floor, you might well prefer to tidy them up later rather than now. And if you don't particularly feel like cleaning your teeth of an evening, why exactly should you have to? It's human nature to evade the tasks we don't really fancy. You can't knock kids for trying.

I'm going to count to three . . .

Regardless of all that, there's something particularly infuriating about a child who won't do what you ask of them. It's not always flagrant defiance: sometimes they're lost in a world of their own or are too busy concentrating on something else to really hear you (although, it's true that their hearing can be highly selective at these moments). But either way, when you find yourself repeating the same instruction for the third time and you still haven't had the response you're looking for, or any response at all, perhaps, it's enough to make steam come out of your ears. It's worth bearing in mind that, sometimes, they may have a genuine reason for avoiding something – perhaps they're reluctant to go to bed because they've developed a fear of the dark, or they don't want to do their homework because they're struggling with a certain subject. Children aren't always good at coming clean in these situations, so it's worth keeping an open mind.

The Problem Shared

What the Netmums say

I think you have to educate them from an early age to do things they don't want to. From day one, I've taught mine to put away something they've finished with before getting another item out.

Admittedly they don't always remember, so I give them a nudge. I tell them that bits will get lost if they're not put away, which usually works. I give lots of positive praise when they do tidy up. And as my youngest copies the older one a lot, she'll often put things back without being asked.

Mary from Bristol, mum to Mollie, five and Connie, two

I try to warn them in advance if I want them to do something, so they know it's coming. I'll tidy up alongside them – 'You do that, and I'll do this' – which usually works well for us. Or I say things like 'I bet you can't put that away before I count to ten/come upstairs/finish what I'm doing'. I do use bribery sometimes with Caitlin – she only gets her pocket money on Friday if her bedroom is tidy. And they both know that getting ready for bed quickly will earn them a longer bedtime story.

I think you have to make things interesting for them and be as inventive as you can. Recently, it was nearly bedtime, and I was having a hard time persuading them to tidy up. So I turned the lights off and said, 'Lets clear up in the dark!' I've never known them tidy up so quickly or do such a good job. They really loved it, and still occasionally ask to do it again.

Although it's frustrating sometimes, I do believe that positive encouragement is better than getting annoyed with them. Mind you, I haven't yet reached the stage when they can really dig their heels in about something. I may feel differently then!

Claire, from Blackwood, mum to Caitlin, six and Abbie, three

In our house we 'do a deal' when things get tricky. The deals in our house are negotiated first, so that the behaviour we want to see is demonstrated before the reward is given. For example, I would

expect my boys to behave nicely while we are shopping and in return they'll pick a treat, which they get once we're back at home. We do a lot of praising and clapping at home as well, and on the whole, the boys are well behaved, so it's worked for us.
Amanda from Chichester, mum to Jonathan, six and Toby, four

We have a 'countdown' clock in our house, so the kids know when tidy-up time is. If their rooms aren't tidy, their pocket money is deducted by 20p a time. We also do deals. I'll say, if your bedroom is tidy before we go out then you can have an extra 50p in your pocket money packet (we give out pocket money in little envelopes so it looks like a pay packet that they've earned!)

I find that they'll usually do what I ask them if I say it with a please and a thank you. They deserve respect too, after all. I treat them the same way they treat me. So if they ignore me when I want them to do something, I turn it round and ignore them next time they want me to do something for them. It makes them realise what they do and how maddening it is.
Leigh from Manchester, mum to Jack, four and foster mum to Toby, 12

It gets harder when you've got a deadline to meet, like getting to school on time, and you don't have time to make a game of it, you just have to get there. I focus on the importance of them doing things for themselves, and explain consequences rather than bribing. My daughter's five now and the techniques that worked at two have started to cause problems. Over-rewarding makes her take stuff for granted and stops her developing judgement and self-control.

The way I get her to do what she doesn't want is by giving limited choices, where I'd be happy with either outcome. (So, for example, 'Do you want to wear the blue coat or the pink one?') I explain the consequences and sometimes I let her experience what happens if, out of defiance, she chooses not to accept my experience but learn from her own.

The best outcomes come through life, so don't try to shield them from that. Also teaching them to accept your authority means there are less battles of will: sometimes it's just a case of saying it and really meaning it. Often I'll count to three and because of my tone of voice I get a response before I've got to two. No one knows what happens when I get to three!

As far as our school mornings go, I created a chart with boxes to tick every part of the routine achieved – dressed, washed, teeth, hair. And I did one for me, too – pack lunch, pick up keys. That way she could see how much we both had to achieve and tick them off as they happened. If she completes hers before we leave she might get a bit of television. But there's no 'prize' for getting it all done – the reward is that she gets to school on time!
Mary from Melksham, mum to Aslana, four

When making requests, I don't give instructions, or ask anything he could say 'no' to! I still provide choice, so he feels like he has some control over the situation, but ones where the outcome will still be the action that was required. So he does what I want ultimately, but still allowing him the power of choice and sense of ownership and control over the events.

He also responds well to knowing what will come next: although his language is good, I still keep my sentences short so that he hears the most important thing – clean teeth, then play with car', for example. If he doesn't want to tidy up, I make a game out of it or sing. These things are working for him, at the moment, anyway.
Darryn from Kingston, mum to Christian, two

If I say to my eldest: 'I would like you to do this, and you have this amount of time to do it in', it normally works. If not, I threaten him with no TV, or taking away a favourite game.

With my youngest, I can still get away with a change in tone of voice. If you ask him to do something you know he won't be keen on but you say it in an excited voice and make it sound like a fun thing to do, he'll be well up for it!
Emma from Bristol, mum to William, eight and George, three

Learning from an early age makes all the difference. They also learn by copying adults around them. I'm very tidy, and I've noticed my son is, too. He's good at stuff like putting his DVDs back in their cases, which

is more than his dad is! We sing the tidy up song from *Doodle Do*, or we 'race' each other to see who can do it the fastest. We do have a few disagreements about turning off the television. I can usually get round this by always offering an interesting alternative: Let's go and bake some cookies, or, Shall we go and play on the slide? Ask me again when he's about ten, though, and I might have a different answer!
Jo, from Cheshire, mum to Alex, four

The Problem Solved

Laying down the ground rules

Kids are more inclined to do the things they don't want to do if they know there's no other option – if they know there might be some leeway, they'll push to see if they can get it. So it helps to lay down the law in advance on those tasks you feel strongly about, and aim for consistency. For instance, if you make teeth-cleaning an invariable element of their bedtime and morning routines, they'll be more likely to accept it as non-negotiable. And if you want them to always tidy up their discarded toys before getting out a new lot, insist they do so on *every* occasion. It's useful to have a mantra for these moments, which you should hammer in at every opportunity, for example: '*Last* game away, before the *next* one comes out.'

Troubleshooting in advance

In all households there are unpopular tasks, which are consistently difficult to achieve, but you *can* make life easier with a bit of forward planning. For instance, tell them as soon as they've turned the television on that it will have to go off in one hour – or whatever the time limit you choose to impose is – or, after a sneaky glance at the schedules, when such-and-such a programme has finished. They may surprise you and click it off on cue, but if you're forced to step in and do it yourself, at least you can say you warned them.

Parenting is a lot like scouting: it pays to be prepared for trouble. As any school morning veteran will tell you, you should aim to have clothes, hair-brush, bags and whatever else will be needed laid out in advance the night before, limiting the available excuses for not getting ready in time. (For some reason, heel-dragging is compulsory in children before 9 a.m., Monday to Friday, during term-time. Which is unfortunate, as it's the one period when you *really* need them to get their bottoms in gear . . .)

The gentle art of persuasion

Tempting as it may be, the least likely way to get an obstinate child to do something is to try and force them. Shouting, swearing, weeping and begging are also worth avoiding because, although they'll probably get you a result eventually, everyone involved will end up stressed out as a result.

When it comes to convincing a child to do something they don't want to, you're better off aiming to be clever rather than cross. You can generally make the unpopular popular by turning it into a game or competition although it has to be said this works better when they're little, before cynicism sets in. If you need them to stop doing something they clearly don't want to, you have to offer a desirable alternative (or at least one you can make seem desirable!) And there's a definite art to making the unappealing seem appealing: a combination of good acting, a positive tone of voice and careful use of words. It comes with experience!

Heads you win, tails you win

Many mums swear by the relevance of choice in these matters. Kids, not unnaturally, don't like to be told what to do because they're independent beings who want to make their own decisions in life. So, whenever possible, convince them that the choice is theirs – just make sure the options you offer will get you what you want, either way. For example: 'Dinner's nearly ready! Would you like to go and wash your hands, or lay the table first?'

Think requests or commands through carefully before you couch them: one useful piece of advice is never to ask them something they could legitimately answer with a no!

If you don't wear your coat, you're going to get cold!

Sometimes you can help a child see sense by pointing out what will happen if they don't do as they're told. This can mean threatening them with a premeditated punishment: 'If you don't put your shoes on in the next ten seconds, I'm going to take away your favourite DVD for a week.' More gentle and just as likely to be effective is talking about the natural consequences they're inviting. For instance: 'If you don't put your coat on, you're going to get cold'. You have to be prepared to follow through on these though – don't suggest it if you can't bear the thought of them goose-pimpled and shivering once they're outside!

Bribery (aka 'offering incentives')

A more positive spin on the game of consequences is to dangle incentives. It needn't be an actual prize, it may simply be the positive results of their actions. For example: 'If you put your coat on you'll be lovely and warm and we'll be able to stay in the park for a bit longer.'

More tangible incentives (also known, sometimes, as bribes) may be particularly effective for older children, who can see through you when you suggest that tidying up their bedroom will be the most fun they've had all weekend or refuse to be fooled by the cheery tone of your voice when you tell them it's time for their bath. The good old sticker chart can be called into play here, and if you have a pocket money system in your house, the promise of a raise (or the threat of it being docked) can be a useful aid to persuasion.

Not everyone agrees that this is a good way of getting what you want, however: some people think that children should be expected to do what you tell them without necessarily being rewarded for it. For those of us with kids that aren't that amenable, there's no shame in resorting to it during moments of desperation. Just don't do it too often, or they'll be driving a hard bargain at every opportunity in the future.

At the risk of sounding repetitive, don't forget that all-important positive praise every time they do what you ask them without a murmur. And remember to be specific when praising, so children can identify what they've done right. For example: 'Well done for turning the television off as soon as I asked, I love it when I don't have to ask twice!' In theory, it will make them more likely to oblige the next time.

Let the little stuff go

A final word on this subject. Only bother asking them to do the things you know they won't want to do if you *really want or need them to do it*. Otherwise, why make work for yourself?

What the experts say

The child psychologist

Children are instructed on what to do for the majority of their day. If you stop and listen to the average mum or dad in the park or in the street you will probably hear a series of instructions – do this, don't do that, stop, go. Sometimes kids just can't be bothered with it, and would rather do the opposite of what they've been told. It's a normal part of being human. And, as with adults, you get some kids who are more 'oppositional' than others. Keep your instructions to a minimum, so that when you do want or need them to do something, your request isn't just background noise, but actually something they listen to.

Children can smell desperation a mile off. If you find you're begging them to do something, or getting quite harassed if they're ignoring you, take a step back and stop trying so hard. If a child doesn't do something he's asked, he's probably going to get more attention in the short term than if he'd obeyed you in the first place, so be aware of making a big deal out of things.

Dr Angharad Rudkin

The mums' life coach

It can drive us to distraction – that feeling that whatever we do, our children just won't do what we want them to. Life can feel like one endless round of nagging and chiding. Bedtime, bath time, school time, getting out of the house: at every turn there are opportunities for conflict.

A dose of realism is essential here. We have different agendas from our kids, and so an element of conflict is inevitable. Babies and children have their own personalities and strong feelings about what they do, and from a very tiny age they're bound to want to follow their own wants and desires rather than ours – whether it's crawling towards the electric socket (again) or shaking their heads vigorously when we try to clean their faces.

You may also find that your children go through phases of being unco-operative. Siblings, too, tend to see-saw in their behaviour; if one's being obstructive, the other may become miraculously helpful and vice versa. So if you're having a day when you can't get them to do anything you want, don't panic – it's not necessarily a pattern for life.

Put yourself in your child's shoes. If someone marched into the sitting room right in the middle of your favourite programme and switched off the television, you might well feel a bit miffed. And if you kept being served food that you really didn't like, you might feel inclined to complain.

A few moments considering things from their perspective could save you a lot of hassle. You might, for example, give them till the end of the programme to turn off the TV or give them five minutes to finish their game before they have to come in from the garden. And giving your children an element of control and choice in their lives – such as asking them in advance what they'd like to eat this week and helping you to plan a menu – can help to make them more co-operative.
Patricia Carswell

The Problem Summarised

◆ Children don't always do as they're told – it's human nature.
◆ Make the important things part of an unwavering routine so they know they're non-negotiable.
◆ Be prepared: know the flashpoints, and give them a warning in advance.
◆ Try the old lawyer's trick and give them two choices (both of which are OK with you!)
◆ Warn them about the natural consequences of their actions. Let them experience them, too.
◆ Incentives and bribery are OK – don't use them too often, though!
◆ Don't sweat the small stuff. It's not worth the hassle.

Planes, trains and automobiles: How to travel happily with children

The Problem

Boredom is our main problem when we travel long distances, and sickness. Also, my eldest is very unsettled in strange environments so we tend to stick to the same holiday destination and try to leave a good day for travelling so that we can stop a lot. We did invest in an entertainment system for the car so they can watch DVDs. I think it's a great invention, especially when you have kids that can't keep still. I love holidays with my hubby and kids, even if they can be hard work. We book a cottage and there are no nightclubs or babysitter services. We spend our days on the beach looking in rock pools, splashing in the sea, making sandcastles. In the evenings we play with the kids and once they're in bed we can have a lager or share a bottle of wine. All this in the UK. Who needs to go abroad?
Mary from Bristol, mum to Mollie, five and Connie, two

No more worries for a week or two

Travelling with children can be a draining experience. With kids in tow, long journeys are far more likely to be boring, tiring, incident-strewn and stressful. Once you're at your destination, there are no guarantees you'll have everything you need and that your kids will settle happily in a strange environment. And even assuming things do go smoothly, holidays and trips away can be hard work: you don't get time off from being a mum, just because you happen to be a long way from home. All of which means that travels with your children can hold dread as well as excitement. Which is a great shame, because getting away from it all, swapping the same old scenery for a new view, and dumping the daily domestic routines in favour of something completely different, can be a happy, healthy and harmonious experience for the whole family.

Don't hold your breath

You can never be sure of a trouble-free trip: if you accept that, it's easier to cope when stress levels rise, and you're more likely to be a happy traveller. But there are lots of things you can do to make it more likely. Among them are forward planning, clever packing . . . and a bit of deep breathing!

The Problem Shared

What the Netmums say

I don't drive, so my little ones are well used to all forms of public transport and they really love the adventure of it all. My best advice is, keep your cool. If you're calm and relaxed, then your children will be, too. I've never taken too much in the way of toys or books to stimulate them – the more you involve your kids in what's going on, the less bored they'll be. On a plane, I'll tell them what's happening: we're going really fast, we're going up into the clouds, etc. Things can go wrong when you're travelling with kids, so you have to be philosophical. I tell myself it will all be over soon, that tomorrow will come, and it could be worse!

Nancy from York, mum to Betty, three and Max, one

I keep a bag of things in the car to keep Alex amused; for instance, small books, a children's mp3 player filled with his favourite songs, a mini magnetic drawing board. We make our own games too, like counting all the different vehicles we see. If it's a really long journey he'll listen to a story CD, and then have a nap. He does notice a difference if we're staying away from home and can get a little unsettled. We try and take his favourite things to reassure him and explain where we are and how long for, and that home is waiting for us at the end of the holiday.

Jo from Mow Cop, mum to Alex, four

Always take a potty for little ones – you can guarantee they'll need a wee when you're miles from a toilet. Also, try to travel when they usually sleep or have their nap. We don't have the luxury of an entertainment system for the car, so we just play I-spy, and take books and colouring pens and plenty of snacks too – raisins, bananas, crisps and juice. There's nothing worse than getting stuck in a traffic jam with hungry kids needing a wee! At least with snacks and a potty some of their demands are met.

Helen from Kent, mum to Rebekah-Eve, four and Amy-Jayne, one

We're lucky as both our sons love travelling and are no problem on long journeys. They have a DVD player, but we also play observation games. And we make frequent stops so we can all stretch our legs. Before we go away, they both choose something to look after their bedrooms whilst we're gone. They usually pick a game, cuddly toy or book!

We always try and make the journey for long trips part of the holiday, too, so we approach it very light-heartedly. Often we'll stop halfway, and stay in a travel lodge for a night. It all adds to the fun.

Amanda from Chichester, mum to Jonathan, six and Toby, four

Max gets very car sick. On long car journeys we plan our route so we come off the motorway and stop somewhere we can picnic and play for an hour. We've discovered some lovely little villages and beauty spots that way.

Because of the sickness he can't read or play with toys in the car.

We take the headrest off the front passenger seat so he has a good view out the front and I sit in the back with him. We also take some tubs with well-fitting lids, in case we don't have time to stop when he's sick.

To keep us amused we have music CDs and audio books. He also loves a good singsong.

Irina from Saltcoats, mum to Max, two

We've travelled a lot with Will, both in the UK and abroad. We find the best way to ensure a happy, stress free holiday for all of us is to ensure that he's happy, and the rest follows. We always do our homework and book places that are child-friendly. We know there's no point trying to take a noisy five-year-old to a smart, adult-orientated resort, for instance. Last year we chose a cruise with plenty of beach stops, and so we could have a little time to ourselves, Will popped in and out of the excellent kids' club. We also love walking in the Lake District. We take Will but we choose walks that have some interest in them for him, and stay in a child-friendly B&B.

Gervase from Bourne, mum to Will, five

I think that any holiday taken with children should be taken somewhere that has kids' activities laid on, so the parents can have some time away from the little angels to do their own thing. Sadly, I reached this conclusion after our last holiday being a complete and utter disaster! I'd say that self catering is a No-Go! Otherwise, when do we mums ever get a break from cooking? Or clothes-washing?

Christine from Kettering, mum to Holly, 12, Chloe, ten and Jack, eight

Holidays can be hard work, especially self-catering, but for those of us who work full-time, it's a chance to be with our children. We've gone to a caravan camp for the past two years and we've had a great time. I guess I'm just someone who believes a family holiday is a family holiday. Personally, I like to take my children with me when out for the evening on holiday – if they get too tired or troublesome, then we just go back to the caravan. On holidays, my husband and I enjoy the few peaceful moments we get when the kids are asleep. I'm old fashioned, obviously!

Maria from Kent, mum to Ben, five and Amy, three months

When we're going away I plan Caoimhe's outfits in advance and put each one (including socks and underwear) in separate sandwich bags for each day, so there's one less decision to make! Also, if your kids are used to sleeping in a dark room, bring a roll of bin bags and sticky tape so you put up some makeshift blackout blinds.

Ciara from West London, mum to Caoimhe, two

Buy lots of cheap little toys, wrap some up, and produce something new every hour or so to keep them amused. Those magnetic boards with magnetic shapes that stick on are great as you don't lose the pieces. Take a little photo album full of pictures for them to look through. We took mini pots of paint and play dough with us and mini crayons, so that the children could use these when we were staying in our rented accommodation. Doing 'normal' things like that helps settle children and keeps them going on a long trip.

Our two actually loved the flight (more than we did!) and were very well behaved. Alex slept for ages. We did have to use lots of our snack stash for him as he kept sleeping through the mealtimes. We took bread sticks, raisins, dried fruit, muesli bars and saved the bread rolls from our own meals.

If you're flying, make sure you ask for the help you need. We found that the aircraft staff didn't volunteer to help much, but once we asked, they were happy to.

Rosalind from Chippenham, mum to Helena, five and Alex, three

My daughter likes to think she gets car sick, mainly because her cousin does and she doesn't want to be left out! Last year we went to the Isle of Wight, and we knew she'd work herself into a state over travelling on the ferry, so we didn't tell her we were going on one in advance; in fact, we didn't even tell them we were going on holiday, and packed secretly. It wasn't until we pulled in at the ferry boarding that we told them: the look on their faces was brilliant. Jessica didn't have time to work herself up, and in the end, she loved the ferry crossing and it worked out much better all round as they didn't have the chance to get over-excited.

Tina from Maidstone, mum to Jessica, ten, Fleur, nine and Daisy, three

I'm a travel agent as well as a mum, so I've had lots of experience in helping families travel with their children. Personally I think flying with children is easier than travelling in the car, as you can give them your undivided attention. I've taken my daughter away since she was five months old and I think it's a lovely way of introducing them to new things.

The most important thing is to keep them in their routine as much as possible, even if you're on a long haul flight. Try to distinguish between night-time and playtime, and feed them when you usually would. Also, bring familiar things, so their new environment doesn't seem as daunting. Start them travelling young and it will soon become second nature.
Jemma from Cardiff, mum to Grace, three

We've been on lots of long travels with our two. Our girls get excited about our trips abroad but they know what to expect now, as we make sure we explain to them both that it will take a long time to get there. We did our first major long-haul flights when Anya was 18 months old and Maija was just three. It was just fine, despite being on planes non-stop for about 16 hours. They were really excited for the first eight hours and the toy bag, nibbles and in-flight films kept them amused, and for the next eight hours they just slept in their seats. My top tip for long haul flights would be to always pay out for seats for toddlers.

I'd also say, don't expect too much from your children. Travelling can be a bit traumatic for them if they're wrenched out of their usual routine and it's easier if you can accommodate their little quirks. We find that we can only see and do about half of the amount of stuff we would have done before the children came along. However, we enjoy it twice as much now. It's so wonderful to see them playing with children they don't even share a language with, and to see them enjoy new cultures. I was nervous about our trip to Japan but now I would say to other parents, just do it. You'll survive, they'll survive. You'll all learn from the experience. And if you approach it with the right attitude you'll enjoy it too!
Karen from Manchester, mum to Maija, three and Anya, two

Travelling with children involves compromise and realistic expectations. I've always loved foreign travel and now I have a son I haven't lost any of my wanderlust. But I've realised that very young children have short attention spans and while you can still go away and have adventures, you have to factor in the needs of your child. Pre-kids I could spend hours wandering around medieval villages or churches, but now I realise kids – especially male toddlers – need to expend a bit of energy. Now, we do what Luca wants in the morning, have lunch and then we go off and explore the things we want to see, within a realistic timeframe, and often using the lure of an ice-cream (a bit of bribery keeps you sane on holiday) for Luca. Sure, it's not always plain-sailing but so far we've been camping in Croatia, travelled around Sardinia and explored the South of France, all with great success. I keep a collection of toy cars in my bag at all times for keeping him occupied in cafés. It helps if you always know when to bail out – that way tempers are kept in check and everyone feels like they've actually had a holiday.

Luisa from Bristol, mum to Luca, three

The Problem Solved

What sort of holiday?

Whatever holiday you plump for, there'll be pros and cons. Self-catering in a villa, cottage, apartment or campsite can work brilliantly for families, allowing plenty of space and flexibility, and ideal if you're going in a group with friends or relatives. Always make sure the accommodation is within easy reach – preferably by foot – of the shops, facilities and attractions you'll require. Drawbacks are having to do the cooking and housework, which can leave some mums feeling barely more relaxed than they do at home. If you can afford it, villas with hotel style facilities such as restaurants and babysitting options provide a lovely compromise. Otherwise, make sure you've a system in place (a rota, if necessary) so that everyone pulls their weight – kids included.

If you're heading for a hotel or B&B, there'll be less work, but less flexibility. Most big hotels or resorts will offer much more than just a room for the night but make sure you know what, exactly, before you get there.

Holidays may not work so well with young children if they involve touring, sightseeing and walking – for obvious reasons. Having said that, adventure holidays with organised itineraries, often to ambitious destinations, are becoming more and more popular with families. It's worth being open to all possibilities – plenty of parents enjoy the same holidays they used to before kids came along. At the same time, be guided by common sense. Go with what you know your personality – and your kids – are likely to cope with!

Forward planning

Some careful research in advance of any trip with kids goes a long way. Wherever you're staying and whatever you're doing, be scrupulous about checking – regardless of what the brochure says – what they have in the way of facilities and equipment, and to what extent the kids will be catered for. Check the small print for details like children's clubs – some aren't open outside the high season, for example. And if you can, talk to people who've been before, or stick to places that have come recommended. You may well find some useful advice on the Netmums.com holiday review forums.

Just in case

Packing is paramount when you're going away with kids. Unless you're travelling by car and you have a huge amount of luggage space, you'll be restricted in what you can take and will have to prioritise the essentials. Make comprehensive lists well in advance and tick everything off as you pack. Keep a count of the number of bags that you leave with, too, in case one gets left behind.

Always take at least a couple of favoured toys, even if you're confident there'll be plenty there to amuse them. If you've room, a duvet, pillow or blanket from their bed will help them feel settled in an unfamiliar place, as well as providing a bit of comfort during the journey. Letting them take their own small suitcase or backpack will help them enter into the spirit of things.

For more detailed ideas on what you may want to pack, check out the lists on www.babygoes2.com.

Are we there yet?

Usually, the most trying aspect of any trip is the journey itself. Children are not always great travellers, it's true: they're not generally keen on being in confined spaces or sitting still, may easily get bored and fidgety and are commonly prone to motion sickness. Having said that, parents who dread and fear long journeys with kids are often pleasantly surprised by how well they work out in the end. Aim to treat the journey as an exciting part of the holiday itself. If they're old enough, let them help to plan it – show them the route on a map and help them look up information on your destination, what you'll find there, and the places you'll pass through.

Some people think it's good to take as many toys and activities as you can manage to stave off boredom while travelling. Others say it's better not to overstimulate them and let them create their own fun. In the end, it probably comes down to the individual child. Other essential items to have to hand are a good supply of snacks and drinks, wet wipes, and a travel potty for little ones.

It's easy enough to say, of course, but a relaxed attitude is essential to successful travelling. Get as much ready as you possibly can the day before and give yourselves masses of time to get where you're going, so you're not rushing, and to allow for unplanned delays. If you're prone to anxiety journeys can be stressful experiences, which the demands of overtired, sticky and fed-up children do little to ease. Simple deep breathing can go a long way to helping, as can a spot of your favourite music on your car or personal stereo. (And if you're on a plane, train or boat, a little something from the bar is always good.)

You can't really expect the same levels of behaviour from kids when travelling as you get at home, so relax whatever your usual rules are and cut them some slack – you'll have enough on your mind without having to lay down the law on misbehaviour. Obviously if you're in a car, the driver needs to be able to concentrate, and on public transport, other passengers need to be considered, so keep noise levels down by providing plenty of other (quiet) distractions.

Pass the plastic bag

Motion sickness is common in children. It's caused when the brain receives conflicting messages from the eyes, which think you aren't moving, and from the balance mechanisms in the inner ear, which tells them you are. The result is nausea and sometimes vomiting. Sufferers may also be sweaty and pale, salivating or have a headache. Various medications are available over the counter, although many aren't suitable for little ones, and alternative treatments include acupressure bands, which are worn on the wrist. There are also a number of common sense measures to try when someone in your family suffers from motion sickness. Get fresh air or ventilation if possible, and avoid greasy foods. Dry crackers or ginger biscuits are said to help.

In the car, drive slowly and avoid sudden or fast turns, and take the most direct route possible – travel sickness is usually less likely to occur on motorways. Allow them if possible to sit in the front seat and encourage them to fix their eyes on the road ahead. (Looking down at something such as a book or a game can make things worse.) Better still, encourage them to close their eyes altogether, and try to sleep. Stop for regular breaks. On a boat, go on deck to get as much fresh air as possible and ask them to focus on the horizon. Or sit in the middle of the boat, where it moves least.

In a plane, try to sit over the wings where it's most stable.

It's a nuisance, but it's worth bearing in mind that travel sickness is just one of those things. Be prepared with plastic bags, a tub with a lid, wipes and changes of clothing. Fortunately, most children (eventually) grow out of it.

Home and away

Some people avoid holidaying abroad with their kids because they worry about the stress of flying, or fear of the unfamiliar. It's a personal choice, but it's perhaps worth pointing out that most families who venture beyond the UK regularly say it's no more difficult – or even costly, in some cases – than travels in this country. And the chance to see other places, people and cultures is a great way to broaden kids' horizons.

Parents who've flown with children often report that it was not the nightmare they feared. In fact, it's often less stressful when a trip is broken into different stages. A good tip if you're going by air is to contact the airline in advance to request bulkhead seats (or get to check-in extra early and ask), which allow a bit more space. Another is to carefully consider whether you're prepared to save the cost of a child's seat by having a toddler on your lap: if you can afford it, pay for them to have a seat of their own.

If you're flying long-haul, prepare for them to be affected by the disruption to their body's rhythms, caused by the crossing of time zones – although it's said that children are less affected by jet lag than adults, for reasons unknown! Make sure they drink lots of water on the flight, as dehydration can make jet lag worse. Once you've arrived, try to slot into the local routine straight away, and get out and about as exposure to daylight is thought to help re-set the body clock. Take it easy for a day or two, as you all adapt to the new time zone.

For European destinations, it's well worth considering ferries or trains as alternative means of transport: the journey may be longer, but on the other hand you've got more freedom to move around and more space to pass the time in.

Call this a holiday?

Congratulations – you've arrived at last. Now you just have to overcome the various hurdles of staying in a strange place, eating strange foods and adjusting to a strange routine for a short period of time. You may need to remember that, while most adults relish the novelty of change, young children can be wary of it. They may be unsettled for a while, even clingy, and you may need to bear that in mind if you had high hopes of depositing them in the nearest creche and nipping off for a bit of couple-time. If you *can* get some time together, fantastic – but it goes without saying that you need to be completely satisfied that whatever childcare is available is reliable, and that it's not advisable to leave children alone in a place they don't know. More often than not, mums and dads find the only way to get a break on holiday is for one to take charge of children while the other relaxes. If you do this, make sure that the balance is fair – otherwise, resentment can rear its head!

In the end, perhaps the best advice for really enjoying a break with the kids is to embrace it as just that, a family holiday. Get it right, and it can be a truly positive experience. You should all come back with a glow – and not just because you're sun-tanned.

What the experts say

The family holiday specialist

There are so many reasons why it's worth going on holiday with your children. A simple change of scene can be invigorating and

stimulating for everyone. And time spent away on holiday is free from
many of the stresses, strains, routines and distractions of everyday life,
leaving parents free to enjoy precious quality time with their children
– even if they do still have to deal with the mundane sleeping and
eating requirements just as they do at home. For many parents, a
holiday reminds them what fun it can actually be to spend time with
their children. Some even come back full of plans to build more
'family' time into the normal home routine. It's also a great way of
introducing children to new and exciting experiences, whether
petting a pony in Devon, or snorkelling in the Maldives. These can be
the sort of shared moments you'll always treasure in the future.
Travelling with children means you notice things you may not have in
a purely adult environment, as you look at the new surroundings
through their eyes and point things out to them.

Understandably, people do have worries about taking children
away – the boredom of the journey, fear of the unknown and not
having all the stuff you need to hand, for example. Then there are
practical issues like what medical facilities there'll be, what and when
the kids will eat, whether they'll cope with the climate and, if they're
little, how their routines will be affected. But children can be surprisingly
adaptable. There'll always be *something* they can eat. Hot weather
can be handled with a few sensible measures. And journeys are usually
fine – you always get there in the end! Oddly, lots of people panic
about little things, like there not being a bath – yet a toddler can easily
be washed in a sink, and an older child introduced to showers. Having
to do things differently for a few weeks is all part of the fun.
Debi Green, Director, babygoes2.com

The Problem Summarised

◆ Journeys with children can be challenging: pack well, be prepared and take
  it easy.
◆ Choose your holiday wisely. Work out what will most suit the whole family.
◆ Do your research: be sure there'll be everything you need where you're
  going.

- Don't shy away from flying or trying something new. It may surprise you!
- At the same time, remember that most kids don't demand much from a holiday. Your time is the best thing you can offer them.

Ten things to take to amuse the kids on long journeys and holidays*

1. Books and comics (unless they're prone to motion sickness).
2. Their favourite cuddly toy (You may want to sew a label to it with your contact details on in case it gets lost).
3. Fuzzy Felts.
4. Crayons and pencils (avoiding felts which stain, if possible), paper and activity pads.
5. Sticker books.
6. Erasable scribblers.
7. Finger or hand puppets.
8. Lidded box filled with small cars, action figures, dolls – whatever they're into at the time!
9. Story and music CDs or tapes. Letting them have a personal stereo is a brilliant idea as it means you don't have to be subjected, too.
10. Handheld computer games. Get them to keep the volume down though!

* With thanks to the Netmums and babygoes2.com

Fit kids: How to help them live a healthy life

The Problem

I've tried everything to help my daughter lose some weight, but nothing seems to work and she often comes out of school in tears because people call her names. The health visitor arranged for me to see a dietician but to be honest, she only told me what I already knew, like cutting down portion sizes and fatty food, eating more fruit, and doing more exercise. I do worry about the effect it will have on her in later life as I'm sure it's putting a strain on her heart with the extra weight she's carrying. I'm trying to get her to be more active and we've started walking the two miles home from school every day. We got her a trampoline and try to encourage her to go on it every day, and I've also enrolled her for dance lessons.

Dawn from Scarborough, mum to Alice, seven and Scott, two

A big issue

The state of our children's health is a huge subject at the moment. According to the headlines, we're raising a nation of couch potatoes, and heading for an obesity epidemic. Worryingly, the statistics back that up: the number of children who are either overweight or obese has increased in recent decades, and is likely to continue to rise. And more and more youngsters are developing conditions that are linked to being overweight, such as diabetes and cardiovascular disease.

You don't have to be an expert yourself to see how it's happened: children are now exposed to a huge variety of unhealthy foods and at the same time, they're generally much less active than they were in the past.

Too much on our plate

Most of us know only too well what the consequences of a seriously unhealthy lifestyle are: in the short term, reduced levels of concentration, energy and immunity. And in the long term, an increased risk of serious illness such as cancer, diabetes, respiratory and joint problems and heart disease. The implications aren't just physical, either. They're psychological, too. A healthy kid is far more likely to be a happy kid.

Their future in our hands

Junk food is everywhere and sedentary activities rule. You could argue that it's hard to swim against such a major social and cultural tide, but that would be a poor excuse. As parents, it's up to us to make sure our kids get their lives off to as healthy a start as possible. It's not rocket science. We just need to dish them up a balanced diet and help them to be physically active, and to make those things part of our ordinary lives. If it's just the way things go in your house, they'll be accepted as normal – and hopefully it will influence them forever.

It's not just the younger generation who stand to gain. We *all* need to look at our lifestyles if we want to live life to the full.

The Problem Shared

What the Netmums say

I've always allowed my kids to use the garden as an extension to the living room. I've never got the car out to take them to nursery or school, or to nip to the shops. I'm a strong believer in walking and I think cars have a lot to answer for. We try to eat healthily but I don't stop them having chips, chocolate and sweets because I think everything in moderation is fine. We have an allotment, so my girls know about growing vegetables and where they come from. They eat all the veg I put in front of them and I think that's because they've helped plant them and watched them grow.

Mary from Bristol, mum to Mollie, five and Connie, two

My boys love LazyTown so they eat Sports Candy (i.e., fruit!) and veg with no fuss. They're both very active and we live right next to a large park which they love walking, riding and scootering through. They've started gymnastics and swimming as well. To be honest they'd rather be doing active stuff than watching TV, which is fine by us. Every morning they have something out of our fruit bowl and we spend a lot of money on it to keep up their interest. We have apples, pears, bananas, grapes and an exotic alternative as well. They love trying new fruits. Our youngest is not so keen on vegetables that are cooked, but he'll try anything raw. Of course, they get chocolate and sweets but normally just once a week of each, and they have a biscuit every day after school – sometimes Jonathan will ask for fruit though, instead!

Amanda from Chichester, mum to Jonathan, six and Toby, four

My husband and I are both overweight so this is a big issue for us. Our son has loved fruit and veg from an early age and didn't have chocolate or sweets until he was nearly two, when he was given them by his grandparents, who felt we were being over-protective! We encourage him to be active, from dancing round to music to playing football and 'chase'. He has a varied diet with treats in moderation. It's hard to monitor what he has when he's with grandparents but I'm not too worried as I know that they always take him to the park to run off steam, too. I'll try never to deny him certain types of food, as I know from experience that when you're an adult and in control of your own diet the temptation to eat 'forbidden' foods is too great. I'd like to encourage him in the future to make his own, healthy choices.

Claire from Worksop, mum to Luke, three

I made the big mistake of using the car a lot from the word go and as a result I have kids who hate walking! If I could go back I'd walk a lot more, and would have persisted with giving them water to drink instead of squash. Walk lots and drink water from an early age, that's my advice.

Linda from Bristol, mum to Becky, 12 and Sam, ten

I'm hoping I've got the balance right. I have to use my car to get to work and drop the kids off so I try to walk as much as possible the rest of the time. They walk a lot with their childminder, too.

Not having a garden is a major problem. I try and get round it with trips to the park. If it's wet, indoor play areas are good. I get in there myself, too, and we have races.

Fruit's easy. I leave it on the table in a bowl for the kids to help themselves. Also, on trips out, tinned fruit is good as it's easy to transport and not too messy, as well as dried fruit like raisins. I sneak extra veg such as swede and carrot into mash.

Kimmie from Newhaven, mum to Joshua, four and Chelsea-Lou, two

When they were little we always had them out on their bikes, walking in the woods, swimming on a Sunday morning. Both of them belong to football teams, and do Taekwon do. My eldest belongs to a running club, my youngest goes swimming. Of course, they both enjoy the PlayStation and TV, but given the choice they'd prefer to be outside, as would my hubby and I. Luckily our house backs onto a park where we regularly meet our friends in the summer, and all the kids play football, cricket, tennis, rounders and climb trees. Even if it's chucking it down we'll walk in the woods and get shelter from the trees, or make a camp. To my kids, this is just their way of life.

Rosie from London, mum to Sean, 11 and Owen, eight

The Problem Solved

Making healthy normal

Many of the principles outlined in the section on fussy eaters (pp. 11–22) apply here too. Give them healthy food from the start and make certain habits ingrained in family life: for example, a bowl of fresh fruit permanently on the table, eating together – and eating the same foods – wherever possible, always having breakfast, sticking to regular mealtimes and keeping snacks healthy.

Setting the right example is vital. If children see that eating healthily is the norm for their parents, they'll automatically follow. And if your own eating habits leave a lot to be desired, having kids is a rock solid reason for changing them. If you have a food issue yourself – maybe you're a binge eater, perhaps you never touch vegetables – you might want to think about tackling it before your children start to follow suit.

One of the easiest ways to eat well as a family is to keep unhealthy foods out of the house as much as possible. If they're not there, no one's going to eat them.

Eat your greens, and other tips

Fortunately, you don't need a degree in nutrition to understand the basic guidelines of healthy eating. Ideally, children (and adults) should eat as wide a variety of food as possible, which means getting a bit of something from every food group – although admittedly, this isn't always easy with a fussy eater on your hands. You can only do your best!

A balanced diet is typically based on a majority of carbohydrate-rich starchy foods such as bread, pasta and rice, with loads of fruit and veg, some protein (fish, meat, eggs, beans and pulses), dairy products (three portions of milk, cheese or yoghurt a day are recommended), and a limited amount of fat.

Everyone knows we're supposed to get at least five portions of fruit and veg down us, as they're a vital source of vitamins, minerals and fibre. Again, variety is good – a useful guideline is to aim for an array of different colours. Lots of mums rely on sneaky ways of upping the F&V quota – adding them to mash, blending them into pasta sauces and hiding them in puddings, for example. But it's better still if they can learn to appreciate fruit and vegetables for the (delicious) things they are. Kids often prefer raw over cooked, so sliced carrots, pepper and cucumber served on the side, as a snack, or an appetiser, are often popular. And fruit is a lot more appealing when it's sliced into segments and presented on a plate. However you serve it though, don't make a big deal out of it or bang on about it being the 'healthy option'. Just make it normal, everyday fodder.

Children also need plenty of liquid throughout the day to keep them from being dehydrated. Try to avoid or limit fizzy drinks and stick with water, milk or diluted fruit juice.

A word on home cooking

Home cooking *is* healthier, there's not much doubt. For a start, you know exactly what's going in – there are usually higher levels of fat, sugar and salt (not to mention additives) in packaged and processed foods. But it does present a dilemma for many of us. We want to give our children good food but we don't always have the time or energy.

It's worth remembering that, often, it isn't any harder or more time-consuming to get a healthy, home-cooked meal on the table than the less nutritional, processed version. For example, you can put a tray of chicken pieces and skin-on potato wedges in the oven in the same time it takes to open a bag of frozen chicken nuggets and oven chips. (And if you need more inspiration than that, there are more examples of low-effort, high-nutrition ideas in the Netmums cookery book, *Feeding Kids*.) It's also a great example to set kids and a great way for them to learn about the joy of food: if you can, get them to put on their aprons and join you in the kitchen. Even if you can't or won't cook from scratch, you can still eat well, with a little attention to what you buy and how you serve it. Be label aware (there's advice on ways to do this on Netmums.com) so you know what the healthier options are, and boost goodness levels by dishing up extra fruit or veg on the side.

A little of what you fancy

None of this means that we should never indulge in the things we love that we know aren't very good for us. In fact, if you tried to ban unhealthy foods altogether, kids would want them even more – and then binge on them whenever they get the chance. Moderation is the key, and for most people, common sense will dictate exactly where that lies. Sweets, cakes, crisps, chips, fizzy pop, takeaways and all those other things which we know come crammed with salt, sugar and fat, should be enjoyed in a limited way, not as a matter of course. Don't make these things seem like 'forbidden fruits', though, as you'll boost their appeal.

Hop, skip and a jump

It's recommended that kids partake in an hour of moderate physical activity every day. And as with healthy eating, the best way to achieve that is to make it an ordinary aspect of our lives. Squeeze it in wherever you can: leave the car behind at every opportunity, take the stairs, encourage them to help with the housework. Balance out their sedentary activities (computers, telly) with lots of physical ones, too. And join in whenever possible – it will help motivate them and be good for you, too. Don't sell it as 'exercise'. Always make it fun, rather than competitive. Go to the park, fly a kite, have a race, play hopscotch, jump rope, walk in the woods, hold an impromptu disco, challenge them to a game of rounders. And if they're keen, encourage them to take up a formal activity or two – not all kids are sporty, it's true, but chances are there'll be *something* out there that they really enjoy. Once they're old enough, you might want to take up a hobby the whole family can do together, such as cycling. Apart from the obvious physical benefits, it's a lovely way to get in some quality time together.

What the experts say
The dietician

The best advice for having healthy kids is to have a think about your lifestyle as a whole family and about the ways you can change it to make it healthier. There's a simple way to cut down a child's 'junk' intake, and that's not to have it in your cupboards. If you don't want them to eat it, don't keep it in the house – that way, there won't be any disputes if they want to eat something that you don't want them to. And I think that's good general advice, not just something I'd say about a child with a weight problem. The whole family will benefit.

Of course, it's fine for children to have these sorts of foods sometimes. But if crisps, sweets and fizzy drinks are being consumed regularly and/or in large quantities they may be displacing other more healthy foods, and causing children to have more fat, sugar and calories than they need. They're better considered occasional foods rather than staples.

Setting a good example is key. Whatever you want your children to eat is what you should be eating. The same goes for physical activity. The best way to have active kids is to be active yourself, and support them in the active things they do. Is there anything your family can do together, maybe going for a walk or having a game of football in the garden? And just trying to include little bits of activity into day-to-day life is important. That way, your children will accept that an active life is a normal one.

It's not always easy working out what's good for them and what isn't. But there are some basic guidelines to bear in mind. Trying to get at least five portions of fruit and veg down them a day is the ideal, although it's something a lot of parents grapple with. Don't nag, or try to force healthy foods on them. Just have them around, make them part of your daily diet. Have a fruit bowl on the table and keep it filled up. Always serve main meals with at least one portion of veg or salad. And make sure you eat them yourself, to show them how it's done! Meal habits are important – do you sit at the table together to eat, at least sometimes, and eat the same foods? It's not always possible for modern families, but it's good to do it as often as you can. Home-cooked food does tend to be healthier, and if you prepare meals yourself you've got more control over what's going in. But we know that, realistically, lots of families these days don't eat this way. If you're going to use processed foods, use the labels to make healthier choices.

Children definitely snack more than they did in the past. There's a perception that they mustn't ever be hungry, but I think it's OK sometimes to hang on until the next meal and hopefully they'll be more likely to eat it. Having said that, *healthy* snacking is an excellent way to get extra fruit and veg down them and boost their nutrient intake.

Helen Croker, Health Behaviour Unit, University of Central London

The Problem Summarised

♦ Generally speaking, children are eating less healthily and are less active these days.

♦ Lots of experts are very concerned about increasing levels of obesity and the rising incidence of serious illnesses that are linked to it.

♦ A healthy lifestyle is something the whole family ought to be aiming for.

♦ Strive to give them a reasonable balance in their diet, with the right proportions from each of the food groups.

♦ Fruit and veg are vital. Five portions a day is the *minimum* we should all be consuming!

♦ Make the 'naughty' stuff occasional, not staple.

♦ Cook from scratch whenever you can. When you buy food in packets, check the labels.

♦ Give 'couch potatoes' a kick up the behind! Get them moving. And move with them.

Factfile: Childhood obesity

It's estimated that almost 28 per cent of children aged two to ten in the UK are either overweight or obese. Apart from the obvious physical risks of being overweight or obese, there are the emotional ones too: kids with a weight problem are often teased, and that may cause them to suffer from anxiety and low self-esteem.

Recognising – and acknowledging – that a child is overweight isn't always easy for a parent, and it's common to pass off surplus pounds in children as 'puppy fat'. However, the truth is that although some children will naturally shed the extra weight as they grow, the majority won't – particularly if they have one or more parents who are overweight or obese, too.

The only way to tell for sure, though, is to measure their BMI. For adults this is a calculation of a person's weight (in kilograms), divided by their height (in metres) squared. However, with kids there are other factors to take into account such as gender, age and growth rate, so it's more complex. You'll need to ask a GP, health visitor or nurse to make the calculation for you.

As anyone who has struggled with their weight long term will tell you, the longer you leave it, the harder it is to get under control. So the earlier you intervene, by introducing them to a more healthy lifestyle, the better. Most overweight children will not need to actually 'diet' (and a child should never be put on a restrictive diet without the say-so of a doctor or dietician). It will usually be a question of introducing a more healthy lifestyle at home. If that doesn't help, a medical professional may suggest a more formal weight-loss plan, make a referral to a specialist, or take tests to rule out a small handful of possible medical causes, for example, an underactive thyroid.

A child with a weight problem will need the right emotional support, too. Never make them feel bad about being overweight, don't criticise them, and don't make them feel they're the only one in the family with a weight problem – make sure everyone under your roof is making changes, too.

Media matters: How and why to keep tabs on television and computer time

The Problem

We used to have the television on all day and my son would watch it most of the time. I do think that he learned quite a bit from it but lately his concentration has lapsed and his behaviour is terrible. So now we have Fun Radio, a station just for kids, on all day and he just watches TV for an hour before he goes to bed. His concentration and behaviour improved dramatically and he plays more with his toys now and uses his imagination a lot more.

Sharon from Uxbridge, mum to James, four

Time to turn off?

In recent years, excessive small screen habits have been blamed for causing or contributing to a whole host of childhood ills: aggression, poor educational achievement, attention deficit disorders, behavioural problems, speech and language delays, depression, anti-social tendencies and even obesity. It's enough to make you reach for the off-switch in alarm.

Research into the subject has drawn varied conclusions but overall, it seems certain that whilst restricted amounts are fine and even beneficial, there *are* risks attached to excessive television and computer habits. In particular, communication experts have strong concerns that the development of children's speech and language can be affected, because they need human interaction to develop those skills, and watching TV or playing on a computer generally hampers that.

However, none of us really need the experts to tell us that it's not a great idea for a child to spend too much of his life glued to the box, surfing the web, or clicking away on his console. Frankly, it's pretty *obvious* that if television and computers dominate his life, he'll be missing out on other opportunities to broaden his physical, educational, social and developmental horizons.

Here is the (good) news . . .

Let's face it, television and computers are here to stay. They're an indispensable part of the furniture in most family homes, and if we're honest, most of us adults couldn't live without them, either.

TV-watching and computer use is ingrained in modern culture: if we denied our children access to the television and computer, they'd be considered oddballs. And, quite apart from anything else, they are a massive aid to mums as they go about the business of trying to get things done – without the telly, some kids would never get their tea cooked, and the ironing would mount up in piles.

Kids need to relax, particularly at the end of a long day's work or play. And they have every right to be entertained and to lose themselves in their favourite programmes, just as we have, as adults. And as for the educational potential of both media – well, the possibilities are endless. So, all in all, there's certainly no question, for most of us, of trying to live *without* our televisions or computers.

As with so much that's controversial in life, the answer lies in finding a sensible balance that weighs up both risks and reality.

The Problem Shared

What the Netmums say

My son is a whiz on the computer already – he's been around them since he was tiny – and I'm sure it will help him at school. He can only have access to a few sites and for a set period of time (I know he can't read but I thought we'd start as we mean to go on). He also has some children's educational CD-Roms. We do let him watch television and DVDs that are appropriate for his age.

TV can be a good thing as long as it's controlled. He picks up lots from it. I'm happy with the balance we have – we also play outside, read books, bake. A little television or computer time won't harm him. However, I'm sure it will get harder as he gets older and realises there's more on his television and computer than just CBeebies!
Jo from Mow Cop, mum to Alex, four

In the morning the television only goes on after they're ready and dressed for school. After school they do homework first then the television stays on till they go to bed. They don't sit glued to it, they do go off and play. I like the fact that the CBeebies channel is quite educational.

As for computers, mine is switched on all day. I have Netmums stored in my favourites and Abbie knows how to open it and how to click on the Nick Jr link. I allow her access to her own username so she can now log in with her own password and play her games. This is normally limited to about an hour at a time. I think it's important practice, as they use PCs quite a bit at school.
Zoe from Sutton, mum to Abbie, five and Jake, three

I don't allow the television in the mornings, but sometimes it's on from the minute they get in from school till they go to bed – although 90 per cent of the time it's playing to itself because they're outside. I turn it off, then they come in and turn it on. I don't let them have access to the PC unless I'm in the room with them so I can check they're not on sites they shouldn't be, and we also have a website filter system so they can only get on sites we allow. Toby's allowed half an hour to an hour three times a week, as well as extra time for homework, and Jack has 15–30 minutes.

We have channel blockers on the television, too, so they can only get the programmes we allow them to watch – kids, geography, history, national geographic and some music channels. There's a PIN number to change to other programmes but we won't be telling them it for quite some time.

Leigh from Manchester, mum to Jack, four and foster mum to Toby, 12

My three kids each have their own computer. However, my son's is kept in the dining room so I can keep an eye on the type of games and sites he uses. I found out a while ago he was on a game you have to be 15 to play. Apparently the boy next door enrolled him! There was also a period when he was receiving 'chat' messages from all sorts of people. We've now put a block on his computer. My middle daughter likes to play games and interact with other kids. However, I still monitor her use carefully and she knows she mustn't give out any personal information. She probably uses the computer for two hours a night, to do her homework and play a game.

As for the television, if the kids are good they can watch it, if they're naughty it's banned. There are a few programmes that they are not allowed to watch – *The Simpsons*, *Dick and Dom*, *EastEnders* and *Coronation Street*. I feel that these are sometimes a bit too close to the knuckle!

We were given a month's free Sky viewing recently and the arguments it caused were unbelievable. It confirmed my view that it would be a very bad idea to have so much choice.

Christine from Kettering, mum to Holly, 12, Chloe, ten and Jack, eight

The TV is on in my house a lot of the day, to be honest. It goes off for eating times and sleep times. He doesn't watch it all day though, we have different activities so we tend to just listen to it. He does have favourite programmes and I don't stop him watching them but as they're normally repeated twice a day he's only allowed to watch them once!

We have a 'film night' every Friday where we put Isabelle to bed and have some Mummy, Daddy and Taylor time watching a film and having a 'picnic'. He still has his bedtime story afterwards. He thinks it's great.

Zoe from Rhondda Cynon Taff, mum to Taylor, two and Isabelle, one

Our television usually goes on after school, until 6 p.m. when Grace goes to bed. We often sit down together and watch *Numberjacks*, *Nina and the Neurons* and *Toddworld*. Then we talk about what we've seen. Grace never has unsupervised access to the internet, although she's competent at getting round CBeebies or Nick Jr. She sometimes plays games, usually for up to 40 minutes, an average of once a week. We also sit at the computer together and search for answers to questions she's asked. I think as long as kids live a balanced life, then computer and TV has its place. But it shouldn't overshadow playing out, board games, chatting and reading.

Louise from Newcastle under Lyme, mum to Grace, four

My son is addicted to his PlayStation, so he's limited to using it only on Thursdays and Fridays. He chills out in front of the television after school for about an hour then he does some homework, if he has any, or he reads to me. I think all kids need time to relax after school, just like we do, when we finish work. Of course, I'd rather he were in the tennis courts with his friends or out skateboarding, but a little bit of everything will do just fine. Also, having daughters aged ten and 13, I have to watch what they watch in the evening. Leanne likes *Hollyoaks* but I think it's dreadful and should be banned!

Clare from Havant, mum to Leanne, 13, Molly, ten and Thomas, eight

We don't necessarily have the telly on every day, although the children usually watch a DVD of their choice at some point. They like *Charlie and Lola* and *Pingu*. They sometimes come into our bed in the morning and watch *Milkshake* so we can lie with our eyes closed for another ten minutes! I prefer something with educational content, but I think children learn all the time anyway. Both children turn it off when asked. In fact, my daughter often switches it off herself and chooses to sit and read books instead, which she says is 'cosier'. Maybe that's because I always sit and read with them. When the telly's on I use it as a chance to get something else done, so I'm not there. Tom would probably watch for longer given the chance, but there's always something else to do when the TV goes off, so he's not fussed.

Cate from North East London, mum to Daisy, three and Tom, one

In terms of quality, I allow my two year old to watch children's programmes that I feel are positive or educational, but also broader programmes such as nature documentaries or cooking shows, which we then talk about. And quantity – I monitor the amount of TV over the course of a week, not a day, as I think it gives a more accurate idea of how much we're watching. An hour a day adds up to seven hours a week, nearly a full day in front of the box! So, I don't have an issue with her watching a couple of hours in one day, but I would count this towards a weekly total. I also try to match TV time to 'mummy' time to alleviate the guilt!

Liz from York, mum to Issy, two and Niamh, ten weeks

Personally, I don't monitor television and computer time, as my son does plenty of other activities each day – swimming, playgroup, soft play, walking, riding his bike, the list is endless. So if he wants to chill out and play the computer or watch TV, then so be it.

Emma from Fife, mum to Kade, three and Jay, four months

My husband and I fight all the time about how much TV our daughter should be allowed. I let her watch more than he does, because it lets me get on with things around the house. She's doing OK at school, but teachers have always said she has trouble concentrating for too long. My husband thinks this is due to too much TV watching – he's quoted the latest research, which says that children under three should not be exposed to TV at all! This makes me scared to leave my eight-month-old son in the same room while the TV is even on, which is a difficult thing to avoid. I'd say she watches about seven to ten hours a week of TV. She also seems to have picked up a lot of 'attitude' from it – she's seven going on 17! She loves the teenager channels and the film *High School Musical*. I do read with her and do her homework with her before allowing her to watch TV. It's difficult, though, when you want to get on with things.

Emma from West London, mum to Aimee, seven and Ethan, eight months

My daughter uses the internet unsupervised, but the computer is downstairs in the dining room where I can keep an eye on her and make sure she only uses sites suitable for her age. We have a parental control system that denies access to anything inappropriate. We have blocks on all chatroom sites too, as I will never allow her to use these, even when she's older. She'll never be allowed a computer in her room, either.

Mary from Bristol, mum to Mollie, five and Connie, two

The Problem Solved

Risk assessment

A huge amount of research has sought to establish the potential effects of too much television and computer time. Different opinions abound, though, and the various research findings don't always match up, making it hard for most parents to know exactly what the risks are.

Many studies have concluded that too much television can be harmful. For instance, US researcher Dr Dimitri Christakis found that for every hour of television watched, toddlers had a ten per cent risk of suffering attention problems later on. His report concluded that children under two should not watch television at all and that children over two should be restricted to two hours a day. And in *Remotely Controlled: How Television is Damaging Our Lives*, psychologist Aric Sigman argues that too much television may stunt the development of children's brains, increase their likelihood of developing attention deficit disorders, and contribute to obesity and depression. He recommends that children under three don't watch television at all, that those aged three to 12 watch no more than an hour a day.

However, many other researchers have drawn more positive conclusions. In 2006, for example, Matthew Gentzkow and Jesse Shapiro of the University of Chicago found that childhood television viewing did not necessarily cause harm to educational or cognitive development, and that pre-schoolers who watched television performed 'marginally better' at school. And a study of infants' and toddlers' television viewing by Linebarger and Walker in 2005 questioned the recommendation that children under two should not watch television at all, finding that some pre-school programmes can lead to larger vocabularies and higher expressive language in one-, two- and three-year-olds.

It's also worth bearing in mind that this is a difficult area for researchers to be conclusive about, as any apparent consequences of television and computer use may also be influenced by other factors in a child's life, such as parental attitudes. Other studies have investigated the possible influence of television and computer games on children's behaviour, particularly where violence is concerned. And some experts believe there is a clear link between the violence children are exposed to on screen and the increase in real violence in our society. In 2005, for example, researchers from the University of Birmingham's Centre for Forensic and Family Psychology reported that the violent imagery they see in the media increases the risk of children becoming aggressive and emotionally disturbed, and called on parents to exercise caution over their children's media consumption. However, other experts point out that these things are influenced by a range of factors, and that what children watch and play on screen form just one part of the overall picture.

So, just how much is *too* much?

There is no official 'recommended daily allowance' (although some campaigners would like to see one), so it's really just one of those things every family must decide on for themselves. One guideline, from the National Literacy Trust, is that the under twos should watch no more than half an hour of appropriate programming a day at most and from three onwards, it should be limited to an hour a day. Researchers Teresa Orange and Louise O'Flynn, in their book *The Media Diet for Kids* (Hay House, 2005), concur that two hours' screen time a day for the over twos is a useful limit to aim for – although it may be helpful to think of it in terms of 14 hours a week, since some days will involve more screen time than others.

Get the balance right

Whether or not you consciously set a limit on screen time in your home, the single most important thing you can do to minimise any negative effects is to make sure your kids do lots of other things, too. It stands to reason that too much of one thing (especially if that thing involves sitting down and staring at a screen), is not ideal for a great many reasons. However, if you know that your child also spends plenty of time talking and playing with their friends, runs around outside, engages with you and their siblings, reads or listens to stories, plays a wide variety of other games and is generally happy, healthy and well balanced, then you probably don't have to worry about imposing drastic time limits. They're doing that for themselves.

What should they be watching?

It's also hard to come up with definitive guidelines on the *sort* of screen material children should be consuming. Fortunately, when it comes to little ones and pre-schoolers, the vast majority of programming for that sort of age group is done with their development in mind: if you stick to age-appropriate shows and television channels, you won't go far wrong. Speech and language experts recommend that for children under two, programmes with low stimulus – something presented by a single adult speaker, for example – and for two- to five-year-olds, anything that encourages involvement and response. However, too much action may be confusing and over-stimulating. If your little one has a favourite film or programme that they like to watch over and over, don't fret: experts say it can actually be a positive thing, because it gives them the opportunity to learn repeated words and phrases.

Remember to turn off the telly, though, if they're not watching it. Apart from being a waste of electricity, it's a distraction that can interfere with developing attention, listening, talking and play. And it gives kids the impression that they can dip in and out whenever they want to.

The viewing habits of older children are just as much a cause for concern.

A significant number of research findings suggest that kids' behaviour *is* influenced, either overtly or in a more subtle way, by what they see on their screens – although the jury is still out on that matter. Plenty of mums are fairly certain, based on what they see with their own eyes, that there is undoubtedly a link.

It's basically down to us as individual parents to decide what's 'appropriate' viewing for our kids and, since there are few official guidelines (other than ratings certificates in the case of DVDs and computer games), it has to be based on common sense. Some people argue that there's not much point in protecting our children from what they'll eventually be exposed to, anyway. If you're going to let your child watch something that's not really age-appropriate, the best advice is watch it with them and help them to put it into perspective – in particular, helping them sort out fact from fiction – by talking about it afterwards.

Of course, it can be very hard keeping an eye on what younger siblings watch if older brothers and sisters have control of the remote – if it's impossible to agree on something that all parties approve of, you may have to negotiate turns and make sure that everyone gets to see what they want to see at some point. If something's on that an older child isn't interested in, that could be the time to suggest they go elsewhere to do their homework, draw, read or play outside. And having a special time – perhaps after smaller ones are in bed – when an older sibling can watch a particular programme or use the computer, is usually a much-appreciated privilege (and often an effective incentive to good behaviour!)

Watching with mother

Of course, most of us don't really have the luxury of time to curl up on the sofa with the kids, much as we'd like to. But the advice is that we do so when we can to make television viewing as beneficial as possible. Try and talk to them during and after programmes, asking questions about what they've seen and discussing it together. And you might want to try using programmes or plots to inspire imaginative play after the telly's been turned off.

The experts all say that it's not a great idea to let a child have a television in their bedroom, for obvious reasons – it makes it harder for you to keep tabs on what they're watching and how often.

Guiding the Google generation

Computers and the internet have huge benefits for children in terms of education and entertainment. The majority of primary schools use them as a teaching aid now and it's certainly no bad thing for a five year old to know their way around a mouse and a keyboard.

But with the pros come a number of cons. As with television, some experts have advised that kids under two shouldn't use computers at all because they may harm development of basic communication skills. With little ones, it's probably best to keep computer use limited to very short bursts. Use the computer with them, and talk together about what you see. The same basic rule applies whatever their age: make computers and electronic toys just one part of a wide variety of other games and activities in their day.

These days, it's not unusual for computer and internet habits to be well established before they're ten, especially if they're influenced by older siblings. Set limits in place early on, and you may save yourself hassle later on when the appeal of MSN Messenger and Xbox really kicks in. If they do chat online to friends, make sure they know the basics of internet safety: never give out personal information, or arrange to meet anyone you've chatted to on a computer. Impress upon them that they must let you know about anything they come across online that worries them. Inappropriate web pages are another worry. There's a wide choice of software that can block or filter out undesirable sites, but nothing's as important as a bit of well-placed parental monitoring. The key is to be involved in their computer use: even if you're not actually sitting at their side when they're online or at their keyboard, make sure you're never far. As with tellies, it's recommended that you keep computers in a family room rather than letting kids have one in their bedrooms.

What the experts say
The campaigner and author

There's no doubt there *are* risks attached to a child having too much screen time. There's been a lot of debate about it over the years but recently a lot of research findings have started to come through which backs up what most parents feel and know instinctively, anyway –

that if a child is in front of a screen too much, it can't be good for them.

We think there are five different areas where the risks of too much screen time lie:

1. The first is behaviour. There's no doubt in my mind that children can pick up bad behaviour from the screen and there's evidence now to back that up. Children's energy levels get out of sync if they've spent hours sitting down in front of the telly. They need outlets for their energy otherwise they get frustrated which means they can be impulsive and rude. They can also pick up and mimic bad behaviour they've seen on screen. In the short term, too much television watching is linked to aggression, disrespect and bullying.

2. The second area of concern is physical well-being. Research shows that the risk of obesity and heart problems may be higher for children who have too much screen time.

3. Thirdly comes relationships. There's a danger that children who spend too much time in front of televisions or computers become hermits and don't know how to relate to other people, either their friends or members of their own family.

4. Fourth is education. There are reports that suggest children's educational performances are affected by out-of-balance media habits, something that teachers have been concerned about for a long time.

5. Lastly, there's the matter of outlook. Do we really want a world where telly becomes the most influential thing in your children's life and shapes their perception of the world, the way they think, and their moral values? Of course not. So it's important for parents to turn the telly off sometimes, or to share viewing with their children and talk to them about what they've seen to help them understand that what they see isn't necessarily an exact reflection of the world. Watching with them when you can is vital, particularly with little ones. Studies show that shared viewing is the most effective way to benefit from it and I'm a great believer in that. Computer use isn't as easily shared, but parents can and should take an interest in their children's online pursuits – and where games are concerned, join in sometimes, too.

Of course, there are masses of good things about television and computers, too. As a socially cohesive force, for one: it's good that they have things to talk about at school and share with their friends who'll all have seen the same programmes, or visited the same websites. To deprive a child of that would be miserable. Also, all children *need* time to chill out, be entertained, and have fun, particularly after school, which can be high pressure and hard work for them. Television and computer use is a wonderful way of winding down. And it can be a great help for busy mums too – there's nothing wrong in using these things sometimes for a little tactical babysitting.

The educational benefits are enormous. And they don't have to be isolating activities – they can promote social interaction used in the right way – boys playing computer games together, girls chatting on a networking site, families getting together to watch a favourite show on a Saturday evening, for example.

The trouble is, there's so much that's good about television and computers and such a wonderful choice, it then becomes difficult to know when to say enough is enough. Our recommended daily limit (as a very general rule of thumb) for screen time is two hours for the over twos. But you have to be flexible about that – they may watch less on a school day and more on a wet weekend. But if you averaged it out over the course of a year and they'd had about two hours of television or computer use a day then that's probably a pretty good average. Most families seem to feel it's a reasonable balance to aim for.

It's a good idea establish limits early on, when you're in a position to be firm about their schedule. Just like healthy eating, it's about instilling good eating habits from the start, so that they actually become part of their normal life and, hopefully, by the time they're teenagers they can recognise for themselves what a healthy balance is.

What they watch is relevant, too. You have to think quality, as well as quantity. But how do you define what's good and what's bad? It's subjective, so different people will have different views. For example, some people think *EastEnders* is depressing and wouldn't want their children to see it, while others think it's good for kids to get a dose of realism.

We think that mums do need to be a bit better at looking at how a specific programme affects their child. We need to become more attentive to the effects of what they're watching – does it affect their energy level, what are they likely to take away from the tone, morals and role models in it? And we need to be proactive when it comes to working out what's good quality, and what's appropriate. But having said that, I don't think there's any harm in watching television purely for entertainment sometimes. We all need to have a laugh and to have fun.

It's OK to celebrate and enjoy television and computers, but the important thing is that they don't become the wallpaper of our lives. A childhood that's one-dimensional and focused largely on a screen isn't a rich childhood. We mustn't let them become so caught up in the wonders of the screen that they don't make time for other things. *Teresa Orange, www.TheMediaDietforKids.com*

The speech and language therapist

Televisions, computers and other screens are a definite part of our world. They offer many opportunities for education, conversation and play. There are also some negative consequences of too much screen time: when children are learning to talk (from birth to around four years), having a constant noise in the background makes it very difficult for children to work out which are the sounds to listen to and which is the noise to be screened out. Even having the pictures of the television with no sound can be very distracting for children who are still learning to focus their attention. Our advice is to turn the television off if it is not being watched, because this will help young children to focus on the communication of the adult and will give them a better chance of learning to listen, understand and talk.

There are lots of television programmes for children, some specifically designed for very young children. This means that they can get involved with characters and stories that they may otherwise not come across. To make the best use of television with young children, parents or carers can sit and watch the programmes together with their children and then talk about what they see. There are lots of things to do together based on what you have seen on the television – perhaps making some of the crafts that are demonstrated on programmes; name some of the food that you share together after some of the characters in the programmes; sing some of the songs together; or involve some elements of the programme in pretend play

with your child. The important thing is to do these activities together – children learn to communicate from interacting with the people in their environment that they have the closest relationships with. Televisions do not interact with children, they cannot respond to what a child is saying, they cannot copy children's noises or adapt the level of conversation so that the child will understand what is being said. Thankfully, people cannot be replaced by an electrical box!
Kate Freeman, I CAN, the children's communication charity

The Problem Summarised

- If you feel confused about the issues surrounding children and screen time, that's understandable. Lots of research has been carried out on the 'risks', but it doesn't all conclude the same thing.
- Without or without help from the experts most sensible parents know that too much television and computer use can't be a good thing.
- It's up to us to set our family's screen time limits. A useful rule of thumb is to aim for no more than two hours a day for children over two. (And some experts say the under-twos should have significantly less than that.)
- Watch with them whenever you can. Talk about what they've seen.
- Think about it carefully before allowing them to have a computer or television in their bedroom.
- Make sure you know what they're watching, playing or logged on to.
- Get the balance right: Don't let television, computers or electronic toys be their only or dominant focus, and make sure they do lots of other things, too.

Don't leave me! How to help a child with separation anxiety

The Problem

Josh is going through this stage. He refuses to get dressed on school days and we have a battle to get his clothes on. He also spends the whole car journey there saying things like 'I'm sorry mummy' and 'I love you', or 'I promise I'll be good if you don't make me go'. It's heartbreaking. But I know that within minutes of me peeling him from my body and escaping, he'll be fine and will have forgotten about me. So I talk to him about the toys there and wonder what he'll have for a snack and what the story will be, to keep him interested and enthusiastic.

Jo from Leicester, mum to Josh, two

When parting is such sorrow

The majority of little ones will suffer at least one bout of separation anxiety at some stage. Usually it kicks in during their first year, at eight or nine months, when they begin to understand that you're leaving a room but are yet to grasp the certainty that you'll be coming back. However, it's also very normal for it to either continue for quite a while, or to return a bit later in response to a new routine, like starting at nursery or pre-school. It may also be linked to seemingly unconnected events that shake their general sense of security – the arrival of a new sibling, or some kind of upset in the family, for instance.

It's a heart-rending thing to have to cope with. But a small child who kicks up a fuss about being separated from his main caregiver is just doing what's normal.

Bye bye, baby

Trying to disentangle yourself from a weeping child who doesn't want you to leave them is a tough thing for any mum to do. But in most cases, there won't be much choice: you may be returning to work or need to be somewhere else, or it may be time for them to test the waters of life without you, at pre-school or nursery, or a social event.

You might feel terrible about leaving your little one's side when they're upset. But needs must. And in fact, it's actually healthy to get a little distance between you sometimes. At the very least, it will make life easier when it's time for them to start full-time school and will need to get through five whole days a week without you around.

The Problem Shared

What the Netmums say

Robert's been fine about me leaving him places such as pre-school or with family members when I go to work. The problem is if I want to go anywhere without him and we're at home. It could just be something like needing to cook the tea and having to leave him in the living room with my hubby – if I shut the kitchen door on him, he screams. He doesn't like me going upstairs without him, so it's hard to get a bath in peace. He'll bang on the door to be let in, and shout or cry for me.

It sounds awful, but I've learned just to ignore him. Or my hubby will distract him by keeping him entertained downstairs.

If I'm actually going out, he's even worse. We've found that if his dad takes him to the door so he can wave to me and I beep the horn at him when I'm in the car, it seems to soothe him.

Sharon from St Helens, mum to Lauren, 15 and Robert, two

My eldest son is almost two and just starting at pre-school. He's been going on visits there for a couple of months, three times a week, but every time I get to the door of the nursery he cries and cries until he goes blue. It breaks my heart, but I've been told to let him cry. When I go to collect him, he's just sitting there watching the other children playing.

I only leave him there for a couple of hours now but I really don't know what I should do. I'm thinking of pulling him out until he has to go to nursery when he's three, but the staff have advised me not to do that because they think if I do, he'll never get used to it.

Ayesha from Leeds, mum to Zayn, two and Ismaeel, one

My daughter used to be very clingy when I dropped her at nursery, although not so much with my husband. The nursery assistants were less than helpful and would just carry on doing what they were doing and I could be stood with her clamped to me for ages. Eventually one would come over and would have to physically pull her away. I'd spend most days at work totally depressed and desperate to get home. Now she's much better and will 'try it on' for a few minutes, but usually gentle persuasion – I'll ask her to draw me a lovely picture for when I pick her up, for example – usually works.

I'm dreading her starting school in case the whole thing starts again – although luckily her dad will be taking her most of the time. I don't recall having any trouble with my eldest, who's always been much more independent.

Alison from Gravesend, mum to Lauren, 16 and Leigh, four

I still get a bit of this from Luke when I drop him off at nursery. I suspect it's mainly for show; however, at the start of the year they had lots of changes in staff and his main carer, who he adored, left. I only found out three weeks later when I enquired about her health, which I was

most upset about. My concern is, how do you tell if they're making a fuss 'for effect' or if there's a real problem they are having with the nursery or their carer, which means they really don't want to be left?
Claire from Worksop, mum to Luke, three

Ava's quite clingy. She started nursery five months ago and it broke my heart to leave her. She'd cry and call out to me when I tried to leave. For the first few weeks, apparently, she refused to move away from the door and stood there with her coat and bag for the whole session!

She's better now and does join in but if I gave her the choice she'd always stay at home with me. Apart from her grandparents, she won't go out with people if I'm not there, too.

It's hard, but I want her to be independent so I try and push her to do new things and play with other children. Hopefully in time she'll be happier to go away from me.
Kate from Bexhill, mum to Ava, two and Elsa, six months

Louis didn't know anyone else in his class when he started school recently, as he had gone to a different nursery, and he cried every day for the first term. He was mostly fine until I said goodbye to him, and then he'd burst into tears and cling onto me. A couple of times he even ran out of the classroom and across the playground to try to stop me from leaving. He also started wetting the bed every night.

I found this heartbreaking at first, and for the first week walked back home in floods of tears myself. Fortunately I met the mum of another boy in his class who had had a similar experience with her eldest son, and she invited Louis to play with her son. Her empathy helped me feel better, too. I'm ashamed to say though that I also felt embarrassed by his crying, as he was the only child in a class of 23 who reacted this way. I felt as though the other parents were forming views about my parenting skill (or lack of!) and about my son based on the snapshots of us that they saw in the classroom in the mornings.

I'm determined to learn from this experience, though, and hopefully make the transition to school easier for Cole than it has been for his big brother.
Joanna from Nottingham, mum to Louis, four and Cole, nine months

When Mollie started pre-school she was a nightmare. She refused to take her coat off, cried the whole time, wet herself, carried her teddy everywhere and wouldn't move from whatever chair she was sitting on. I found it really hard. The pre-school gave me the option of pulling her out, but we spoke and finally agreed that it wouldn't achieve anything.

It took a good six months before she was really settled. But I'm pleased I went through all that emotion with her. I actually think it was good for her – she's very outgoing now. I'd advise anyone in the same situation not to give in, however hard it gets.
Mary from Bristol, mum to Mollie, five and Connie, two

Caitlin went through this aged two. It started after I went into hospital overnight for the first time. Overnight, she turned into a nightmare and it lasted for a year. She was OK if I dropped her anywhere – nursery hasn't been a problem as it was always me taking her and picking her up. But she wouldn't allow anyone, even her daddy, to take her away from me at home. She'd become hysterical, crying until her face was swollen, being sick and choking. Many a time my mum and dad, who'd regularly taken her out in the past without a problem, had to bring her back, or I'd have to go and collect her, because she was getting so upset.

It seems to be stopping now, thankfully. She went out for a walk with my sister recently and was absolutely fine.
Donna from Manchester, mum to Caitlin, three and Lucy, two

I went back to work part-time when Lewis was five months old. To save on child minding fees, my mum had him for almost a year and this has made him very close to her. I never had any real issues with leaving him with her. When Lewis started nursery at almost 18 months they were wonderful and he settled very quickly. But then his dad and I split up, and I had to go back to work full-time.

I feel guilty about leaving Lewis and I think he can feel this, as he has days where he screams and asks me not to leave him. The girls in nursery have to cuddle him for me and stand him at the window so he can wave; sometimes even then he reaches out for me as I'm driving off. He tends to be worse after a long weekend or when he's spent

some time with his dad but he normally settles down after I've promised to pick him up, and that I'll play football with him later.
Kerri-Ann from Wellingborough, mum to Lewis, three

Emma started nursery at five months old when I went back to work, and she's never shown a bit of separation anxiety. But we've really struggled to get Samuel to settle since he started at nursery two mornings a week. I've come very close to giving it up as a bad job at times, but recently he finally seems OK. He still cries at first when I leave him, but I find the best way to deal with it is to be quite firm and say: 'Mummy is going now. I'll be back soon,' give him a kiss and hand him over to the brilliant nursery staff. I know he's fine, because by the time I get to the top of the corridor, he's stopped crying. It's not easy sometimes, but I'm pleased we've persevered with it, as he really does enjoy himself once he's over the initial separation. He's getting better at it, although I think it may take a while longer before he gets to the stage where he'll let me go without crying.

My advice would be to persevere. I've noticed the change in Samuel since he started nursery. He's more confident and much more willing to leave my side at playgroups.
Fiona from Doncaster, mum to Emma, four and Samuel, two

For the first term and a half after starting Reception, my daughter made herself physically sick every morning. To start with she wasn't allowed to stay in school but once they realised she was ill and it was just anxiety, she had to stay, often in sick-stained clothes.

It was very stressful and I dreaded the morning. She'd be fine until we reached school and then she'd just make herself sick on demand. Lots of reassurance and a reward chart seem to have done the trick, although she still gets anxious some mornings.
Sarah from London, mum to Cara, five

Separation anxiety is something we've dealt a lot with. Our eldest son is adopted and was four when he came to live with us, and as you can imagine there were a lot of issues, separation being one of them. Two things we found that helped were, leaving little notes in his packed lunch or pockets for him to find. And putting some of my perfume or hubby's aftershave on a piece of cotton wool, which we put in his pocket so if he became anxious he could have a sniff of a familiar scent.

Another thing that was recommended to us is to get a small stone and cover it in kisses, while they watch, and then they can keep it in their pocket and get it out for a kiss if they need to. We had a family friend who was a dinner lady at his school, and she used to keep a pocketful of my kisses so he could claim them from him at lunchtime.

If we're going on a night out and leaving the boys with a sitter, we leave my purse with the eldest so he knows I have to come home as without it I have no money!

Amanda from Chichester, mum to Jonathan, six and Toby, four

The Problem Solved

Be prepared

Kids cope better with separation if they're given plenty of warning, so talk about what's going to happen well in advance, and don't ever let it come as a surprise to them that you won't be around for a while. And when the time comes to try out a new setting, or get to know a new caregiver, always make sure there's some kind of settling-in time – most nurseries, child-minders and pre-schools will offer an acclimatisation period, with one or more short trial visits to allow a child to familiarise themselves. When you think about it, who wouldn't cry if left in the hands of someone they've never met before or in a place they've never been?

Try to let them practise life without you in little ways before you cut the apron strings in a major way. If they've never been away from you for very long before, make sure they try it first in a comforting context: an overnighter with Grandma, for example, or an afternoon spent at a friend's house.

No looking back

Don't prolong the agony, hard as it may be. Say goodbye, and walk away. Don't attempt to sneak off when they're distracted – it could increase their sense of abandonment.

As ever, your own attitude is all-important. Try not to cry or show them you're upset, too, and stay positive – remind them of all the good things they've got to look forward to that day. If it's a new arrangement, they may have doubts that you are really going to come back for them, or they may need to know that their 'security blanket' will be coming back soon (even if, at three or four, they are somewhat more rational creatures than they were at nine months), so reassure them that you'll be returning later on.

Some caregivers are happy for you to stay a while, but most agree it's better to bite the bullet and head off straight away. And once you've gone, be gone! Resist the temptation to linger or return. Phone in half an hour to check things are OK if you must, but they almost certainly will be: if there was a real problem, you'd have heard about it.

Cope, don't cling

You may feel just as pained as your little one on leaving them, a feeling compounded by guilt and misery because of how upset they are. In most cases, you really won't need to feel bad about leaving them. The majority of children, however many tears they may shed when you wave goodbye, will be fine once you've gone. Any good caregiver will know what to do and say to reassure them, and distract them from their misery.

If their distress is more intense or prolonged, they may need a longer settling-in period than you bargained for – for some children it will be months rather than days or weeks before they become accustomed to you not being there. Take heart in the thought that they'll get there eventually and, in the meantime, remain upbeat. At times, a clingy child can feel like an embarrassment, and even an annoyance. Try to see things their way, and think of it as a good thing: they love you, and they don't want you to go.

Separation anxiety . . . or something else?

If a reluctance to be left appears out of the blue, when they've previously been fine, they may well be upset for a reason, which you'll need to thrash out with whoever you've left in charge. There's always a chance – although hopefully only a small one – that they don't like their carer for some reason. So if they're letting you know, either verbally or through their behaviour when you leave them, that they don't want to go somewhere then you may need to do a little digging to find out why. Get as much information as you can by talking to your child and by spelling out your concerns to the carer or staff in question. Talking to other parents can be helpful, too.

There's also the possibility that an emotional display is not caused by real distress: what seems to be genuine separation anxiety is in fact a little play acting on their part, undertaken to make you feel guilty for having the gall to leave! If you know your child, you'll probably know which is the more likely.

Big school, big deal

Although they'll probably have normal collywobbles, the majority of children should be happy enough without a parent around when the time comes to start primary school, aged four or five. Separation anxiety may still strike though, particularly in children who aren't used to being away from their parent for long stretches, or if there's an underlying cause for unhappiness which may destabilise them, such as a new sibling or unhappiness at home.

In a very small number of children, it can become a real problem. They may cry, cling to you, beg to be taken home or claim they are sick (or even be sick). In these cases you'll need the support of a sympathetic teacher, who can help ease them into life behind the school gates. As a mum you may be able to make things easier by staying positive, and keeping any distress or worry you're feeling yourself well hidden. And giving them a little object – something the teacher doesn't mind about that won't be confiscated – to remind them of you can be hugely comforting.

Otherwise, it's probably a question of biting your lip and being patient while a difficult but temporary period of their life runs its course. Bear in mind that children will adapt at different times and paces, so you shouldn't worry if your child is one of those who's finding it a bit difficult. It doesn't mean they've got something wrong with them! If it happens well into a school term and they've been fine before, it's probably a fair indication that all's not well. You'll need to gently persuade them to come clean about what's on their mind, whether it's a child bullying them, a teacher they don't get on with or struggling with their schoolwork, and be prepared to go to the school for some help.

There are some more ideas about how to help them settle when they start school for the first time in the factfile, p. 314.

What the experts say

The child psychologist

It's perfectly natural for a young child to feel separation anxiety – after all, when you're little, it's just nicer being with your mum – or dad – than anyone else. There are also some fundamental reasons for it. We're wired to display more attachment behaviour – i.e., sticking close to our parent figure – at certain times, for the sake of our own safety. It's all about the basic fear of being left alone and whether you'll be able to survive on your own and we all experience it to one extent or another – babies, children and adults rationalise this primitive need to stick close to safe things in different ways, but the fear is still lurking underneath.

Sometimes, in more complicated scenarios, a child will want to stick by Mum because they're worried about *her*, either because of illness or because of some difficulty at home. We all go through 'adverse' life events at times and it's a very natural consequence for us to be a bit less certain about things afterwards, so it might be worth bearing that in mind if a child doesn't seem to want to leave you. How long separation anxiety goes on for and how intense it is probably depends on the individual child, the nature of their attachment, and the relationship with their caregiver. Some children are better at reassuring themselves and distracting themselves from the worry of separation. If they think that the world is basically an alright place then they may protest a little bit when separated, but basically they'll be able to get on with it. Others may suspect the world is a dangerous place and something awful is going to happen to them if they're separated from their carer, so naturally they'll do anything they possibly can not to be separated.

Usually they are temporary difficulties but they can become

reinforced by parents' behaviours – clinging to them, for example, crying into their hair or lingering on the nursery doorstep after you dropped them off, anything that might make the child feel their worries are justified – and obviously that will only make the situation worse.

It can be heartbreaking to untie a clinging child from you and walk away, but you may have to ask yourself why it's so heartbreaking. Is it to do with your own needs and insecurities – do you want to stick close to them, or feel guilty going to work, for example? If so, then you may need to be a bit tough on yourself. You need to convey the message that the child will be OK and that you will be OK when separated. Separation anxiety is exactly that: an anxiety caused by being apart from someone predictable and loving. So, providing the child with information about what will be happening, giving them a chance to familiarise themselves with people and places and providing predictability can be useful too. Establish a routine for leaving them and stick with it, for example, say to them: 'I'm going to take you to the door, give you two kisses, then I'm going to go.' Talk to them about what you're going to do once you've picked them up and you're back together again – for example, 'After I've picked you up from nursery, we'll go to the shops to get some food for tonight.' This gives the clear message that the time apart is only temporary and provides a longer-term view.

Once a child is past the age of seven or eight and already well established at school it becomes more unusual if they're worried about not being with their mum. If it's a new behaviour, it may be that they're having a tough time at school, perhaps being bullied, not getting on with their teacher or struggling with their work. Talking with the teacher about what can be done to make the start of the day more predictable may help, and get their support in identifying the problem. Otherwise, it may be because they have worries at home. You'll need to work out what these are as a family and then tackle them.

Dr Angharad Rudkin

The Problem Summarised

◆ Separation anxiety is very normal. A bout in their first year is almost to be expected, and they may well go through it during their pre-school years.

◆ Leaving a little one can be hard when they're miserable. But they'll almost certainly be fine when you're gone. And it's got to happen some time!

◆ Help them cope with separation anxiety by making them well prepared and well informed about where they're going and when.

◆ Don't linger or look miserable yourself when you say goodbye. It's better not to look back.

◆ Sometimes, separation anxiety occurs when something more serious is up. You may need to be tuned in to all possibilities.

First class: How to help them settle in at school

1. It can be hugely reassuring if their new school is familiar to them. Even if there's no formal opportunity for them to look round (and most schools should be happy to arrange this), try to attend any fêtes, productions or sporting events staged at the school in the weeks and months beforehand. And practise the journey, however you'll be making it.

2. Talk lots about all the positives of being a school student: how 'grown-up' they'll look in their uniform, how many new friends they'll meet, and how exciting it will be to learn so many new things.

3. Read storybooks about starting school and talk through the characters' experiences. You should find a choice of titles in your local library.

4. Try to arrange for them to meet at least one other classmate who's starting at the same time, if they don't already know any. The school may be willing to help you make contact by forwarding a note, or you could approach anyone with a friendly face at prospective parents' evening, if the school holds one. Otherwise,

members of the local mums' grapevine may be able to point you in the right direction.

5. Involve them in preparations for the start of term. Let them help when you buy uniform and equipment, and try them out in advance if they want to. Lay it all out together, the night before.

6. Be strong, happy and positive (even if you feel like weeping!). They'll take their emotional cues from you.

7. Make your goodbyes brief if possible. Let them know you'll be back to pick them up when the school day is over.

8. Remember, even distressed children will usually settle pretty quickly once they're distracted. Most early year teachers will know exactly how to do that in a kind and sympathetic way.

Beating the bogeyman: How to fight their fears

The Problem

My son was scared of the dark and complained he could see things moving around his bedroom at night. He'd spook himself out and then couldn't sleep. However, he shares a room with my other son who hates having the light on. So I bought him two battery operated 'touch lights' and he now has those on when he goes to bed. We turn them off when he goes to sleep and then if he wakes up he can just turn it on as it's right next to his bed. This seems to do the trick and as they're portable, he can take them with him when he goes to his granny's.

Rebecca from Poole, mum to Jaymes, eight and Joshua, seven

A frightening thought

It's completely normal for kids to feel fear or to worry about things, sometimes to an exaggerated degree – it's all part and parcel of normal development and a completely natural part of our emotional make-up as humans. It can even be good for them because once they've felt fear they can learn ways of coping with it, and then they can use these coping strategies in the future. They tend to feel fear more often, and more intensely than adults, because they can't reason and rationalise so well, and because they have active imaginations!

Fears vary throughout different stages of childhood. Common fears in children up to the age of six include strangers, animals, loud or sudden noises, being left alone, water, the dark, monsters and ghosts, the toilet, dogs, spiders, storms and balloons. Beyond six, their thinking becomes more rational and they fear things like imaginary creatures less but may have more 'real' worries such as school, death or injury and failure.

Why worry?

Whilst sometimes irrational, specific childhood fears can also be triggered by bad experiences – being bitten or barked at by a dog, for example, might lead to a general fear of dogs.

And there's another explanation: children often pick up the same fears and anxieties that their parents have.

Fears in childhood are almost always temporary and in most cases, won't be a major cause for alarm and will go away, eventually, of their own accord. But neither should they be underestimated: if a child is frightened of something, however irrational, they have a very genuine need for your help and support so that they can overcome it.

The Problem Shared

What the Netmums say

My eldest had a panic attack during dinner one day, which was really scary as I thought she was choking. When she'd calmed down, she sat on my lap and told me that she'd developed this fear (but had kept it inside) over the last couple of months, after hearing me talk about a little girl who died choking on a cocktail sausage. I'd told all four girls one dinner time because I wanted Naomi to eat more slowly, but Becks had really taken it to heart. I felt terrible!

I explained to her that it was an incredibly rare thing to have happened and the fact that it had been reported proved that. And I phoned the doctor for advice – he told me that as long as she was eating something, to let it take its natural course. She had another couple of panic attacks at school over the following weeks at lunchtime and once in a morning assembly, but she's heaps better than she was. My worry now is that it turns into some kind of eating disorder, so I'm trying not to make a major issue out of it.

Rachel from West Sussex, mum to Rebecca, nine, Naomi, eight, Sophie, six and Charlotte, four

Mollie absolutely hates the dark. We tried letting her have a nightlight but that didn't seem to help matters so now we tend to just leave her light on until we go to bed, when we'll switch it off. If she wakes, we have to go through the whole thing again.

Mary from Bristol, mum to Mollie, five and Connie, two

Ever since he had a nightmare about Fireman Sam's helicopter, Jack has had a kind of love/hate relationship with them. He clings to me if he hears one and I have to make sure that his bedroom door is shut tight at night to stop them from coming in. Yet, when he saved up his pocket money, he chose to buy a toy Fireman Sam's helicopter!

He also has a fear of cars, which is worrying. We saw a girl get hit by a tram in Blackpool. She was OK, but it was obviously traumatic, and Jack has been scared of cars ever since. He keeps asking what it feels like to be hit by a car, what it sounds like to be hit by one, and he's very scared in car parks. His sleep has been awful lately because of his nightmares.

We're just answering his questions, reminding him it's very rare to be hit by a car, and trying to change the subject. I'm hoping he will gradually forget it.

Jen from Chorleywood, mum to Jack, three and Theo, four months

My eldest daughter developed a big phobia of bees and wasps at the age of about five which she still has. Picnics and outdoor eating became a nightmare, with her often just up and running if anything should fly by her. She still reacts in an extreme way to wasps. I have a similar phobia, but manage to control it a little more and wonder if I've somehow transferred my fears to her by my past actions.

Sindy from Severen Beach, mum to Amelia, 15, Star, two and Talitha, three weeks

Bradley is scared of lions, although I have absolutely no idea why! I might be in the kitchen making dinner and he'll run at the safety gate and try to jump over it, saying that the lions are getting him. Sometimes he'll panic, and refuse to move because of it, or he might cry and say it's going to get him. He's also woken up from dreams, saying that 'the lions put water in his eyes'.

To be honest, we just humoured him. We discovered a soft toy lion on the wardrobe and wondered if that was what had scared him, so we made a big thing out of throwing it in the bin. He's been fine since then.

Kerrie from Brighton, mum to Bradley, three

Sam's always been really sensitive to noise and hates going into loud situations that he has no control over. When he started school, he was really scared of playtime, although it no longer holds any fear for him now, thankfully. But he still hates things like the vacuum cleaner, and fireworks, and sits with his hands over his ears. We've since found out he might be dyspraxic, and sensitivity to loud sounds is a factor in that.

When he was small we either avoided the noises or made it fun for him. Thanks to the *Teletubbies* and their noo-noo, the vacuum wasn't so scary. And as he's got older we've listened to his fears and explained how noise can't hurt him. Noises at night are made into a game – we get him to listen carefully for different sounds, so that he doesn't feel overwhelmed by the noise as a whole.

We've tried to desensitise him to fireworks, but not made a big deal if he wanted to stay under the kitchen table and last year he actually went outside to watch the last big rocket go up, so he's getting there!

We've listened carefully to why he's scared, and tried our best to reassure him. We've not gone out of our way to avoid noisy situations as I think that would have just prolonged any problem and luckily that seems to have worked. Shame he's not scared of his own noise!
Donna from Rotherham, mum to Samuel, six and Emma, four

This sounds silly, but Joey has a fear of warm or hot food. Even if it's just slightly warm, he gets upset. I think it probably stems back to when we went out for dinner once, when he was about 18 months old, and we ordered him a child's lasagne. He put some in his mouth and it was really hot and he got very upset. For a while his food had to be stone cold before he'd touch it, so we'd have to put it next to the window before serving it. We also taught him to blow on it to cool it down – these days he will eat food warm, but only if he's cooled it down by blowing on it first!
Ellie from Pembroke Dock, mum to Joey, two and Grace, nine months

Jack was having bad dreams about a red dragon and a dinosaur chasing him so we gave him a 'magic wand' to put under his pillow because, as we all know, dragons and dinosaurs are scared of magic. The dreams stopped. Unfortunately we left it at my sister's so he had a night without it and was in our bedroom at 3.30 a.m., crying because the dragon was back. We had to borrow another 'wand' from Toby until his other one could be sent back.

I think it's important not to show a child that any fear or phobia they have is silly or not real, because it *is* to them. I go along with whatever's bothering them and find that a bit 'magic' can work wonders.
Leigh from Manchester, mum to Jack, four and foster mum to Toby, 12

Alex suddenly developed a fear of the vacuum cleaner. It never used to bother him, and he's always been the kind of child who laughs at scary things. However, one day I went to vacuum his room when he was in the cot and he had an absolute screaming fit. It happened every time I vacuumed after that, and then it evolved into him screaming every time he even so much as saw the vacuum cleaner. I started leaving it on the landing and letting him 'investigate' it himself. He'd click the button on and off when it wasn't plugged in. Then I moved to vacuuming with him in the room, but would talk him through what was happening, for instance: 'Mummy's going to turn it on now. It will make a big noise, but it can't hurt you.' He was still very fearful, but at least he was no longer screaming! Then one day I got my husband to be in the room and I made a game of it, getting the nozzle and pretending to suck daddy up the vacuum cleaner, which Alex thought was hilarious! After doing this a couple of times, he even started holding his hand out so he could be sucked up too.

Now, he's happy enough to be in the room when I am vacuuming, and although he's still a bit wary of the noise he still likes to be 'sucked up' by the nozzle, and loves it when daddy is! Maybe it was a little bit cruel, but I felt it was better to re-introduce him slowly than to keep him away from it and compound the fear.

Tracey from Teesside, mum to Alexander, two

The Problem Solved

Tackling terror

Always acknowledge a child who is scared. Don't dismiss or tease, however daft their fear may seem to you as a rational adult. Give them comfort, and humour them, whenever necessary. It's important to talk to a child about what's worrying them, and help them put it into perspective and see reason.

If there's a simple solution to a pressing worry – leaving a nightlight on, for example, if they are scared of the dark, or taking a different route to the park if it means avoiding the house with the very noisy dog, then make use of it. Fearful children aren't being 'soft' or oversensitive. They're just going through a very normal phase of childhood.

Most fears slip away on their own. But sometimes fears can worsen with time so it's always worth keeping an eye on them. And if a fear is presenting a real problem or beginning to affect them practically – for example, if they've become so afraid of water they will no longer get in the bath – they may need help in overcoming it permanently. In that case, you could try a little 'gradual desensitisation'. This means taking little steps towards confronting their fear, until they reach a point where they are no longer sensitive to it. So you might present a child who's too scared to get in the bath with a few inches of bubbly water to dip their toes in, and increase the volume of water bit by bit over time. If dogs bother them, you could start by looking at some in a picture book or DVD, before introducing them to a real one, who you know is extremely docile.

Keep fear at bay

Some things are very obvious sources of fear for children – scary movies, or frightening fiction for example. Avoid them if you know they're likely to cause nightmares. And where necessary, help them understand that they have nothing to fear from what's not real. Horrifying headlines from real life, on the other hand, can't be explained away as fantasy. Of course, you can't shelter children completely from the realities of the news, and you should certainly answer questions truthfully if they ask, but it's worth trying to limit their exposure to it. And since children might not be able to put the doom and gloom of news headlines into perspective, they'll need some help in understanding that life is not nearly as terrifying as it may seem.

Don't keep your fears in the family

Fear is by no means confined to childhood – lots of adults have anxieties too. And it's very common for us to pass them on to our children, often in spite of our best efforts not to. Children are very perceptive and, even if it's not obvious, they may pick up on your body language if you so much as bristle when a spider scuttles across the floor. As far as we possibly can, we need to do our best not to show it if we don't want our children to inherit the very same fears. If you struggle with a fear or phobia, it may be a good time to seek professional help in overcoming it – there are lots of techniques which can be very effective: for instance, exposing yourself to the feared thing gradually, rationalising your thoughts about the frightening thing and learning to relax in its presence.

What the experts say

The child psychologist

It's very normal for children to have all sorts of fears. And these fears differ as the child grows up and thinks about different things. When they are very little it tends to be fear of separation and unpredictable noises. Then just before they go to school they tend to be worried about strangers and animals (and sometimes separation, still). As they approach eight they'll get more anxious about monsters, the dark, and dying, and will be quite superstitious. This is the age of 'magical thinking' when children believe that they might actually be able to influence their fate by not walking on the cracks in the pavement! And as they get older, then anxieties tend to be based around friendships, doing well at things, and death or losing someone they love.

Adults are very good at finding ways of overcoming their anxieties. They set themselves little routines and have 'safety behaviours', which are the things that we do to make us feel safe – if you're scared of heights you will try to avoid being high up, or you'll do things such as not walking to the side of the cliff, or not looking though a window or gripping very tightly to someone's hand to make you feel better. And of course, we can also have a stiff drink if we want to! Children don't have the control or choice to do these things. And they don't have the brain capacity to work out what it is they're worried about, and talk themselves out of it. But it's also a developmental stage for them. There's something dramatic and enlivening about intense feelings and children can find them quite exciting, in a way. This isn't to say that all of these feelings are particularly pleasant. But it's one way that they can learn and grow.

Recent research suggests that one of the strongest predictors of anxiety in a child is whether their main caregiver is also anxious. There's a genetic as well as an environmental component to this – basically you're born with a predisposition to getting more anxious than others, but also by being brought up by someone who is constantly thinking about dangers and risks then the child will also be thinking in this way.

For some children, having a horrible experience can of course cause intense anxiety. Otherwise, children will have the 'normal' range of anxiety throughout their lives.

Bad news and scary films will tend to worry those who are worriers anyway, so maybe it's worth protecting these children from too much adverse media – it can be hard finding the right balance between exposing them to the news to allow them to ask questions and digest the information that sometimes bad things happen but people cope, and showing them so much that they overload their brain and feel really overwhelmed and frightened. Keeping an eye on the kind of things they are watching or reading to make sure they're age-appropriate, and being approachable so that the child can ask you if they are worried about something are the main things. But this all depends on your ability as a parent to reassure the child sincerely. If you're anxious yourself this is harder to do. Hence there can be a cycle of anxious kids, anxious parents.

It's important to acknowledge their fears; to talk about them, and to keep asserting the message that these fears are normal, but not necessarily realistic. A child needs to know that you, as their parent, think that they are safe. Information can help reduce anxiety by providing a rational argument against their emotional reaction. But you need to make sure this is provided in a child-friendly way and know when to stop if they signal to you that they've had enough information – too much, and they may end up processing none of it because they've got into a bit of a panic about it all. If a fear develops into a phobia and is seriously affecting a child's functioning, or family life, then you should think about seeking some professional help. This could be through a school nurse or counsellor, or by referral through your GP to the local Child and Adolescent Mental Health Service, or CAMHS – the section of the NHS that exists to help children with any sort of psychological or psychiatric issue.

Dr Angharad Rudkin

The Problem Summarised

- Fears and anxieties are a very normal part of growing up.
- They tend to vary with age and usually disappear on their own eventually.
- They may be completely irrational, that is, there's no apparent reason for them.
- Or a nearby grown-up may have passed them on. If you fear something, or if you are an anxious person generally, don't show it.
- And sometimes they're triggered by a specific incident.
- Always acknowledge a child's fears. They're real to them.
- To overcome a problematic fear, try gently exposing them to it.

Give me strength: What to do if they're being bullied

The Problem

It's hard to know what bullied children should do. My daughter was bullied at primary school, and at first her teacher and I told her to ignore the bullies, which she did. But they just carried on.

Now, I think that victims of bullying should fight back. Teachers and parents can only do so much. It's up to the child to protect itself, especially if their teacher is aware of a situation, but doesn't deal with it. The child has the right to defend itself, and should.

Christine from Kettering, mum to Holly, 12, Chloe, ten and Jack, eight

A big, bad problem

Bullying's been around forever, but it's widely feared to have reached epidemic proportions these days. Figures from Childline, the NSPCC-run telephone counselling service for children, give an indication of how bad things have got: more than 37,000 UK children a year call seeking help because they're being bullied. To put this figure in context, the total population of 0–16-year-olds in the UK in 2005 was 12.4

million (Office for National Statistics). And Kidscape, the child safety charity, estimates that around 60 per cent of children have experienced the problem at some time or other. But those figures only relate to the reported incidents. There could be many others who have suffered in silence.

Professor Al Aynsley-Green, who was appointed Children's Commissioner for England in 2005, believes bullying is one of the most significant issues facing children today, and has said that he blames our wider society, with its culture of violence, for the fact that it is so widespread now. Technology is also thought to have contributed significantly, with mobile phones and the internet making it an insidious problem that, for the victims, means there is no escape.

Pick on someone your own size

A child who's being persistently bullied may suffer in a number of ways. Their self-esteem and confidence takes a battering, their eating and sleeping habits and general health may be affected and their schoolwork go downhill. They may be withdrawn, depressed and begin to have behavioural problems themselves.

It can be devastating to find that your child is being bullied, often compounded by frustration and anger when you struggle to get the situation resolved. With the problem as rife as it is, it makes good sense for all parents to be armed with some basic bully-busting guidelines.

The Problem Shared

What the Netmums say

My daughter was bullied by a boy at primary school and it went on for several years. She was chubby then, and he called her names. He also punched her in the face once. The school weren't much help, to be honest. Her class teacher dealt with the problems really well but when she moved up a year, the new one was less supportive. I did see the head a number of times and even threatened to remove my daughter from school. I was really worried about the effect it was having on Lauren. At one point, she even said she didn't want to be alive anymore.

Thankfully the bully went to a different secondary school. Lauren sees him around from time to time and he still calls her fat, even though she's slim now. But it doesn't bother her anymore – she can fire off a quick comment back to him now.

Sharon from St Helens, mum to Lauren, 15 and Robert, two

Luca was bullied at school for almost a year by a rather boisterous classmate who was twice his size. He'd come home with huge bruises on his legs, chest, ribs and arms. We encouraged him to talk to the teacher, but it fell on deaf ears. Then one day he came home with the bruised ribs. We rang the headteacher, and she spoke to my son and the bully. She rang back and said the boy had promised not to do it again, but the following day, our son came home with a huge bruise on his shin. My hubby went straight to the head with my son. The boy lost a week's playtime, and my son now avoids him where possible.

I can't think of anything worse, than to go to school and be physically abused by someone in that way. The boy's parents obviously didn't see a problem in his behaviour. It's truly shocking. Teachers need to nip it all in the bud sooner.

Susan from Bradford, mum to Luca, five, Leo, three and Poppy, 18 months

My daughter has been bullied at school for more than a year and the school don't seem to be doing anything about it. The child who's responsible has bullied other children in the past, and the school is aware, but it seems they don't want to admit they have a problem.

She didn't tell us for about three months that she was being bullied as her nan had just died and her granddad was terminally ill, and she felt we had enough to deal with. She finally told us after the child had made jokes about her nan dying. He'd also punched her, spat at her, kicked her, shut a drawer on her hand, and smacked her on the head with a stick.

I've spoken to her teachers and they agreed to try and keep a look out, but the bullying's still going on. My daughter hit him back the other day, and even though I don't like the thought of her hitting another child, I can see why she did it. I think that schools need to take more action when it comes to dealing with bullies.

Emma from Swindon, mum to Bethany, seven, Robbie, two and stepmum to Owen, 18

It was heartbreaking when Sam was bullied in his first year at school. It was hard enough sending him to school for the first time without the thought of him getting hurt while he was there. It got to the stage where every day he'd be coming out of school with a new bruise. Annoyingly, when we went to speak to the teacher, she said she didn't want to label any child as a 'bully', although she did admit this boy was lashing out daily. To me, that's bullying. She said that Sam was the focus of this child's anger because he's so friendly, and kept going back to make friends. The boy who was hitting Sam did have other educational and behavioural problems too, but you can only be so understanding. When Sam started not wanting to go to school, we felt enough was enough and told him to stand up to the boy. He was too scared to, as he thought he'd get into trouble. Then we told him to stay away from the boy completely and we told the teacher this too. We also warned her that if it continued, we couldn't tell Sam *not* to hit back, and that we'd be keeping a list of every incident Sam told us about.

It turned out that the child was mainly attacking Sam and other children during the dinner hour, so he was eventually excluded from school at lunchtime. Thankfully it's now settled down and they're actually friends now.

Donna from Rotherham, mum to Sam, five and Emma, three

Mollie got bullied in her last year at pre-school. It started when she befriended another girl, and this girl's best friend wasn't happy about it. She told my daughter not to go near her and pinched, slapped and pushed her. As soon as I found out, I confronted the pre-school staff and demanded to know what was being done to curb the problem. I had weekly meetings with the nursery head and was given a full incident sheet every week. Although I don't think the situation went away completely, it was brought under control.

Mary from Bristol, mum to Mollie, five and Connie, two

We have a success story. My son transferred to a new school in Year 3 and was verbally bullied by another boy there. This boy had been bullying other children in the school, including two that I knew about (one had been removed from the school by their parents). I spoke to the teacher and left it with her to sort out, but the bullying got worse. My son didn't want to get up for school and we often ended up arriving late. Finally I rang the school and asked for an appointment with the head. We had a meeting that afternoon.

My son was believed without question, and was given the opportunity to talk about his feelings about the behaviour of the other boy. The school provided someone to work on confidence building with my son. It worked. We don't know what they did with the bully, but he got help too. They are now coming to the end of Year 4 and the two boys are the best of friends! So there's always hope.

Mandy from Buckingham, mum to Joseph, nine and Dominic, six

I was bullied at school 16 years ago, and I can't believe that in all that time no one has managed to come up with a system that proactively deals with bullying and stops it. The trouble is that there is still this mentality that it's almost a 'rite of passage', that it's just part of everyday school life. Schools seem to get terribly embarrassed by the mere suggestion that they have a bullying issue and are unwillingly to take a stand. I think there should be tough punishments for bullying someone. It's my biggest fear for Sam, that he'll be bullied. I know from my own experience that the pain doesn't stop as soon as you leave the school yard for the last time.

Chelle from Poole, mum to Sam, one

The Problem Solved

Keeping an eye out for the signs

It's not always obvious when a child is being bullied as, in many cases, they won't want to admit to it because they are embarrassed, or fearful of the repercussions. Usually, though, there will be little indications that all is not well – changes in their behaviour or eating patterns, for example. You can read more about these in the factfile, p. 338.

Once you've managed to get the truth out of them, be careful not to promise you'll keep quiet about it – you'll need to take action, so tell them so. But reassure them you'll get it sorted out.

How to 'bully-proof' your child

Some children are more pre-disposed to being picked on than others, perhaps because they are smaller or less confident than others, or because there is something about them that's slightly different, but most fall into a bully's path by being in the wrong place at the wrong time. Often, they are children who belong to a loving family and have been taught to be nice to everyone.

Sadly, bullied children commonly find themselves locked into a cycle. If a 'victim mentality' sets in, they lose confidence and then they become a target for continued bullying.

Experts agree that one of the best things you can do for a child who's being bullied is to help them deal with the problem by themselves, by boosting their confidence and courage. Bullies only really operate when they're sure they'll have the upper hand, and they're unlikely to come back to someone who stands up for himself.

First though, be sure to find out exactly what it is they're being bullied about. It well may be something you can help them to change – a habit such as nosepicking, for example.

Strength in numbers

Sometimes, ignoring a bully can work. Bullies love a reaction and if they don't get one, chances are they'll give up. Another piece of good advice to give them is just to keep out of the bully's way: tell them to avoid being alone or in places where you know they'll be, and stick with a group whenever possible.

It's common for victims of bullying to become withdrawn, so help them to be sociable and to focus on the good friendships they have, which can be a great source of strength when the going gets tough.

Make sure yours is a home where they feel confident about talking: let them know they can tell you anything so that if they need to, they will. And it's worth talking about bullying even when it's not specifically affecting them. Bullies feed off the approval of their peers, so make sure your kids know that it's not acceptable. Encourage them to stand up for someone who's being bullied, or to give them support whenever possible.

Just say NO!

You can help a bullied child defend itself by arming them with the right attitude and language. Help them devise some non-aggressive one-liners to keep up their sleeves. They don't have to say anything particularly clever – the way it's delivered is more important. For example: 'I may be short-sighted, but at least I'm not mean!' And if nothing more eloquent comes to mind, they could try what Kidscape suggests and loudly repeat the word 'no'. You can help them practise at home using role play, re-enacting certain scenarios to help them work out how and what they're going to do and say if they need to.

Body language is all important: encourage them to stand tall and make eye contact when they're facing a bully. But don't advocate an aggressive response. Two wrongs don't make a right, and besides, they may end up in trouble themselves.

School rules

Schools have a duty of care to their pupils and these days, they are all required to have an anti-bullying policy. Be firm in wanting action, but don't put the onus entirely on the school – see it as something you have equal responsibility for sorting out. As ever, keep calm and remain civil: you're more likely to get the help you're looking for. And be positive about any solutions they put forward, even if you don't think they will help much.

While some schools boast a 'zero tolerance' line on bullying, many prefer to take a 'no-blame' approach. It can be hard to accept this if you know that another pupil is making your child's life a misery, but unless you're prepared to remove them from school, you'll have to go along with school policy. The truth is that the majority of bullies act the way they do because they are themselves unhappy. They will quite possibly – although by no means necessarily – come from a home where parental love or guidance is lacking, or there may even be violence. This doesn't excuse their behaviour, but it does go some way to explaining it.

Talk to their class teacher first and go to the head if necessary. Find out what the school's anti-bullying policy involves. Put your concerns in writing. Request a meeting and ask for an investigation – make a follow-up appointment a week later to find out the results. If the bullying continues, keep a careful note of what happened, when, in a diary.

If bullying goes on over a long period of time or involves incidents such as theft, serious physical assault or has a racial or sexual element, and you don't get the help you need from school staff, take the matter further by writing to the school governors, local education authority, your local MP, or if necessary, the police. If things get very bad and your child is very unhappy, you may want to consider a change of school.

You cannot simply withdraw a child from a school, though: you must put it in writing and by law you're required to see they are educated so you'll need to get them into another school or teach them yourself in the meantime. Some time away from school may help them to get back on their feet, but you can't just keep them off for long periods of time because they're being bullied – it would be considered an 'unauthorised absence'. A sympathetic GP may provide a sick note if they feel it would be beneficial.

What if *your* child is the bully?

If you find out it's your child who's the bully, try to stay calm and deal with the situation without anger, however furious you may feel. Piece together the truth by talking to everyone involved, and by asking for your child's take on the situation. Reassure them that you love them, even if you aren't pleased about their behaviour. Bullies are often unhappy about some aspect of life, so if something's troubling them, you'll need to establish what – if they're coping with a difficult time of life such as a divorce in the family, it gives them a reason (if not an excuse) for taking their troubles out on someone else and you'll need to take that into account. If it's a one-off incident, be lenient. But if they're repeating the behaviour, you need to be involved in making it stop by issuing whatever 'consequences' you deem appropriate. More importantly, help them to empathise with their victim and to understand why bullying is wrong by talking the situation through. And encourage them to make amends to whomever they've bullied by apologising, and trying their best to be friends.

As with everything else, the messages we pass on in everyday life are vital. If it's possible your children ever see you, or other influential adults, in the act of bullying someone else, remember that you can't expect better from them. Aim to get across the message, at every opportunity, that violence is never acceptable.

What the experts say

The anti-bullying campaigner

Unfortunately bullying is more widespread than ever. I think this is partly because children don't have many good role models anymore, and it's considered cool to be cruel. Also, technology means there are better means of bullying each other – you can get at people pretty much constantly whereas before it could only ever have been at school or in the street, perhaps.

It's pretty devastating being bullied. At its most extreme, it can cause victims to feel suicidal, with everyone disagreeing about the best way to handle things. Some of the parents who come on our courses say that they have almost come to divorce over the stress. Because in 99 per cent of cases the bullying is not their child's fault, the guilt and anger over this unfair situation leads to all kinds of blow-ups and tears. Of course, if the school does nothing or, worse, blames the victim, the resulting angst exacerbates everything.

If you suspect your child is being bullied ask them directly what's happening. Agree on a course of action with them. If it's happening at school, you have to let the staff there know in some way. Talk to a teacher you trust, and ask to see the school's anti-bullying policy. If the incidents are happening regularly, keep a written diary of what's said or done, and when. Most cases *should* be fairly simple to sort out. But sometimes schools can be defensive, and reluctant to admit that bullying is going on. Don't be put off if you don't get the support you're looking for straight away, keep putting pressure on until the situation is resolved. And be prepared to take strong action if need be. If you have to take your child out of a school, then you must. Whatever you do, if your child is really distressed, don't leave them in an untenable situation. Unfortunately, some children have committed suicide because they could not cope, so better safe than sorry.

Most importantly, encourage your child not to think like a victim – urge them to pretend they are confident and strong when facing a bully, even if they're quaking inside. A child that's being bullied will need a huge amount of emotional support. Keep telling them you love them, and that you're on their side, and reassure them that the bullying is not their fault.

Michele Elliott, Kidscape Director (www.kidscape.org.uk)

The child psychologist

It's natural to feel angry and emotional if you find out your child is being bullied, but it's important to stay calm. Anyone can get themselves out of a bullying situation with effort, time and support, and children who've dealt successfully with bullies when younger develop a good set of skills to use throughout their lives when dealing with potential bullying situations in the future. As a parent you need to let them develop these skills whilst keeping a watchful eye on their well-being. Don't rely on the school – if that's where the bullying is taking place – but take control yourself. Encourage your child to stand up to a bully. Not by physically hitting back, because they could end up in trouble themselves, but by standing tall and using assertive language. Use role play to practise going through what they will say or do when the bullies next approach. Approaching the bully's parents might help if you know them and you think you'll get a calm reaction, but it's probably best avoided as there's a good chance they'll be on the defensive.

It's true that some children are more susceptible to bullying.

Often bullying starts because someone's a bit different, but how a child copes with that is down to their own self-confidence and it can end up being a vicious circle – if a child start to believe they're fat, or stupid, the bullies can see they've exposed a weakness and may keep on bullying. Getting a reaction is the biggest feeder of a bully, so if a child is one of those who wear their hearts on their sleeve then, sadly, the bully will come back for more because they can see they are having an effect (a desire we all have, but thankfully most of us can get it from being nice to people rather than nasty!)

If you find out that *your* child has been bullying, remember that they'll need help and support, too. If they're bullying it will usually mean that they're unhappy about something themselves so you'll need to work out what. Or it may be that they've got in with a peer group and got strung along. It's also worth remembering that bullying can be just an experimental phase youngsters go through. Calmly get their side of the story and talk things through, perhaps involving their teachers. Bullying is unacceptable though, and children who do it should experience the consequences of their actions.

Dr Angharard Rudkin

The Problem Summarised

- Bullying is an increasingly widespread problem, so if your child is affected, they are not alone.
- Bullying can cause serious misery, short and long term, for victims, and much concern for their parents.
- Some kids are more susceptible to bullying, but anyone can be bullied.
- The best thing you can do to help a bullied child is to teach them ways of standing up for themselves.
- Be sensitive for signs that they're being bullied. They may not tell you it's happening.

Factfile: Is your child being bullied? Key signs to watch for

- They come home with cuts, bruises or torn clothing. Their possessions or money have disappeared. They are unusually moody or withdrawn, or are picking fights at home.
- The standard of their schoolwork drops or they can't concentrate on homework.
- They seem reluctant to go to school, don't want you to leave them there or feign illness.
- They're off their food.
- They aren't sleeping well, or are having nightmares.
- They're withdrawn and lacking in confidence.
- They are tearful for no apparent reason.
- They don't want to talk about reasons for any of the above, or give unlikely explanations.

Confidence tricks: How to help a shy child out of their shell

The Problem

My daughter has been extremely shy since she was very little. She'll only put her hand up in class to answer a question, and as soon as the teacher asks her to answer she puts her hand down and whispers the answer to her best friend! I've enrolled her in lots of different groups and classes to try to help her come out of her shell, but to no avail. I try not to let it worry me, but there are times when I cry because I really don't know how else to help her become more confident with others. What makes it worse is that my other daughter is a total opposite. I'm sure that Ceddina often wishes she could be more like her sister.

Amanda from Selby, mum to Ceddina, seven, Arianna, one and Xander, four months

Come out from under there!

Shyness is a very normal characteristic of early childhood – after all, the world's a big place when you're small. For some, shyness will be shed as they grow older and gain confidence. For others it will remain a long-term trait, right into adulthood.

Shyness may be caused by a combination of factors but commonly it will have been passed on to a child by their parents. As with most of these things, no one's sure whether that's genetic or by example, or a bit of both. It may also be shaped by other sorts of parental attitudes – where they are over-protective, for example – and other family relationships, such as those with domineering siblings.

A drawback in life?

Parents of a shy child may worry that it will affect their ability to socialise, their performance at school, and even their chances of getting on in life – particularly if they are shy themselves and they know from experience the drawbacks it can have. There are lots of ways that you can gently support a child who's shy. But the first piece of advice to take on board is to put the issue into perspective: there are many worse things that a child could be! Shyness isn't a defect or flaw that must be eradicated. It is a character-istic, which, if they don't grow out of it early on, they will need a little help in coping with.

The Problem Shared

What the Netmums say

We've been worried about Jack's shyness. Both my husband and I suffered from shyness as children, and were keen to instil as much confidence in our son as possible. We always took him out to new places, encouraged him to talk to people, and he's been at nursery part-time since I went back to work when he was six months old. Despite all this, he's still very shy in situations he's not used to – for example, at nursery he'll refuse to do anything new, and he doesn't like to go into a shop he's never been in before. He moved to upper pre-school recently and after a few weeks it became clear he wasn't joining in with any of the structured play or any of the adult-led activities such as yoga, cooking, French and music. After a few weeks, I sat down and had a chat with him and he said he'd rather just put his head down and not look at the teacher instead of joining in. I spoke to the staff at nursery, and they said that, as he'd just had a baby brother, they didn't want to push him.

I asked him if he'd join in for a sticker, and he was keen, so I spoke to the nursery and they drew up a sticker chart. So far, it's worked a treat. On the first day he got a sticker for answering his name at register time (I hadn't realised it was that bad!) and they made a real fuss of him. A few weeks later, he's doing everything and elsewhere the change has been amazing. He chats to my friends, will pay for things in shops, and is just more confident in every way.

Jen from Chorleywood, mum to Jack, three and Theo, four months

Ava is shy. She won't join in with the children at nursery and always wants to be with an adult for security. At toddler group, she wants me to play with her and won't go and find toys on her own.

If someone talks to her she'll hide behind me and won't look at them. At home, she has loads of confidence and is really loud. I think she's just a person who likes to stand back and check out a situation before she dives in head first. She's cautious and wouldn't want to be in a situation she didn't like so she won't try it, just in case.

I've been taking her to more groups and encouraging her to interact, and we've also had children round to play. She's more confident in her own home. I think she feels more in control. Perhaps she'll always be this way to some extent, but as long as it doesn't hold her back then it's not too much of a problem. I'd hate to see her with no friends because she's too shy to make them. But we give her loads of praise and tell her how great she is if she does something on her own or talks to someone new, so hopefully she'll get better as she gets older. She isn't quite three yet, after all!

Kate from Bexhill, mum to Ava, two and Elsa, six months

Being shy has been a constant battle for me my whole life. So I try and take Daisy to as many places as possible, and encourage her to

join in with everything. This invariably means I have to join in too, but I force myself to do it for her sake. I hope that she'll be outgoing and bold, which most of the time she seems to be. I think a big part of being shy is down to personality. I just don't want her to be too nervous to walk into a shop half the time in case someone looks at her, like I am.
Katherine from Nottingham, mum to Daisy, two

My second boy is boisterous at home and loves playing with his brother but a year after starting he's still reticent about going to nursery two days a week. We no longer go to music class or Tumble Tots as it became a waste of money – he just wouldn't join in. He's the complete opposite of his brother, who's articulate and sociable. But then, why should he bother to make friends when he has ready-made entertainment at home in the form of an older brother?

Last week I was speaking to a GP friend about how it worries me, and she said that he's just a one-to-one person who takes a while to warm to people. I'm trying not to worry. Why should I try to shape him into someone that I (and society) think is the best model? People react badly when they speak to him and he hides or scowls – I can see a marked difference in the way people respond to him than how they were with his brother who would giggle or chat or grin. Maybe I should stop apologising for his shyness and reluctance to join in. It's not a problem for us!
Paula from London, mum to Thomas, five and Gabriel, two

Shyness is nothing to be ashamed of. Have you considered what a strange place our adult world can be for kids? Everything is so new and daunting, and they're surrounded by adults telling them what to do the majority of the time! My little girl is shy but it's OK, I know it will come. She has other fantastic qualities, and a great sense of humour. I don't want to become angst-ridden or try too hard on her behalf, because she'll pick up on it. I can remember everyone pointing out how shy I was when I was little, which just made things worse! What's the big hurry? They've got the rest of their lives to work on 'people skills'. My eldest was a bit shy as well, but has become a lot more confident since starting school. Give it time.
Sadie from Woking, mum to Eleanor, six and Eve, three

We enrolled Adam into a local drama group to build his confidence, and he's not as shy as he used to be. For the first few classes he cried, and didn't want us to leave, so we stayed with him, trying to coax him into joining in. Now he goes in alone quite happily and we've seen a difference, as have staff at his nursery. He's more likely to speak out now, and join other kids in play. He still takes a back seat, but I think that's just part of who he is. When he arrives at nursery he always has a ten minute sit-down, and looks around to see what's happening before doing anything. I think it's part of a person's personality, and that there's nothing wrong in being a bit shy.

Adelle from Glasgow, mum to Adam, four

At home, my son is outgoing, cheerful and very talkative, but as soon as he's with other people he clams up. He won't even talk to friends who've known him since he was little – some have never heard him utter a word!

Both my partner and I were very shy as children but are now socially quite confident so we both recognise how painful it can be, whilst realising that it can change with nurturing. I have painful early memories of first days at nursery. My son starts soon and I have to make sure I don't pass that feeling on and that I can help him see it as a positive and fun adventure.

I have seen tiny breakthroughs recently. I heard him talk to a friend of mine while I was out of the room so I only hope it's the shape of things to come. He's such a gorgeous little chap at home. I want other people to be able to enjoy his funny conversation and cheeky grins!

Corinna from Brighton, mum to Orlando, three

All three of my children are quiet, especially at school, where they hate putting hands up to answer questions or join in with discussions. My twins have always had problems with this, and teachers constantly tell me they want them to join in more. But you can't force this (as I know from experience, being shy myself). I think teachers could help more by drawing the shyer children into discussions without them realising. Jack is very boisterous at home and anywhere he feels safe, but was quiet at nursery and to begin with at school where he would watch and weigh things up before joining in. Recently, to increase his confidence, he's been taken out of class for 'circle time', where a small group have got together and played and done activities and games. It really seems to have worked for Jack, and he's now much more confident in school. He'll never be the life and soul of the party, but hopefully he'll keep his newly gained confidence and build upon it. I hope so, as I know how disabling shyness can be.

Jenny from Northampton, mum to twins Adam and Kayleigh, 12 and Jack, five

The Problem Solved

Like parent, like child

As ever, example is everything. Our kids absorb the messages we put out like sponges, so if one or both parents are shy, slightly anxious or lacking in confidence, there's every chance they'll have a child who is, too.

We need to demonstrate social confidence to our children if we want them to be socially confident. If you've always lived with shyness, having young kids can be a great reason to tackle it – it's hard to avoid social situations when you're a mum, even if you wanted to, and conversation rarely dries up when other mums are around. Playgroups, parties and get-togethers are good opportunities for children to make strides into a social world, but they'll need some support from you at first, which means you're going to have to meet people and go places with them! So helping your child to come out of their shell may be just the thing you need to come out of yours a bit, too.

Social services

It's better to help shy children face up to their demons, not to hide from them, however tempting it may be to make life easier for them. Don't deliberately keep them away from social situations or try to 'protect them' from the big bad world! At the same time, never force or push a shy child into anything that's genuinely upsetting for them.

Take them to new places and try out new things. Shy children are usually happier on home territory, so it's a good idea to initially invite one or a small handful of friends round to your place for them to get to know before plunging them into a group situation. Before setting off for playgroup or any other gathering, give them plenty of warning about where you're going and who'll be there. Don't be dismayed if they seem overwhelmed when you arrive. Give them a little help in breaking the ice by instigating conversation or play with another child on their behalf. And don't forget to show them how it's done by making friends among the mums, too. When they're a bit older, structured activities or a class which will give them something to focus on alongside the possibility of making friends can be good. They may need gentle encouragement and support in getting over the hurdle of the first few sessions, though.

Doing what it says on the label

If there's one thing shy children don't need, it's being reminded of how shy they are. So avoid 'labelling' a shy child – it may compound the problem and make them feel even worse, causing anxiety and lowering their self-esteem.

It can be frustrating and embarrassing if a child refuses to respond to another adult's questions, or they stick to your side like a limpet at playgroup because they're too nervous to get stuck in. But don't hold it against them, and don't be influenced by adverse reactions from other people by trying to make excuses for them or forcing them into a response. Just change the subject, if you need to.

Let's hear it for shy kids

All kids need to be listened to, but shy kids particularly so. Give them time and space to be heard, especially if there's a lot of noise going on in your home. Be patient and empathetic. If you're shy yourself, you'll know how it feels. If not, you'll have to do your darnedest to put yourself in their shoes!

Encourage them to try little things, paying in shops, for example, or introducing themselves to a new friend and praise them lavishly when they do so. And don't forget to celebrate and focus on their other qualities. Being shy hasn't stopped a great many people achieving a great many things!

What the experts say

The child psychologist

Shyness is certainly a temperament trait that can be inherited from parents. We haven't figured out how much of it is genetic and how much is 'environmental', in other words, copied from our parents.

We're all used to seeing small children who are struck mute when faced with an adult they don't know well, or those who hide behind their parents' legs. This sort of behaviour will tend to diminish over their first few years at school. Usually what will happen is that shy children will find their feet somewhere along the line, often through a sport or activity which boosts their confidence and helps them to overcome their shy tendencies. So these children don't inevitably become shy adults at all.

Some children are confident and noisy at home and only shy in public or with people they don't know well. That's because we all feel home is familiar and at home there's also predictability – we know who's there, we know what usually happens and when. Parental examples can also be relevant: children who have slightly anxious parents may get a very clear message that there are risks 'out there'. And sometimes shyness occurs because a child is worried about negative evaluation by others and is overwhelmed by worry about being judged.

Simple shyness *can* hold back a child, though. For example, in the classroom, the shy child may not put their hand up to answer a question and therefore not come across as bright as their peers. They may be less likely to put themselves forward for new situations, joining the scouts or a dance class, for example, and therefore not develop the skills and miss out on the fun these sorts of activities provide. However, with the right kind of guidance from their parents, shy children can still make friends and enjoy activities that are perhaps less socially pressured.

You can do a lot of practical things to help gently encourage a shy child to be more outgoing. I'd suggest doing it very gradually, though, starting by inviting one friend over for half an hour at home, then moving to more friends, more time and then outside the home.

We all have hopes for our children based on our own regrets, so it can be a difficult thing for a shy parent to have a shy child. The thing to remember is that the majority of children will find their way through all of this with a bit of guidance and good mentors. If a mum is shy, then she could ask her partner, a family member or friend to help them both get out and try new things.

It's worth remembering that other characteristics sometimes get confused with shyness. Sometimes it's simple caution that causes a child to hang back – they may want to be certain about new people, places and situations and need a bit of time before they dive in, which is no bad thing. Or they may just be quiet and reflective types, who happen to prefer their own company.

It's very hard to know how much of a hindrance shyness can be in life. But I do think that what we make of our child's shyness is very important. For instance, if you accept it as a given and let the child go nowhere and do nothing (where you hear a parent say, 'Oh, they don't do that kind of thing because they're shy', for example) then you could be facilitating the shyness into a real barrier to life opportunities. Better to acknowledge that the child is shy – and therefore less likely to run head first into new, demanding social situations – and give them gentle support and encouragement to help them discover that these things may be enjoyable once they've tried them.

Finally, let's remember that shyness isn't necessarily a disadvantage. Shy children tend to be great observers and take a lot in. They give themselves more time to think about things and often become quite thoughtful people. And they will usually have great empathy for other shy people and will tend to go out of their way to help them – dependent on what extent they have overcome their own shyness!
Dr Angharad Rudkin

The Problem Summarised

- Shyness is a perfectly normal trait in childhood, which a child may or may not grow out of.
- Shy children are usually that way inclined because of family influences.
- It needn't be a major concern. But it may hold a child back socially, and

sometimes impacts on their progress at school. So shy kids may sometimes need a little help in overcoming their shyness.

◆ Set the right example by letting the child see you at ease in social situations.
◆ Avoid labelling a child as 'shy' – they may well fulfil the prophecy!
◆ Help them make friends and be at ease in social situations by gradually introducing them to a social life.

Living with loss: How to help a child cope with bereavement

The Problem

I was distraught when my dad died recently. I had to tell my daughters that their beloved Grampy had died and that they wouldn't see him again, and they both reacted very differently. Rosa refused to listen and has 'blanked' the subject ever since, even though she was very close to Grampy. If the subject does come up, her standard response is that she's 'tired' and wants some quiet time. Isabel was very open about her feelings, often telling me that she was feeling sad about Grampy, but putting him in the ground was a nice idea as he loved being in a garden, and we could plant flowers for him.

To be honest, I've found the reaction of my youngest much easier to deal with. We can have a cuddle and a cry when either of us feel the need, and she allows me to talk about him. Rosa I have found very difficult. I'm worried that she's afraid of showing emotion in front of me in case I cry. She was the one who looked after me, cuddling and comforting me when it was all happening, and I really think that she's worried about causing me more distress. I've suggested that she might talk to her daddy or teachers, but nothing so far.

Sarah from Woodstock, mum to Rosa, five and Isabel, three

Matters of life and death

Death is something that touches all of us, sooner or later, and the time will come when your kids need to know about it. A significant number of children will, sadly, have to cope with the trauma and sadness of bereavement. And even if they never have to face the loss of someone they're close to during their childhood, they'll inevitably hear about death from somewhere, and will probably want to ask questions about it. It's not a subject where the answers come easily. But we need to provide them, as best as we can.

Helping a child to grieve

The needs of children aren't always met when someone dies, perhaps because the adults around them may be grieving too, and because children often give the impression that they're doing OK. But children are affected by death just as profoundly as adults, even if they don't necessarily show it – they may appear more resilient because they tend to flit between feelings of sadness and normality. Kids can and do manage the death of someone important without any long-lasting problems, but only if they have lots of love, support and information to help them do so. Evidence shows that the majority of children who are helped during bereavement come through the experience without significant consequences.

The Problem Shared

What the Netmums say

I lost my son when he was two days old. While he was still alive, Holly came to visit, and we were honest with her all the way, using words she understood. She was with us in the hospital when Joshua died, and took it all in her stride. The nurses offered to take her away to play, but instead we asked her what she wanted to do. She wanted to cuddle her brother and say goodbye, sitting on a chair on her own as she was his 'big sister'. She told him to be a good boy and play nicely with Rusty, my aunt's dog that died. She was very upset that we were crying, so we reassured her that we were OK. She then asked to play with the toys in the parents' room!

So I believe in telling the truth. If someone explains any other way they will fill in the gaps themselves. I also believe it helps with the grieving process. They have to understand it's OK to be sad and upset, and can cry if they want to. She accepts Joshua has gone to heaven and has been to his grave, if only to play with the wind chimes in the tree.

Tina from Uxbridge, mum to Holly, five

We lost both my mother-in-law and father-in-law in a horrific road accident. My five-year-old daughter adored them and she's older than her years, so there was no option other than to tell her the truth. She knew there'd been an accident so when she asked how Mommar and Gang-gang were, I told her what had happened, and gave her big hugs and kisses.

At first there were a lot of tears and questions which I've always answered honestly. Whenever she cried I'd listen to her and hug her. Then I would bring up a happy memory of Mommar and Gang-gang, which would usually bring a smile back to her face.

Nearly eight months on she still wakes in the night, cries for them, and says how much she misses them. I've tried to keep it simple, but honest. We aren't religious but I've said Mommar and Gang-gang will be watching over her and wouldn't want her to be unhappy.

I don't think there's a right or wrong way to deal with bereavement in children. It's hard enough trying to deal your own grief and your partner's, whilst holding it all together for the kids. So far we all seem to be holding it together, becoming stronger, taking it one step at a time.

Kelly from Nottingham, mum to Katelynn, five and Jak, three

My mum died recently, completely unexpectedly. I didn't hide anything from my daughter – I was determined she wouldn't be excluded from this intense, emotional family period.

She came with me to see Nana in her coffin. I explained to her that Nana had died and that she would look like she was asleep, but that she was never going to wake up again. I wasn't mawkish about it, nor did I even mention anything about not being frightened, I just let her take it in her stride. Which she did, admirably.

I haven't hidden my tears from her and nor have I used sentimental or confusing language and euphemisms. I'm a Christian, but I think talk about heaven and angels is too big for little children to grasp. I haven't said things like 'We've lost Nana', or 'Nana's passed away'. I don't think they're helpful.

I took her to mum's funeral and explained it was like going to church, but not so much singing, and that the funeral was about saying goodbye to Nana's body. I also explained that just because Nana had died it didn't mean we couldn't love her any more and she found this very reassuring. I particularly didn't want her to be excluded from my mum's funeral as I recall my grandpa's death when I was seven and not being allowed to attend the funeral or memorial services. I was gutted, and felt that my love for my grandpa didn't matter at all.

Children shouldn't be excluded or 'protected' from this very normal part of life. They are almost definitely going to lose relatives, parents, and possibly friends at some stage and I think normalising this process is invaluable and strengthening for them.
Trish from London, mum to Alex, 17, Pip, four and Peter, one

My son lost his dad, my ex, to cancer, when he was nine. When the end was near, we took him to New Zealand, where his dad was living, to say goodbye.

We were very unsure whether to take him to see his dad's body before the cremation service, but eventually we decided to go (my current husband and Molly went, too). He put a tiny teddy bear in the coffin, and we tucked in a little letter we'd written together to say goodbye. We also took a couple of photos, which we have kept in case he wants to see them one day. (He's now nearly 14, and his memory of events has become pretty hazy, but I know there may come a time when he wants to revisit the experience.) We stayed for the funeral, obviously, and all did our best as a family to help him through a really sad and difficult time.

Grief is an ongoing process. There are many different ways to work through it, and each child or situation, I guess, will need to be handled a little differently. We talked very openly about everything that came up: heaven, cancer, spirits, cremation, coffins.

When we got back to the UK, I bought a special candle that we lit each month on the anniversary of his dad's death, and we'd always sit round it and chat. After a few months, his interest waned a bit, so we then mutually agreed to just light the candle on the anniversary of his dad's death each year.

But of course we still chat about his dad sometimes. It's just a part of our family history. Sam has a special Memory Box, in which he puts anything and everything to do with his dad, and I have a few other memories put away, which he can access when he wants.

Deb from Egham, mum to Sam, 13 and Molly, six

Before my dad died of cancer, I explained to the children that he wasn't well, and was very weak, and I encouraged them to give him gentle cuddles. While it was hard for them to see him like that, I felt it was important that they spent time with him and were as involved as much as possible. I made sure they came to the funeral and were a part of the whole thing, and before the funeral they were busy debating among themselves whether it was Grandpa that had gone to Heaven or just his soul. At the funeral they saw him in his casket and even kissed him good-bye. After the burial, they agreed among themselves that Grandpa's body was in the ground but that his soul, which is the bit that makes him, is in Heaven.

Sophia from Paisley, mum to Emily, five and Daniel, three

My mother died slowly, over six months, and was in much distress and pain at the end. I had no one else to look after my children during the daytime, so Henry, then two, witnessed almost everything.

He made lots of comments like, 'Grandma did shout a lot, and then she did die.' At the time we had to go with his level of understanding. Later, he asked why she couldn't get mended. Then he asked why the medicine didn't work, later still he asked why she 'did get cancer'. I think that Henry kept reprocessing the memories he had, but then his reasoning and understanding would advance with his age and he'd need an 'upgrade' on the last explanation he had been given.

After a year of intermittent 'upgrades' and painful reminders, such as, 'Mummy, have you got no Mummy now?' he settled on my explanation that Grandma had gone back to being a star. And I also explained that we leave our body behind. This was not because of a lack of religion, but for simplicity. I asked him which was better, to stay with us but be sad and in pain, or to go back to being a star, and he said being a star again was better. Hopefully when he's older still I can introduce some thoughts about heaven and so on, but for now I know he wouldn't understand why he couldn't visit her there!

Yvonne from Cheadle, mum to Henry, four and Oliver, two

In the space of one year, my children lost their grandmother and both their grandfathers. They must have thought our whole family was being wiped out. It's always so hard to know what to say to kids when someone dies. We've told them that when you die, you become a new star in the sky. So every time you look into the sky at night, the brightest star is someone who has just died. The other stars are all the grannies and granddads and other people that have died.

We visit the cemetery every month to put flowers on their graves, but we call these 'memory boxes', because when we go there, it's to tell and show our dead relatives that we still remember them. Although my kids did once get a bit puzzled when a television programme mentioned how to make a memory box, for your keepsakes!

I've tried to explain that people die, because their bodies can't work properly any more and the doctors can't mend them. The bodies close down and in the end the bones are put in a special box, but the person evaporates into stars.

Christine from Kettering, mum to Holly, 12, Chloe, ten and Jack, eight

The Problem Solved

Response to death

Children may respond in different ways to a death. Their age is relevant, as understanding of death generally increases as they get older. Very young children, under five or six, for example, find it hard to grasp the permanence of death, so they may need to be told many times to gain an understanding that a person who dies is *not* coming back. Other influencing factors on the way they react to a death include the relationship they had with the person who has died, how they died, the reaction of other family members and the effect it has on the family as a whole, and their own personality.

While a child may be upset about a death, it's also normal for them to show little outward grief. And they may hop quite suddenly from one emotion to the other. Initially, they may show shock and disbelief, and won't be able to take it all in. They may feel guilt – wondering if the death was somehow their fault. They may also feel anger, particularly if the death was sudden. And they may become very anxious that they will lose someone else they love, or that they will die, too. All these things are normal and will require plenty of reassurance.

There may well be other, wide-ranging consequences, including bedwetting, nightmares or trouble sleeping, a loss of appetite, bad behaviour, anxiety and clinginess, or problems with schoolwork. Bereaved children may suffer from a loss of confidence, or be depressed. Usually, these things will be temporary but they may go on for many months, or they may go only to reappear later.

Whatever the timescale, they'll need a huge amount of patient support to help them through and build their strength back up again. Most importantly, they must be allowed to react in whatever way they choose to, and express their feelings however they feel the need.

Physical touch can be very reassuring at times like this, so hug and kiss them as much as they'll let you.

Honesty is the best policy

People with experience in this area say that we should be open and honest with children about the matters of death and dying. We may want to protect children from the truth if it's painful, because talking about death or a dead person can be very hard, particularly if you're personally affected. But the truth, however difficult, is better than uncertainty. Children almost always understand more than we give them credit for. So they'll pick it up when something is wrong, even if they haven't actually been told.

Always give them whatever information they need – but don't be afraid to say you don't know if you don't know the answer. Make explanations simple if you can, be consistent in what you say, and repeat yourself if necessary. Let them ask questions, as often as they want, and answer them as truthfully as possible. Always use the correct language, not euphemisms like 'they passed away' or 'we've lost them', which they may misunderstand the meaning of.

Life after death?

There aren't clear guidelines on what to say to a child about what happens after death. It depends on the circumstances and on the child. These things will clearly be influenced by your personal beliefs. Even people who aren't particularly religious tend to say comforting things about heaven, angels and stars when talking to a child about death. These thoughts may be reassuring, but if you go down this route, you also need to make it clear that whoever's died is not coming back, because people don't *physically* live on after death and it may be confusing for a child if they're led to believe otherwise.

It may be better to let them know, truthfully, what you think happens, but that no one knows for sure, and that different people have different feelings on the matter – research shows that children just want truthful answers, so don't promise anything that you can't back up during awkward questions later. You could also ask them what their thoughts are – and let them know it's OK to believe whatever *they* want to believe.

One thing we *can* say with confidence is that one part of a person always remains behind, and that's the memories we have of them.

Preparing for death

Where possible, children should be given information gently and sensitively, prepared and given a chance to talk about a death that is anticipated. If they have a chance to spend some time with the person who's dying and to say goodbye, that can be really helpful as memories will be what they're left with.

Lessons in loss

Chances are a parent helping a child through bereavement will be mourning the very same loss themselves. It's important at times like this to give yourself time to grieve. Don't hold your own grief in for their sake – you, and they, need to let it out and express it. Draw on all the help you can from friends and family, and consider seeking professional counselling. There are details of some relevant organisations listed in the back of the book. If you are overwhelmed with grief, they may need some time and space to feel normal again, if that's what they want to do. In these cases, it can be useful for a child to spend some time elsewhere, with good friends or relatives. However, it's worth bearing in mind that many children will prefer to remain in their own home, however sad things may be, because it's where they'll feel the most secure and comfortable.

Losing mum or dad

The loss of a parent can, inevitably, be devastating for a child, particularly if the death was sudden. As well as all the usual feelings of loss and sadness, children who lose a primary carer can feel anxious and insecure – they may worry that their remaining parent, or whoever is looking after them, will die too. And they may worry about smaller practical matters, such as who is going to make their tea, or get them to school on time. Helping a child through these issues, particularly if you are grieving yourself, is not something you should attempt alone. An organisation like the Child Bereavement Trust [contact details are listed in the Appendix, p. 388] will be able to offer support and advice.

Final respects

Many anxious adults would prefer to shield a child from the sight of a dead body but for many children it's a positive thing – as long as they've been well prepared beforehand – because they can see for themselves that a person has died. Likewise, it can be a healthy thing for a child to attend a funeral. (Unless they are very scared or upset by the idea, and of course they shouldn't be forced to.) Funerals offer an important chance to say goodbye, and can help acceptance of their death by marking the beginning of life without that person. It can be helpful for a child to be involved, perhaps by putting something special in the coffin, lighting a candle or choosing a poem or hymn. They'll need plenty of warning though, about what and who will be involved.

If they don't go to a funeral, it can be a nice idea to hold some sort of alternative memorial or ceremony elsewhere or at home to show that the child's love for and their relationship with the deceased is important.

Never forget

Remembering the dead is a vital part of the grieving process, so it's a good idea to keep talking about the person who's died, look at photos, and keep and handle their possessions. Sometimes children want to talk about a person, but aren't sure that it's OK to do that and need to be given 'permission'.

Creating a 'memory box' is a good idea, as is marking an important anniversary with a quiet ceremony or a little ritual like lighting a candle, or a special discussion. As time goes on, memories may fade, and they may need to be reassured that that's OK, too.

What the experts say
The child bereavement counsellor

It's true that children are sometimes overlooked after someone has died. It's usually because they don't tend to exhibit grief in the same way adults do and it won't always be recognised that they are grieving, too. Often, children feel all the emotions of grief but they don't really understand them. So one minute they are very upset, and the next they can be asking what's for supper. Adults can misinterpret that. They think if they're fine one minute, and not the next, they may be putting it on. But children oscillate between feelings very easily. Very often, they can't stay with the pain of grief. Another possibility is that they don't always express what they're feeling because they don't want to make it worse for the adults who are grieving around them. And there may be other indications that they're unhappy which aren't always obvious – if they're playing up or being naughty, for example, it can be their way of calling out for attention.

Most parents or carers will do as best they can, and most children do manage to get on with their lives after the death of someone they were close to. But grief can seriously impact on children. If they get helpful care at the beginning of a bereavement and in the first few months afterwards – i.e., they are told the truth, allowed to talk openly and to remember the person who has died themselves, and their old lives and routines are kept as close to normal as possible they are more likely to have a full and normal life in the long term. Even the loss of a parent does not necessarily mean they will end up 'damaged', but it does depend hugely on the support they get from their surviving parent, or whoever is left to care for them. Parenting a child who has lost a parent is one of the hardest things a person will ever have to do. I would say that it's vital for anyone in this situation to get some counselling to help them through it.

It's very important to talk to them openly and honestly, not in a hurried way, and down at their eye level. If they ask a question, always stop and talk about what they've asked. Sometimes they only ask something once, and if they don't get a response they might be too worried to bring it up again.

You'll need to use language that's age-appropriate – a four year old and a fourteen year old will need very different explanations. But it's often surprising how much they can grasp: even very little children can understand that when you die, your body doesn't work any more. And that's something that you need to make very clear to a child – they need to know if a person is dead, they are not just 'asleep' and they are not coming back. That way, it won't be worrying or confusing for them when they hear that the body is going to be buried or burned.

Where possible, and you have the chance to, you should prepare a child for someone dying of a terminal illness. If someone they love is not expected to live, you need to be honest and tell them exactly what's happening. If the death is sudden, the crucial thing is to tell them as soon as possible and as clearly as possible.

You don't have to give the precise details, but they need to know what happened.

Keeping memories alive is a very important way to help children through bereavement. Memories help us to hold on to a person that's died in a helpful way and to move on in our lives without him.

Jenni Thomas, Founder and President of the Child Bereavement Charity

The Problem Summarised

- The loss of someone they love can have a profound effect on a child, so it's important to help them in the right way, with love and support, so that they can grieve naturally.
- They tend to show different responses to death from adults and often move quickly from one emotion to another.
- Honesty is absolutely the best policy. Tell them the truth, in language they will understand.
- Don't tell them anything you don't believe yourself. If you talk about heaven, angels and stars, be clear that the person isn't coming back.
- Let them express their grief however and whenever they want.
- It can be a positive thing for them to see a body or attend a funeral, if they choose to.
- Memories are all-important. Help them to create and cherish theirs.

Handle with care: How to keep them safe (and when to let them go)

The Problem

My biggest fear is that my children are taken or that something awful happens to them. Now my eldest son is getting older I know the time will soon come to let him go to the shop by himself. He's an intelligent boy who knows not to talk to strangers or to go with anybody. I guess I'll just have to trust him and worry the whole time he is gone, even though the shop is only five minutes away.

My husband and I find it frustrating that children cannot have as much freedom any more. Gone are the days when you could leave the house after breakfast and return for dinner, all before reaching the age of 11! We sometimes wonder if there is actually a greater problem with child abduction, or if it is just the media making it seem that way.
Zoe from Woodbridge, mum to Connor, nine, Jack, seven, Lucy, six, Amber, four and Kitty, eight months

Our worst nightmares

It's in our very instincts as loving parents to want to protect our children. Who hasn't been gripped by fear in the night, worrying that something bad might happen to them?

Once in a while, something unimaginable happens to someone else's child and we hear about it in precise detail via the media, fuelling our fears and making us ever more determined to keep our own adored family out of harm's way.

We all know perfectly well that the probability of something awful happening to a child from a caring home is small. But of course, that doesn't stop us worrying that it will.

Time to sever the apron strings?

Some people think we're all worrying *too* much. According to The Good Childhood Inquiry, an ongoing major survey being carried out by the Children's Society, just under half of adults believe that 14 is the *earliest* age at which children should go out unsupervised, and a third of eight- to ten-year-olds have never played outside without an adult present.

There are fears that we're becoming 'helicopter' parents, hovering anxiously over our children's heads, and in doing so, stifling their freedom, limiting their chances to form friendships, and ill-preparing them for the risks of real life by creating a false sense of security.

It seems that as with so many other issues in parenting, we're faced with the difficult task of finding a balance, somewhere between our passionate desires to keep them safe, and their need for independence.

The Problem Shared

What the Netmums say

We live in a very nice area in a quiet cul-de-sac with a lovely green in the middle but I still don't let my children out alone, at all. We have a back garden so they can have all the fresh air they want there. They're old enough and sensible enough to go out alone and there's a shop a five-minute walk away, with no roads to cross, but I won't let them go alone. If I put petrol in the car, I take the children into the kiosk with me to pay.

I know I'm a bit extreme but I really don't care what other people think. My eldest wants to walk alone when she starts secondary school and I know I'll have to let her. But I dread that day.

Andrea from Derby, mum to Emily-Rose, nine, Lucy, eight, Korben, six and Tyeran, four

Striking the balance on extending the apron strings has always been a concern for me. My son was always telling me that 'so and so is allowed out on their own', but until recently he wasn't, and that was the end of it! Since he turned 11 though, I've allowed him more independence. Last year, we were renting a house across the road from a park. All the other kids in the street would go over and play so I allowed Nathan to, as well. They always went in a large group, he had time limits for coming home, and he had his mobile phone, so he was contactable. I felt this was a really good transition period as he was learning the responsibilities of independence, in a relatively controlled environment.

His senior school is a 20-minute walk away and he usually makes the journey with friends. He also goes out with his mates after school and at weekends. He has to tell us specifically who and where he's meeting, and text or phone when he gets there, or when they move on to somewhere else. He has a time to be home, although that can be negotiable! He knows that if he wants his independence, he abides by our rules, and luckily it seems that most of his mates are in the same position!

He's very sensible and I fully trust him in the house on his own. My main concern is unwanted attention from 'inappropriate' adults. I've told him that if, God forbid, he should ever find himself in an uncomfortable situation he is to kick, scream, fight and swear as loud as he can.

When I was growing up it used to cheese me off that my brother seemed to have more freedom than me, even though he was younger. Obviously now I have a daughter of my own she won't be allowed out of the house unsupervised until she's at least 30!

Sam from Fareham, mum to Nathan, 12 and Lucy, eight months

I have a real panic about keeping my daughter safe. She's just turned five and I have terrible visions of her being taken. I've even withdrawn my permission for her to go to the shops with her school.

Maybe it's because she's the baby, but I just can't relax and even have panics in the night, in case someone tries to get in and take her. I can't seem to stop worrying about it.
Claudia from Tunbridge Wells, mum to Olivia, five

My boys are eight and seven and I don't let them out on their own. A few months ago they got scooters and were nagging to be let out to ride them on the path outside the house. I let them, but stood watching them the whole time. If we go shopping they come with me, and they are never left in the car, not even if I'm just popping into the bank. They are never without adult supervision – to my mind they are not yet responsible enough to look after themselves and as their parent, it's my job to make sure they are safe. It's not worth the risk. I'm honest with them about why they're not allowed out on their own (even though a lot of their friends are) and they have to accept the way I feel. I don't believe it's being over-protective, it's about them being safe. They'll have plenty of time to go out on their own when they're older.
Rebecca from Poole, mum to Jaymes, eight and Joshua, seven

At the moment mine are too young to go out by themselves, but in another year or two I will have to start letting my son out on his own, as he'll need to get used to doing things by himself before going to secondary school. My problem with letting them do things alone is that I have an irrational fear of 'stranger danger' – even though I know that this thing is extremely rare and probably no more prevalent than when I was a child – and also, I worry about the traffic, which I know is probably more realistic! I grew up in New Zealand, where I rode my bike to school from the age of six, played in fields with the neighbourhood kids all day, and went on 'Famous Five' style excursions, all without adult supervision. Unfortunately there's no way I could let my children have that sort of freedom here. We live in a village where the cars come screaming through at 40–50 miles an hour and have no regard for pedestrians or cyclists.

Perhaps in a year or so Robert will be able to go to the park at the end of our road with friends, but I'll probably give him a mobile for emergencies, and so that I can contact him if necessary.
Rowena from Groombridge, mum to Robert, seven and Anna, five

I've always taught Kade to remember the dangers of roads and car parks. However, I've taught him how to behave in and around such places from an early age, too, so he is not afraid of them. He knows to hold the buggy when crossing the road, not to run around in car parks, to stop at kerbs, to look for traffic, and listen carefully to what Mummy is saying. However, I'm always right behind him as there's always the occasional idiot behind the wheel.
Emma from Fife, mum to Kade, three and Jay, five months

I hate the idea that my boys might spend their childhoods cooped up in my car while I drive them to 'safe' places, because the media continuously bombards us with images of very upsetting but very rare things that can happen to children. Of course, kidnapping is a parent's worst nightmare, along with anything else that might cause them harm, but it's just not going to happen. It's a one in a million chance. They're much more likely to get hurt in a car crash.

Most children who are assaulted or murdered know their attacker but these things don't make headlines. Neither do the thousands of children killed or seriously injured on the roads. These are all tragedies and we must do all we can to stop them, but panicking is not the way.

As your child grows up, you have to teach them to look after themselves so they can manage if they are away from you. Whether it's coping with a bus trip to school, going to the shops by themselves or just knowing how to ask for help if they get lost in the park, if we don't give them the freedom to be a little bit independent then they could really come to harm once they are older.

I'm sure some people will say I'm an irresponsible parent, but I really hope my children will get the chance to enjoy themselves safely, and sometimes that might mean I'm not holding their hands *all* the time.
Naomi from London, mum to Josh, five and Toby, two

My daughter has just turned eight. At that age, I was walking alone to school with my sister, playing out in our road and going to the shop. I was always sensible, though, and was educated in road safety and stranger danger by my parents and at school. I know the time has come to start letting Charlie have a bit of independence so that she's not vulnerable when she reaches 11, that magic age when children are suddenly expected to be safe making their way to secondary school.

Unfortunately, she's been so bombarded by stranger danger messages that she's actually scared to go out by herself. When I sent her and her friend out to play in the large communal garden where we live, they returned after five minutes when a delivery man appeared, saying they'd seen a robber. Nothing could persuade them to go out again. When we go shopping, my daughter clings to my hand in case someone tries to abduct her. At home, she puts the chain on the front door.

I'm not so worried about abduction, it's the traffic that scares me. Recently I witnessed an 11-year-old boy in his first week of secondary school being hit by a car. Teaching them road sense is vital.

Denise from London, mum to George, 13, Charlie, eight and Ellie, five

Somehow, we parents have to find ways of giving our children freedom to explore life, without putting them in unnecessary danger. We need to give our children the chance to test their instincts sometimes, and make sure as parents that they're guided to develop *good* instincts, for example, about strangers.

It *is* hard, trying to work out how to teach them to differentiate between stranger danger possibilities, and being open, friendly and helpful to the world at large. But I don't think that each family shutting itself away in a cotton-wool enclosure is a good way to 'evolve' as human beings. How do we learn humanity, if we shut ourselves off from each other more and more?

My husband and I are convinced we have to expose our children to some (calculated) risk, to allow them to form and grow and test themselves, and to be fully-fledged little human beings. Oh how difficult it is though, in today's world, to work out where to draw those risk lines.

Deb from Egham, mum to Sam, 13 and Molly, six

My girls are, as I'm sure all children are to their parents, the most precious things on earth!

But whilst I have a duty of care to them and an overwhelming urge to protect them, they don't 'belong' to me. They need to develop independently of me, learn to be safe without us (when that time comes) and be aware of how to protect themselves. In comparison to friends' children, my four-year-old has great road sense, is confident and is 'sensible' enough to understand that whilst she shouldn't talk to strangers or go anywhere without telling us, not all strangers are bad – they are mostly just people we don't know.

Life is such a game of chance that if you worried about everything, you'd never do anything or go anywhere . . . and what kind of life would that be for a child? I don't want to frighten my girls and make them scared to live a full life; I intend to equip them with a bit of sense which, alongside their own intelligence, I hope will keep them safe from most harm.

Given that life can throw the unexpected in our paths at any time, I intend to keep my fingers firmly crossed instead of twiddling them with worry. There's a massive middle ground between not being protective enough and being over-protective and hopefully we'll strike that balance. I love them to pieces, but I also love watching them explore, learn and gain confidence in their world.

Kirsten from Winchester, mum to Evie, four and Livia, one

My son is three and I let him out to play with the other kids as I live in a cul-de-sac and there's lots of other kids around. I'm always out watching him though, as there's a river and a busy road 300 yards from our house. Perhaps in a few years when he's older and wiser I'll allow him to venture further than our road by himself. But there will have to be boundaries.

Victoria from Dalbeattie, mum to Nathan, three

The Problem Solved

Risks and reality

It's another one of those things that are easier said than done, but we need to put some perspective on the matter. Cases in which a child is abducted get massive publicity precisely because they are so rare. The risk of abduction or attack by a stranger is very small indeed, and it's important to keep that in mind, because otherwise we run the risk of living life in fear and of passing that fear on to our children. According to the most recent available figures from the Home Office, nine children were murdered by strangers in 2004–5. There were 377 child victims of attempted abduction by strangers in 2002–3, and 59 cases involving the 'successful' abduction of a child (63 per cent of whom were returned to safety within 24 hours – of the fate of the remaining 37 per cent, there is no information available). To put these figures into perspective, there are 12.4 million children aged between 0–16 in the UK.

Equally, kids – when the time is right – do need to know that various risks exist and that, in the event of that worst-case scenario coming true, they ought to know what to do about it. So it's finding the right balance between arming them with the right information, and scaring them.

What they need to know

As soon as they're old enough to understand, establish a basic safety code. For instance, make sure little ones know they must always stay by your side when you're out and about. Issue a few guidelines about what they should do in the event of getting lost – agree on a meeting point where you can both head for if you get separated. Remind them there's safety in numbers and that they should always stay where there are people around. If in doubt, they should head for the nearest responsible-looking adult (a shop assistant, anyone in uniform, or a mum with kids are good bets).

Without making them fearful and paranoid, it's important to get the message across that it's better not to talk to strangers and certainly that they should never, ever go anywhere with one. As soon as they are able to, they should commit their address and phone number to memory, and know how to make an emergency call.

When do you let them go?

As children grow up, the matter of when and where to let them explore their independence can be an enormous quandary for the parents. Although the law states that parents can be prosecuted for 'wilful neglect' if they leave a child alone 'in a manner likely to cause unnecessary suffering or injury to health', there are no specific rules about when you can safely leave a child alone in the house, or let them walk to the shops or to school. These decisions are down to individual parents to make judgements on and naturally, they'll be influenced by factors such as where you live, and how sensible your child is.

There are some guidelines, suggested by relevant organisations. The NSPCC, for example, says that in most situations, children under about eight shouldn't be out alone and should always be in the care and sight of an adult or an older, mature, trustworthy child. The society also advises that young children should never be left in a car or outside a shop, and that in a crowded place, they should remain by an adult's side. As for leaving them alone at home, the NSPCC's view is that 'most' kids under 13 are not mature enough to cope with an emergency and should not be left alone for more than a very short time. The Children's Accident Prevention Trust says that children over ten can usually be safely left alone for short periods of time if there is 'no alternative'.

But these are just guidelines. Ultimately, these decisions are down to us as parents.

Sensible precautions

If you *do* ever leave a child under ten alone in the house, bear in mind the basic rules: tell them not to answer the door unless they're sure they know the caller, take away any obvious risks such as matches, make sure they have food and drink so they're not tempted to use the kettle or cooker, and leave contact details for a reliable nearby friend or relative that they can contact for help if necessary.

When it comes to letting them venture beyond the house, your decision will of course come down to what you know of your area and community, and how much you feel you can trust your child.

If in doubt, talk things through with friends and family. They may not have a definitive answer, but they may have some helpful opinions.

Stop, look and listen

Figures from the Child Accident Prevention Trust (CAPT) show that around 29,000 children under 16 were hurt on our roads in the year 2005. Of those, 156 were fatalities and more than 11,000 were pedestrians, 69 of whom died.* So there's not much doubt that traffic represents a very significant risk to our children's safety.

Official advice, from the Department of Transport, is that children under eight had difficulty dealing with traffic and should never be let out alone. CAPT goes a little further, warning that children don't have the ability to accurately judge speed and distance of traffic until they're 11.

Regardless of that, they are never too young for us to start instilling good road sense into them and, although they will probably be taught some road safety skills at school, the responsibility for that comes down to their parents. As ever, teach by example and make sure they know when, where and how to get across roads safely right from the start. Then, when the time is right to loosen their reins, you'll know you have done your utmost to prepare them for it.

What the experts say
The children's safety campaigner

In some ways, the world is a less safe place these days. For one thing, there's more traffic, and for another, there's less community spirit, so adults are far less likely to get involved if a child is in difficulty. But in terms of stranger danger, no, the world is no more dangerous than it was, and we should be no more worried than our parents were. And if we tell our children it's such a dangerous place that they can't go anywhere without us, it's going to make them afraid to go out alone and less likely to develop the skills they need to get along in the world.

*(Source: CAPT)

It may even turn them into perpetual worriers, too frightened to have fun, and that would be a shame.

Our children are not likely to come to any harm of that sort – in fact they are more likely to be hit by lightning than to be abducted by a stranger. But we still need to make them aware of the possibility. We need to teach them skills and strategies for dealing with potentially dangerous or harmful situations rather than keeping them in, watching television and becoming couch potatoes, because it seems the safest option. As for when to let them go, that's not something I can prescribe. It's down to each parent, based on their child's maturity and the neighbourhood they live in. But in the same way that we teach them about crossing the road, how to swim, not to play with matches and other important things they need to know, we can bring in the knowledge that they may need to be safe from some people.

Of course, pre-schoolers are unlikely to ever be out of sight of a responsible adult, and at that age, there's no need to frighten them with facts about the big, bad world. Once they're five or so, though, it's time to start giving them the information they need in a calm, non-frightening way. So, you should talk about how they shouldn't talk to or go anywhere with anyone they don't know.

When the time comes for them to venture out alone, you can start to teach them about their personal safety, and make it clear that they have a right to protect themselves. There are many useful things you can tell them, for instance, that it's OK to yell and run towards people or a shop if they feel threatened, that they should stick in a group where possible; always let you know where they're going and with whom, and that, if they feel they are in danger, it's OK to break all the rules – for instance, if it comes to breaking a window, or to kicking, screaming, shouting and swearing if they need to, that's all right.

In the end though, there's no getting round the fact that as a mother, you'll be worrying about your child for the rest of your life. It's normal – it comes with the placenta.

Michele Elliott, Director, Kidscape

The mums' life coach

I don't know a mother who hasn't given this issue a lot of thought. It only takes another headline about a lost or abused child to get us wondering if the same could ever happen to our own child, and to share for a moment the horror of the parent whose child has vanished in a shopping centre or been physically harmed.

It's absolutely right to think long and hard about this issue. One of our primary functions as parents is to keep our children safe. At the same time we owe them an equal duty to prepare them for the adult world. These two aims often conflict, and there are no black and white answers. We may know that, statistically, the chances of something dreadful happening to our kids is tiny, but we also know that if that something should occur, its consequences are heart-stoppingly awful.

Talking about it to other mums can be helpful; you can voice your concerns and find out if others share your opinions. At the same time it's important to come to your own conclusions based on your own instincts and judgements. No one else knows how trustworthy your child is, and a stranger who doesn't know your area can't judge the risks for you.

Many mums find that the best approach is to introduce freedom gradually to their children. They might, for example, stand outside the local shop whilst their child goes in alone to buy a comic, or watch from the end of the street while he runs to post a letter. Others get their children to take the first steps towards independence with a child of a similar age; there's a bit more safety in numbers. Like learning to walk, baby steps are easier than big ones.

Patricia Carswell

The Problem Summarised

- It's natural and normal to be fearful for our kids' safety, but for our own sanity, we need to take a rational view of things if we can.
- Children need a certain amount of independence from us to grow, explore and form friendships.
- There are no set rules about when it's OK to let a child venture out, or stay in, alone. These judgements are down to the individual person.
- If you're unsure, talk to other mums, friends and family members and take their views into account, if it helps.
- We need to avoid frightening our children, whilst arming them with the basic knowledge and safety advice they need – a difficult balance to find!

Giving guilt the elbow: Why we need to stop worrying and give ourselves a break

The Problem

I feel guilty almost every day because I wonder if I should play with my children more, but I try not to let it overwhelm me. The thing is, I need some time to myself and I don't have any help, so, in order to take a breath I have to let my kids occupy themselves sometimes. Otherwise, I'd be going mental and that wouldn't be any good either, would it?!
Alexandra from West Sussex, mum to Paul, two and Jacob, seven months

Welcome to motherhood

So, we've established that it's not always easy being a mum! In fact, let's face it, there are few roles in life that present us with quite so many emotional and practical challenges on such a frequent basis, over such a prolonged period. (Or many that are as rewarding, either, which is just as well, because it helps to balance things out a bit!)

You'd think, what with all the problems kids throw at us, that we would aim to give ourselves a break and get through the experience as best as we can, without feeling bad about it when things go – as they are prone to – a bit pear shaped. But often, we don't. Instead, we allow ourselves to succumb to the guilt, pressure and anxiety that looms so large among modern mums attempting to parent to perfection and often be a valuable addition to the workforce, too – and in doing so, we just make a hard job harder.

Your best can't be bettered

What is it with mums and guilt these days? We seem to feel guilty about, and worry over, a vast range of issues that, in most cases, we really shouldn't. And yet it's not that surprising. In our competitive modern world, the pressure to be 'good mums' comes at us from all angles: from the mass media, from other people, and, perversely, from the impossible standards we insist on setting ourselves.

Caring mums *want* to do the right thing by their children, whether it's feeding them as well as we can, helping them deal with the ups and downs of their social lives, or guiding them through difficult behavioural phases. Unfortunately, these things don't always come easy, and there are a lot of negative forces out there, conspiring to make us feel bad about that.

We need to give ourselves a break. If we're doing as best as we can manage, then that's the best our children could possibly hope for.

The Problem Shared

What the Netmums say

We live in a society where television programmes are constantly telling parents the correct way to do things, and promising that we can make our children angelic in a week (yeah, right!). These shows just tap into parents' fears that they're not doing it all correctly!

I often worry – in fact, I'm a born worrier. I look at my perfect little girl and wonder how on earth I haven't messed it all up so far. I feel guilty if she doesn't eat her dinner, and stressed when she's still up at

9 p.m. But she's just being a typical two-year-old. When you're a parent you have so many different people telling you what to do and how to do it. Funnily enough, it's we mums that place the guilt firmly on our own shoulders. And we all do it. Working mums suffer guilt for spending time away from their kids, stay-at-home mums feel guilty if they aren't running round the house with a duster in one hand, singing 'a spoonful of sugar'!

I'm not a child psychologist. I can't make her eat food she doesn't like. I have no magical powers that will make my house clean itself. And sometimes I need a break. But I love her and I try my best. What more could anyone ask for?

Lauren from Ashford, mum to Kearsney, two

Yes, I feel guilty and, at times, a failure, too. I hated being pregnant and when he was a newborn I felt like I could have given him away. When he fell off the bed I cried for days, blaming myself.

I felt bad about returning to work and cried every morning when I dropped him off at nursery but we needed the money. Each day I still leave him with tears in my eyes. Not that he's bothered!

I feel awful when I'm grumpy the next day after a bad night with him. Recently I smacked his hand and it still haunts me to this day, as we'd vowed never to smack him. His dad was angry with me and I was annoyed at myself. I cried myself to sleep that night and weeks later, I still feel guilty.

Dyanne from Dunfermline, mum to Luke, one

My second son has been diagnosed with a hearing loss from birth and the feelings of guilt I have about that are overwhelming. He was inside my body for nine months – what did I do wrong to cause it? I also feel guilty now that the new baby will need more time and attention and this will take away from my older child.

I think all parents feel guilty for one thing or another. My elder son goes to nursery two mornings a week and if I do something I know he would enjoy while he's gone, I feel guilt that he's not with me – even though I know he's probably having a lovely time.

Nicola from Gomersal, mum to William, two and Joseph, three months

This is a subject close to my heart. I was feeling so guilty after my second son was born, about everything. Not having enough time for my eldest, not paying the new baby enough attention, not coping like I thought I 'should be'. I'd be sitting in the living room in the morning feeding the baby, and when I heard my eldest son's footsteps I'd be overcome with a wave of nausea because it was the beginning of yet another day where I was riddled with guilt, and would have to fight that battle with myself that could not be won. This went on for a long time, until I realised I had to move on. I was doing the best I could. So if I'm having a bad day, I tell myself I am a good mother, I do my best everyday, and that I love my kids.

Emma from Fife, mum to Kade, three and Jay, five months

I seem to have constant guilt about my son. My boy's father left when he was just six weeks old and I felt guilty for a long time that he didn't have a dad around. I felt guilty that it was just me and that he would never have a 'normal' family life! As it turns out, he's the happiest little boy I know and is not affected at all. And yet I still feel guilty. I feel guilty that I have to work full-time, and guilty for the amount of time he has to spend in nursery. I tend to overcompensate for my guilt by giving him everything he wants, but then I feel guilty that I've spoilt him! I feel guilty if I'm overworked and tired, because then I don't have the patience to play with him. Then there's food guilt – working full-time means I don't have the time or energy to cook from scratch.

My new partner tells me that by doing my best I am doing enough. However, I'm still not sure I'll ever stop feeling guilty! Even though he now has a better life than the one originally planned, I'll always feel guilty that it didn't turn out to be 'perfect'. Will it ever end?

Terri from Sutton Coldfield, mum to Aiden, three

I sometimes feel paralysed with guilt at the end of the day. Did I play enough with my son? Did he get enough cognitive, physical, visual, tactile, aural, emotional, mental stimulation? I didn't grow up with younger siblings and it's all so new for me. All the advertising for special toys and information on 'normal' child development makes me feel quite pressured to create a genius. I lost a component of one of his toys the other day and I actually wept from the guilt and the feeling that I had really let him down! What really helps is to remember that cave mums probably didn't have time to stack blocks for hours each day; they just got on with it. And I remember that really all he needs is to be with me, whatever I'm doing, and that's already pretty exciting for a toddler! I forget to worry and then activities like reading books and singing together become a lot more fun, for both of us.

I must say, my mother *tries* to make me feel guilty about co-sleeping, extended breastfeeding, carrying my son in a sling, taking *all* that time to prepare fresh food every day, but these are things I have never felt guilty about! Maybe it's just a philosophy/generation gap. I suppose everything is alright if I'm following my instincts (when I have them!)

Anna from Cardiff, mum to Pippo, 18 months

I remember someone saying once that as a parent 'you feel guilty when you do and guilty when you don't'! Well, they were right. Becoming a parent opens the doorway to a whole new world of emotions that you never knew you had.

My real feelings of guilt started like so many other mums, when I had to return to work when our first daughter was five months old, to ensure we could pay the bills. When our second child was born I felt overwhelming turmoil that swung from one direction to another. One week I was feeling guilty about the fact I could no longer spend the same amount of one-to-one quality time with Lucy and the next I was feeling guilty that I'll *never* be able to spend the same amount of one-to-one time with Cara that I did with Lucy! Not to mention feeling guilty about not having the time, energy and money to spend with my husband that he deserves.

I feel guilty for feeling resentful at times that I don't get the opportunity to pursue any of my hobbies any more, so that I sometimes feel like I've lost my individuality. I feel guilty that I can no longer put in the time, money and effort into my friendships that I once could.

Every day I feel guilty about the little things too. If I do that bit of housework I'll feel happy it's been done, but then I've neglected the children in order to do it. If I spend time with the children I feel guilty that my husband comes home to an untidy, non-hoovered home!

The way I justify these feelings of guilt is to remember these simple facts: I am not Wonder Woman, never was and never will be. Parenting is a journey of discovery that doesn't come with guidelines or perfect children.

Every day I try my hardest to do my best and do the right thing by everyone I love. My girls will never want or need for affection, reassurance, advice, room to grow or love and that's all that really matters. I am not alone in thinking and feeling all these things!
Wendy from Southend, mum to Lucy, two and Cara, seven months

I always feel guilty, but perhaps it's Mother Nature's way of helping me to make my children a priority. Compared to some women I have a very privileged lifestyle with a supportive husband, family and friends and a very good childminder. But it's still easy to feel down about not doing enough or not doing everything correctly. I need to sit back sometimes and look at this little miracle I've brought into the world, especially while the going's good. You never know what's around the corner.
Liz from Rotherham, mum to Eimear, one

Like every other mum, I've developed extra guilt about everything; from whether I spend enough quality time with my kids, to whether I should have given them a packet of chocolate buttons.

But I got fed up with feeling guilty, it's a destructive emotion, so I've turned it around (or at least I'm trying to!). Whenever I feel guilty about something, I stop and tell myself that either I *should* feel guilty as I have made a mistake (and it's OK to make mistakes, provided that we learn from them), or I accept whatever it was that I did was OK and get on with my life. We all have to compromise, sometimes. It's easier said than done, but I feel more positive approaching it this way.
Liz from Leeds, mum to Issy, two and Niamh, three months

Oh, gosh the guilt thing. It's like a snowball isn't it; small at the start of the day but rolling downhill all day gathering more snow and ends up the size of a small planet by bedtime!? There are just so many things one could feel guilty about. Are my children happy? Are they having fun? Do they feel loved and secure? When they are so small, how can I be sure? I ask these questions, and a million more, all the time! I feel guilty the house goes to pot when I'm spending all my time with my son and daughter and then when I eventually get round to household chores and errands, I feel guilty that I'm not spending time with my children. What do you do? I've accepted it's part of the whole parenting package and I just ignore it. Parenting's for life so I guess the guilt thing will be for life too – I may as well just get used to it being there, no matter what I do!

Sara from Chesham, mum to Sam, three and Emily, one

Yes, I have loads of guilt. I feel guilty because I found it so hard to manage three kids aged five and under. I don't think Homestart was running in those days, which is a shame, as I could have done with a shoulder to cry on or a helping hand. I wasn't a very happy mum and always so stressed.

I feel guilty now, too, for wanting to run away when the kids are constantly screaming and each wanting my attention. I want a bit of 'me' time occasionally. I feel guilty for not wanting my third child and then when he was born, feeling an overwhelming love for him, which made me feel so guilty, thinking I could have lost him!

I feel guilty for having to care for my father when he had a stroke, which meant that my youngest child took second priority. I feel guilty for 'wishing' my children were older, so they could do things for themselves and now that they can, I wish I could have the precious younger years back again.

I feel guilty for being at home all day, while the kids are at school, when there are so many mums who have to go to work and can't be at home when the kids get in. Lastly, I feel guilty that my kids have so much, when there are others that have so little.

Christine from Kettering, mum to Holly, 12, Chloe, ten and Jack, eight

I used to feel guilty that I'm not as good as my mum was. When I'm having a bad day and haven't done the 101 jobs I wanted to do I think, 'How did my mum cope? She had four kids and a job as well'! I think too much emphasis is put on being a supermum, and having a perfect house, well-behaved children, job etc. You just have to do the best you can and if someone else thinks it's not good enough then it's their problem and not yours!

Janey from Leeds, mum to Nicole, 15 and Nevaeh, two

I think all mums feel some sort of guilt as we all wish to do the best for our child. I feel guilty that I didn't go back to work so we can't provide much financially for our son, and I feel guilty that I spend a lot of time on my business – I'm self employed and that means we don't have the security of a regular pay check. When he's at nursery I feel guilty that I'm not providing his care and when he's home I feel guilty because I don't provide the fun environment he has at nursery! I feel guilty that he doesn't have a set schedule and bedtime routine as his dad works shifts but then I think I would feel more guilty if I made him go to bed earlier and he didn't get to see his dad.

When we have an 'at home' day I feel guilty when I lose my patience (and sometimes temper) with him, which is why I try to take him out a lot. Because we are out all day I feel guilty that I never get around to the housework! But then, which would he prefer? A mum who's cleaning all the time and shouting at him for getting in the way, or a mum who hasn't done any ironing since he was born and who takes him to the park for the afternoon?

Claire from Worksop, mum to Luke, three

The Problem Solved

Stop trying to be Supermum

Motherhood is relentlessly hard work, both physically and emotionally. And that's before you've taken the rest of your life into account – we also have other relationships to manage, homes to run and in many cases, jobs to go to. Whoever coined the phrase 'life juggling' was spot-on, and the truth is that sometimes it's just not possible to keep all the balls in the air. Never feel bad about that. You're a human being, not a super hero.

Go easy on yourself, whenever possible. So you're too tired to make tea from scratch? You don't have to. The kids next door are academic high fliers and yours are closer to average? Who cares! Parenthood isn't a competition. There are no prizes. But there is a goal, and that's happy kids, living in happy families. You won't reach it if you're forever striving to be the perfect mum because you'll be too exhausted and stressed out by your efforts.

When all's said and done, you only need to provide children with a few basic requirements for them to thrive. They need you to love them, and to show that you love them. A bit of guidance is helpful. And a reasonably healthy lifestyle is a plus, too. Everything else is a bonus.

It's OK to be angry

A small number of mums are endlessly calm, always patient, and never lose their temper. The rest of us lose it on a regular basis. Children – bless their hearts – can be stubborn, irrational, defiant and infuriating, and all families have their flashpoints. But anger's OK. In fact it's more than OK, it's normal. And what's more, it's healthy, because it's better to blow your top than to keep anger under your hat, where it may fester. Be sure to tell yourself this next time you lose your rag and you feel bad about it. When it does happen, be sure to smooth things over with them – it's a good life lesson for children to see reconciliation at work. And always remember that your children will be forgiving. You should be, too.

Give yourself a break

Know your limitations, and give yourself a break sometimes – figuratively as well as literally. Squeeze in some me-time wherever possible – if you have to stick the kids in front of the television to do so or find money for a babysitter from the week's child benefit – so be it. Get out with the girls once in a while, and let your hair down. Treat *yourself* to something nice, for a change.

Maybe you feel you shouldn't, because money's short, or there's too much else to do. But you should try, whenever possible. In the long run, anything that makes you happier will make your children happier. And anyway, it's the least you deserve.

We're all in this together

One of the best ways to feel better about yourself as a mum is to talk to other mums. When the chips are down, it helps to remember that somewhere nearby, another mum is struggling, too. Sure, there are one or two 'alpha mummies' out there who make the rest of us feel bad. They are few and far between. Don't be tempted to compare your life with another mum's. Just get on with yours.

Solidarity among mothers is a force to be reckoned with, so make your mum friends, and value them. And it doesn't matter whether we work full or part-time, or are at home with our children. We're all basically in the same boat. We should be sailing it together.

What the experts say

The mums' life coach

Guilt is the mother's favourite buzzword; it crops up in countless conversations between mothers. Mums are incredibly hard on themselves, and often demand nothing less than perfection, beating themselves up for the slightest failing.

It may be natural, and it's easy to convince ourselves that we need guilt to make sure we're doing the best for our kids, but the truth is that guilt is generally not a good thing. It makes you turn in on yourself and can affect your happiness and your self-esteem.

It's really important if you're prone to guilt to make a conscious effort to be less hard on yourself. Think about how you'd feel if you were being that critical of someone else – it wouldn't be nice, would it? So the next time you're feeling guilty about something, make a point of lowering your standards a little and giving yourself the benefit of the doubt.

It's also essential not to get into the habit of comparing yourself with other mums. However well the mothers you meet might seem to be doing, you can bet your bottom dollar that there's some area of their lives where they feel they're doing a rotten job.

Often when a mum is feeling guilty she hasn't actually done anything wrong. She may be mistaking the emotion for something else entirely, such as regret or anxiety, or may even just have got into the habit of assuming it's her fault when things go wrong. If you find yourself feeling guilty a lot of the time, run through a quick check on your feelings. Have you really done anything wrong? Can you give yourself the benefit of the doubt? Might you be confusing your feelings with some other emotion? If you're not in the wrong, let yourself off the hook. Analysing is good, but only for so long.

If on the other hand you know you have done something wrong – and let's face it, we all make mistakes in our parenting – don't panic, and don't beat yourself up. Deal with it. Apologise if there's someone to apologise to, and remember that children have big hearts and are endlessly forgiving. Make amends if you can. But then leave it. Martyrs don't make good mothers.

Patricia Carswell

The Problem Summarised

- Guilt is a widespread emotion among mums these days. But it really shouldn't be!
- Modern life is full of pressures, and the business of parenting particularly so.
- Don't try and be Supermum. None of us are perfect parents, or can even hope to be.
- Don't attempt to compare yourself to other mums. It's your family.
- Give yourself some time off whenever you get the chance.
- Don't beat yourself up when things go down the pan or your temper hits the roof. That's life.
- Other mums can (or should!) provide a guilt-free zone. Make friends. Keep them. And remember: we're in this together!

Appendix: Recommended reading and useful organisations, companies and websites

Activities

Recommended reading

I'm Bored! and *I'm Bored . . . Again!* by Polly Beard and Suzy Barratt (Bloomsbury, 2003, 2005)

Aggression/sibling squabbles

Useful organisations, companies and websites

Transforming conflict
The Restorative Justice Organisation.

Web: www.transformingconflict.org

Bedtime problems/night waking

Recommended reading

Teach Your Child to Sleep by Millpond Sleep Clinic (Hamlyn, 2005)

Useful organisations, companies and websites

Millpond Sleep Clinic

Tel: 0208 444 0040

Web: www.mill-pond.co.uk

Bedwetting

Useful organisations, companies and websites

ERIC (Education and Resources for Improving Childhood Continence)

Tel: 0845 370 8008

Web: www.enuresis.org.uk

Bereavement

Useful organisations, companies and websites

Child Bereavement Charity

Tel: 01494 446 648

Web: www.childbereavement.org.uk

Cruse

Tel: 0844 477 9400

Web: www.crusebereavementcare.org.uk

Winston's Wish
A charity helping bereaved children and their fanilies.
Tel: 0845 203 0405

Web: www.winstonswish.org.uk

Recommended reading

Muddles, Puddles and Sunshine by Diana Crossley (Hawthorn Press, 2007)

Bullying and safety

Useful organisations, companies and websites

Bullying Online
Web: www.bullying.co.uk

Childline
Tel: 0800 1111

Kidscape
Tel: 08451 205 204

Web: www.kidscape.org.uk

Recommended reading

101 Ways to Deal with Bullying by Michele Elliott (Hodder Mobius, 1997)
When Your Child is Bullied by Jenny Alexander (Pocket Books, 2006)

Fussy eating

Recommended reading

Children's Food Bible by Judith Wills (Collins, 2004)
Feeding Kids: The Netmums.com Cookery Book by Judith Wills (Headline, 2007)

General issues

The following organisations and websites offer a range of useful advice on all sorts of child and parenting issues

BBC Parenting

Lots of useful advice on all sorts of parenting issues from the BBC's website.

Web: www.bbc.co.uk/parenting

Netmums

One of the web's most popular online parenting communities, offering advice, forums, local information and lots more.

Web: www.netmums.com

Parentline Plus

An independent charity offering online parenting advice plus a free, confidential telephone helpline.

Tel: 0808 800 2222

Web: www.parentlineplus.org.uk

Parents Centre

A Government-run online resource offering information and support on a range of parenting issues including education and childcare.

Web: www.parentscentre.gov.uk

Good behaviour

Recommended reading

Tidy Your Room: How to Get Your Kids to do the Things They Hate by Jane Bidder (White Ladder Press, 2006)

Grandparents

Useful organisations, companies and websites

The Grandparents Association
An organisation offering support and advice to grandparents.

Tel: 08451 205 204

Web: www.grandparents-association.org.uk

Growing up too fast

Recommended reading

Toxic Childhood: How the Modern World is Damaging Our Children and What We Can Do About It by Sue Palmer (Orion, 2006)
De-toxing Childhood: What Every Parent Needs to Know to Raise Happy, Successful Children by Sue Palmer (Orion, 2007)

Manners

Useful organisations, companies and websites

Public Image Inc
Web: www.publicimage.co.uk

Media exposure

Recommended reading

How to Stop Your Children Watching Too Much TV by Teresa Orange and Louise O'Flynn (Hay House, 2007)
The Media Diet for Kids: A Parents' Survival Guide to TV and Computer Games by Teresa Orange and Louise O'Flynn (Hay House, 2005)

Web: www.themediadietforkids.com

Personal relationships

Useful organisations, companies and websites

The Parent Connection

Web: www.theparentconnection.org.uk

Relate

Tel: 08451 30 40 16

Web: www.relate.org.uk

Schooling needs

Useful organisations, companies and websites

Advisory Centre for Education

Tel: 0808 800 5793

Web: www.ace-ed.org.uk

Independent Panel for Special Educational Advice

Web: www.ipsea.org.uk

National Parent Partnership Network

Web: www.parentpartnership.org.uk

Speech and language worries

Useful organisations, companies and websites

I CAN

An organisation working to suuport the development of speech, language and communication.

Address: 8 Wakley Street, London EC1V 7QE

Tel: 0845 225 4071/020 7843 2510

Web: www.ican.org.uk

Talk to Your Baby

A campaign run by the National Literary Trust.

Web: www.talktoyourbaby.org.uk

Afasic

A charity offering support and advice to families affected by speech and language problems.

Web: www.afasic.org.uk

Index

You can buy any of these other titles in the netmums series from your bookshop or direct from the publisher.

FREE P&P AND UK DELIVERY
(Overseas and Ireland £3.50 per book)

FEEDING KIDS   *Netmums with Judith Wills*   £14.99

Feeding Kids includes 120 easy-to-prepare and delicious recipes provided by Netmums members that will fit perfectly into your busy family life.

HOW TO BE A HAPPY MUM   £12.99
Netmums with Siobhan Freegard

How to be a Happy Mum identifies the top ten stresses mothers have to cope with and offers sound advice on how to overcome them from other mothers who have been there, done it and lived to tell the tale.

YOUR PREGNANCY   *Netmums with Hilary Pereira*   £12.99

Your Pregnancy is an invaluable source of mum-to-mum insights and practical know-how from Netmums members, which will make you feel as though you have your very own antenatal group in the comfort of your home.

BABY'S FIRST YEAR   *Netmums with Hollie Smith*   £12.99

Baby's First Year is packed with peer-to-peer guidance and tips from the members of Netmums as well as key medical and developmental information from the experts to help you through the first crucial months of your baby's life.

To order, simply call 01235 400 414
visit our website: www.headline.co.uk
or email orders@bookpoint.co.uk

Prices and availability are subject to change without notice.

To become part of the Netmums community, log on to www.netmums.com.

netmums